UTSA DT LIBRARY RENEWALS 458-2440 DATE DUE

GAYLORD			PRINTED IN U.S.A.

Surviving Russian Prisons

Surviving Russian Prisons is dedicated to
Alasdair Campbell and Rosemary Piacentini
and also to the memory of my father,
Andrea Piacentini

Surviving Russian Prisons

Punishment, economy and politics
in transition

Laura Piacentini

WILLAN
PUBLISHING

Published by

Willan Publishing
Culmcott House
Mill Street, Uffculme
Cullompton, Devon
EX15 3AT, UK
Tel: +44(0)1884 840337
Fax: +44(0)1884 840251
e-mail: info@willanpublishing.co.uk
website: www.willanpublishing.co.uk

Published simultaneously in the USA and Canada by

Willan Publishing
c/o ISBS, 920 NE 58th Ave, Suite 300,
Portland, Oregon 97213-3786, USA
Tel: +001(0)503 287 3093
Fax: +001(0)503 280 8832
e-mail: info@isbs.com
website: www.isbs.com

First published 2004

ISBN 1-84392-103-0 Hardback

British Library Cataloguing-in-Publication Data

A catalogue record for this book is available from the British Library

Typeset by GCS, Leighton Buzzard, Bedfordshire
Project managed by Deer Park Productions, Tavistock, Devon
Printed and bound by T.J. International Ltd, Trecerus Industrial Estate, Padstow, Cornwall

Cover photos © Laura Piacentini. Top left: 'Zhilaya Zona' (prison living zone at Omsk;
top right: classroom in the educational colony for girls in Ryazan, Western Russia;
bottom: prison buildings at Omsk; bottom: rusting train sitting on a track inside the
prison colony at Smolensk.

Contents

List of tables and figures

Acknowledgements

I would like to thank the ESRC for providing an award (number R00429825847) for funding the main study on which this book is based. Thanks also to the Department of Applied Social Science at the University of Stirling for providing financial assistance for a research trip to penal colonies in eastern Siberia in 2003.

The debts that accrue in any piece of writing can be considerable; they are the more so in a research study of this type as I depended on the expertise, patronage and kindness of a great number of people in the UK and in various locations throughout Russia. I first wish to thank Dr Yvonne Jewkes for her enthusiastic support over the various stages of writing this book and for her very useful comments. I would also like to thank my colleague, Dr Reece Walters for his sound advice and great support. Since the book is based on my PhD, I would like to say 'thank you' to my PhD supervisors Professor Roy King and Professor Alexander Solomonovich Mikhlin in (respectively) the UK and Russia for backing the research. I am very grateful to General Alexander Illych Zubkov who, when he was Deputy Prisons Minister at the central prison authority in Moscow in 1999, did this research a great service by sending me to Siberia. I am indebted to Colonel Alekseii Vasilievich Voronkov, Junior Prisons Minister, who granted me unlimited access to Omsk and Kemerovo prison regions in 2003 and who responded cheerfully to my many requests for an interview. I am indebted to the prison chiefs of the Smolensk, Omsk and Kemerovo regions (respectively, General Anatolii Alekseivich Sahkarov, General Yurii Karlovich Baster and General Valerii Sergeivich Dolzhantsev) for generously supporting the research.

Looking back, I am amazed that all the prisoners I came into contact with, and who were incarcerated under extremely difficult physical conditions, were so open to the research. I would like to thank all of them for sharing their thoughts on imprisonment. I am grateful to the dozens of prison officers and their families for supporting my research and my needs as best they could, and for their tolerance and many kindnesses particularly as I was the first Westerner to visit the prison colonies. Thanks also to Valerii Abramkin, Director of the Moscow Centre for Prison Reform, for organising interviews with survivors of Stalin's Gulag. At the International Centre for Prison Studies in London, Professor Andrew Coyle and Anton Shelupanov provided thoughtful insight into human rights in Russian prisons. Special thanks to Nataliya Radievskaia, who helped with some of the translations.

I would also like to thank a group of people have given me fantastic encouragement at various periods. In alphabetical order: Aurora Alvarez, Hillary Bradshaw, Pat Carlen, Nils Christie, Howard Davies, Claire Davis, Rhian Evans, Brian Irvine, Laura Irvine, Andrew Jefferson, Emma Maddocks, Dominique Moran, Karrie Munro, Igor and Irina Nishchita, Judy Pallot, Jenny Parry, Konstantin Petrovich, Alan Prout, Muzammil Quraishi, Paddy Rawlinson, Deborah Ritchie, Viktor and Rita Shambulatov, Valya and Andreii Shildov, David Smith, Caroline Thomas, Tanya and Marina Varlashina and Roy Walmsley. Thanks to Brian Willan for being an enthusiastic and efficient publisher. As usual, I received enormous support from my family.

Finally, very special thanks must go to Alasdair Campbell whose unflinching support and wonderful humour kept me sane throughout this adventure.

Introduction

What do Russian prisons look like? Who is sent to prison in Russia? How is punishment allocated and administered? Few of us pause to answer these questions not least because the traditional domain of criminological research is in English-speaking countries and Western Europe. This book aims to answer some of these questions by embarking on a journey that begins by exploring how the prisons have survived the collapse of the USSR, and ends with a discussion of global penal politics. Indeed, this is the first book to be published in the West on penal practices in the contemporary Russian prison system that is an original English-language publication.[1]

Given this hitherto exclusion, it is hardly surprising to find that there is only a handful of Russian-speaking Western criminologists conducting empirical and theoretical research on Russia's vast and complex prison system. I have worked in the area of Russian prisons since 1997 and I have been interested in Russian culture since around 1992. These interests have led me deep into that country's prison life. I have mastered Russian and lived in the natural setting of prison colonies. I have shared vodka with prison officers as they mourned the sorry state of their nation and I have been an honoured guest at musical concerts performed by prisoners. From my unique experience of prison research in 15 prison establishments, I have formed the view that imprisonment, and specifically prison labour, is ingrained in the psyche and in the social lives of Russian people. This was graphically illustrated in the spring of 1999 when broadcasts appeared on Russian television marking the two-hundredth anniversary of the birth of Russia's greatest poet, Alexander Pushkin. Vivid images of modern-day Russians in real-life settings reading aloud Pushkin's poetry were broadcast. Groups of children were shown playing and singing lullabies by Pushkin. During rare moments of rest at work, doctors appeared on television screens recounting their favourite Pushkin poem while market vendors debated the most poignant lines of Pushkin's poetry. In other words, Pushkin was everywhere. Most striking out of all the broadcasts was a series of images from Butyrka prison in Moscow and Kresty prison in St Petersburg depicting groups of prisoners reflecting on how Pushkin's poetry has enriched their lives. Russian prison authorities were unconcerned about broadcasting images from these prisons, described in 1994 by Nigel Rodley, the Special Rapporteur on Torture to the United Nations, as: 'An appalling reality with no daylight, fresh air and where all detainees suffer from swollen legs and feet due to the fact that they must stand for extensive periods of time and where skin disease is rife.' And later by Walmsley in 1996 as: 'Demoralising places, uncomfortable physically and psychologically and where the stench is unbearable due to over 80% overcrowding.'

Evidently, national pride prevailed and concerns over exposing the inhumane conditions in the penal system were secondary. In some societies such broadcasts could be regarded as exploitative or scandalous (the propensity towards punitive populism in England, argues Reuss (1999), serves to present prisoners as undeserving of any artistic or cultural stimulation). Yet in Russia, the decision to include prisoners into the broadcasts was justified by a senior prison official as: 'Entirely normal since prisoners' labour contributed significantly to building and maintaining Soviet society'.[2]

In order to understand this remark fully, it is necessary to place it within a historical context. The Soviet Union has had a long history of forced prison labour,[3] as did Germany and wartime Japan (Gutman and Berenbaum 1994). It was in the Soviet forced labour camps – the Gulag[4] – where prisoners were to make a functional contribution to maintaining a carefully constructed image that embodied Soviet *identity* as a viable socialist political economy in two closely related ways. First, throughout the Soviet period, prisons were major pillars supporting the Soviet command economy. Prisons did not in themselves sustain the Soviet economy, but their economic contribution was significant, none the less. Through a 'policy of colonisation' forced labour was used to develop natural resources – from timber and coal to diamonds and gold – in inhospitable northern and other Siberian regions where wage labour was considered too expensive by the regime. Secondly, there was a reformative value to labour: persons judged enemies were isolated and forced to work while being politically indoctrinated. This two-pronged function of imprisonment formed the basis of a century-long penal identity that aimed for social cohesiveness and the survival of the state through various social control measures.

One of Russia's greatest living novelists and best-known living political dissident, Alexander Solzhenitsyn, spent eleven years in concentration camps. Solzhenitsyn's memoir, *The Gulag Archipelago*, a prison memoir classic that is both touching in its humanity and shocking in its graphic detail of prison camp life, warns that Russia will struggle for generations to rid itself of a 'Gulag mentality' because forced labour was incorporated into the Soviet Union's nascent manufacturing base and burgeoning ideology. The Moscow Centre for Prison Reform (MCPR) is emphatic in its call for the Russian government to commemorate the Gulag. Valerii Abramkin, MCPR's Director, argues that the legacy of Soviet prison labour has yet to be fully addressed by the central prison administration because the topic raises hard questions about the brutalities meted out by the Soviet regime.[5] The situation of acknowledging that a massive penal empire exploited citizens is made considerably more complicated by the fact that there is yet to be a consensus on the extent of prison labour throughout the Soviet period. Much of the discourse around prisons in Russia is constructed as historical narrative and is conducted by historians who endeavour to explicate the nature and scope of Soviet prison establishments. According to Bacon (1994), prison labour grew quickly in the early twentieth century in the Soviet Union, but it became a gigantic operation from 1930 onwards. How many *zeks* (prisoners) were incarcerated? What was the extent of forced labour? How many died in the Gulag? Firm figures are as impossible to come by in these areas as are Soviet economic growth rates. Any official data are likely to be imprecise due to the practice of falsifying official records, leaving considerable latitude for legitimate debate and disagreement. Even so, by the 1980s it became indisputable that prison labour was not incidental but was central to the maintenance of Soviet political and economic ideology, expanding on an incomparable scale from an estimated 30,000 inmates held in six camps in 1930 to nearly 2 million prisoners in 1931 and reaching a figure in the region of 5 million by 1952 (Tucker 1992: 173).[6]

The most telling testimonies reveal that the contribution of prison labour to preserve Soviet identity was particularly significant during the Stalin dictatorship (1926–53) when deviance was manufactured in order to create a factory of workers, or perfect proletarians, as they were caricatured. The regime dispensed fear through the arbitrary use of crime legislation which led to the creation of a disciplined society – probably the most controlled society of the twentieth century –

subservient to a version of Marxism/Leninism that had been supplanted for political ends. We see the human face of prison life in Russia where stripped of any human qualities that might have permitted a positivistic approach to tackling the causes of crime, prisoners symbolised the human machines that maintained the centralised economy and Soviet sensibility. We also see evidence of an interesting association between prison labour and the net centralised state income in ways that were similar to the development of work in the industrial prisons of nineteenth-century England or late modern American jails (Hochstellar and Shover 1997; Christie 2004). Although millions of prisoners were released following Stalin's death in 1952, the successive post-Stalin leaders upheld Soviet penal discourse where prisons were to articulate state power and state ideology. Thus, the prison population remained high at between 1 and 3 million prisoners until the late 1980s (Amnesty International 1980). The prison population rate per 100,000 of the general population then dropped from 660 in 1979 to 353 in 1989 (Christie 1996: 31).

When the Soviet Union collapsed in 1991 so too did Soviet penal identity because the penal system was no longer connected to the larger structures of ideology and political economy. In the ensuing turbulent transition period, what was once centrally managed and controlled had fallen apart. It became obvious that the penal system could not continue to exist in its previous form. In the 1990s the penal system was reorganised, triggering a process of reform that is ongoing. Of keynote is that penal reform has coincided with Russia's entry into the Council of Europe which is intended to lead to integration into the European Union. Consequently, new legislation was introduced that aimed at making regimes more humane; the rights of prisoners have been safeguarded; and legal and judicial reform has accelerated so that conditions are brought into line with international standards. Apart from improving human rights and instituting a rule of law, there is the serious problem of how prisoners should occupy their time. And if we recall the comment made by the prisons' minister about the prisoners who were caricatured as the heroes of the USSR, an interesting question arises: now that prison labour can no longer be described as a defining element in national identity, what are the forces that come together to define the present-day penal system as an ideological manifestation of state power and as a punitive sanction?

Aims of the book

It is against this background that the book offers two separate but intimately related aims. First, the book intends to uncover how the collapse of the Soviet penal system has impacted on the use and organisation of prison labour in two geographically disparate prison regions. Put crudely, the Soviet Union was an exceptional state where the distorted vision of Marxism/Leninism led to prisons functioning in ways beyond their typical role of instilling a panoptic order. The principal task of the prison system was political correction and forced labour. So when the Soviet Union fragmented, this would invariably impact on penal policy (whether there would be a hangover from the Soviet era, as might be expected, or whether ideas from other penal systems would surface and what forms these ideas might take).

Secondly, the book is also concerned with how the Russian prison system protects its prisoners from exploitation in how it administers punishment. As I will show, this is a problem for most prison systems where prisoners are expected to work. However, given the history of forced prison labour in Russia and its current 'movement' towards Western models, the issue becomes more seductive. Precisely how prison authorities are sustaining an overpopulated under-resourced prison population in the current climate of transition while claiming to be moving towards better standards of care and treatment of offenders will be critical in determining Russia's position at an international level. And if the trend towards greater private sector involvement is happening in Russia, as it is across Europe, what form will this take and most crucially how will this impact on maintaining human rights?

Themes

Three themes emerge from this book which will contribute to the ever-topical concern and developments in punishment and their relationships to economy and politics. First, in bringing together the voices of prisoners, prison officers and prison officials to reveal how penal practices and policies are interpreted and administered, the book will attempt to show how prison systems are governed in societies undergoing turbulent ideological transformation and upheaval. Criminal justice systems in transition have been largely studied in terms of the physical conditions and violations that emphasise material circumstances rather than overarching penal norms. The Russian prison system could, therefore, provide a critical test case of how societies in the twenty-first century operate prison systems amid periods of transition and social change. Secondly, through a description of how prisons function on a day-to-day basis, the book debates sources of knowledge on penal discourse in transitional states and the permeability of prison systems to the importation of ideas from elsewhere. For example, I am interested in investigating how custodians and captives come to develop ideas (are they imported or are they indigenous?) on what a modern penal system should look like. Thirdly, the book broadens the political dimension of prisons by exploring how current practices comply with international regulations designed to promote positive custody and humane containment. The strength of Russia's national regulations and laws is open to 'Western' scrutiny and this is of growing importance to prison authorities as well as prison specialists who are expected to ensure compliance with international standards in justice. Looking beyond the Gulag model that characterised punishment in twentieth-century Russia, the book will ask whether what is happening in contemporary Russia is indicative of a movement towards a globalised (Western) penal ideology that is based on convergence rather than difference. This book's final imperative is to utilise Russia as a model for understanding new global agendas: how penal policy is transferred across time and space; *what* is transferred; and the constructed links between penal policy and globalisation (processes and policy convergence).

It is perhaps worth noting at this early point that modes of penal development vary tremendously in the West and distinction should be made between Anglo-American and European modes. I do not wish to invite the assumption that the expansion of penal systems has been uniform across Western societies, for example. Nor is it the case that there has been a more generalised shift towards more punitive measures, as the continued investment and experimentation in community-based initiatives in the UK show us. Different forms of social, political, economic and cultural developments display variations in penal practice and penal policy in the West. In this book I pay attention to these distinctions, although my position is with locating trends in penal development in Russia within a global context where Russia is looking westwards to norms such as the European Prison Rules (1987) and the United Nations Standard Minimum Rules for the Care and Treatment of Offenders (1955) for classification of its penal system. In this regard, where I refer to 'Western' or 'the West', I am presenting a classification of homogenisation that can be located in industrial nations that exercise political, economic and cultural influence.

Plan of the book

This book continues with the methodological context for the analysis of the empirical data in Chapter 1. The chapter describes how a personal interest in Russian literature evolved into a large-scale research project inside Russia's prisons. The chapter describes how ethnographic techniques produced intimate research experiences that created the opportunity to reflect on gender practices and the importance of advanced knowledge of language and culture when conducting international prison research. In this book, what determines the 'reality' of what prison is like in Russia (and indeed, what determines the contours of this book) are the voices of prisoners, prison personnel and senior officials. Given the very abstract and supplanted official discourse that characterised penality in twentieth-century Russia, it would be unwise to base this prison study on other types of 'reality' (reports and penal documentation).

Chapter 2 sets the stage for a discussion of prison labour in post-Soviet Russia by 'making connections' between the historical literature on prison labour in Russia, the sociological literature on prisons and the contemporary context. Broadly speaking, I discuss prison labour as a penal sanction with its own distinctive characteristics: an identity that is mediated by prevailing political, economic and cultural conditions. The first part of the chapter describes the history of Soviet prison labour before considering Marxian theories on the role of prison labour in the establishment of political economies. This part of the chapter includes an analysis of the complex linkages between prison labour, punishment and the structure of Soviet political ideology. There is a discussion of how the utilisation of prison labour for developing burgeoning political economies raises questions of prisoner exploitation. I continue with this point in the second part, where I offer a criminological account of current political and economic issues in the use of prison labour in contemporary international prison systems. This part also includes an analysis of the current movement to contract out services in respect of the international rules designed to protect prisoners. It introduces the relevant international and European legislation which Russia has subscribed to since joining the Council of Europe in 1996.

This book, as the title shows, is principally concerned with developments in *penal punishment*, the *penal economy* and in *penal politics* in Russia and how each exists in the reform process. Indeed, as Malia (1999) and Olienik (2003) separately argue, one of Russia's mysteries lies in how the overly powerful political and economic structures created the penal miasma. Chapters 3 and 4 are mainly descriptive, gradually building up the evidence on which the subsequent analysis chapters are based. These two chapters deal with changes in punishment and changes in economic practices in Russia. In Chapter 3, each region visited is taken in turn to allow for effective and systematic comparison. The findings on the type of prison labour, its organisation, the methods employed, perceptions from staff and prisoners on prison labour, levels of outputs, the percentage of prisoners who are working, alternatives to work and interviews with those involved in providing additional forms of treatment, are presented. Particular attention is paid to how the decentralisation of the Soviet prison system has impacted on penal ideology whereby the system has evolved from a centralised single-concept penal theory into what I characterise as the 'new penal identities' that are differentiated and where direct political patronage varies. Chapter 4 presents additional findings on the use of prison labour at the sites visited and is supported by further findings gathered from a third prison region in Kemerovo, eastern Siberia, that I visited in June 2003. Although ostensibly prisons are expected to reform as well as punish, prisoners now have to work in order to live and not for the sake of the economy. Indeed, the fact that they have to do this and the manner in which they do this are precisely because of the collapse of the old economy. Central government funding, resources and support are no longer guaranteed and so it is left to the regions themselves to provide for, and sustain, the prison system. Additional resources are provided through a system of barter. This chapter compares the array of barter arrangements in the prisons visited.

Analysis of the findings forms the basis of Chapters 5, 6 and 7 and the aim is to carry the debate beyond Russia and into a discussion of how penal systems are governed in societies in transition. Chapter 5 focuses on explaining the *penal ideological shifts* in punishment and offers a conceptualisation of the path of development of penality in contemporary Russia. Utilising the Russian prison system as a case study of a social system facing an 'identity crisis', I argue that, following the collapse of the USSR, the Russian prison system has evolved over three separate periods that draw on resources and influences from marketisation, religious doctrine, socialism and the state. Thus, the penal colonies are forging links with the local geographical and cultural spaces. I use a theoretical vocabulary that I characterise as 'occasions of penal identification'. Utilising this framework I contend that in the immediate wake of the monumental collapse of the USSR, the prison system functioned according to an unknown discourse (the first occasion). Subsequently, Russian prisons functioned through the hybridisation of familiar penal discourses (re-embedding local narratives with Western constructions) which rendered policies and practices as 'legitimate' (the second occasion). I introduce the third occasion and I argue that the management of prison systems according to a universal application of human rights might be illustrative of a movement towards a globalised (Westernised) penal ideology. This is explored further in Chapters 7 and 8.

Chapter 6 draws attention to the changes in the *economy of imprisonment* through an analysis of the findings presented in Chapter 4. The extent to which the *necessity* of at least some prisoners having to work to survive might breach international covenants banning the exploitation of prisoners is discussed. Current uses of barter might mean that the prison colonies have become self-sufficient economies and this might lead to the maintenance of a very high prison population. Such a priority might be given to this that it subordinates other aims (treatment). However, the utilisation of barter may mean that prisoners are more likely to be engaged in work like that which they might do on release and so prison labour is arguably rehabilitative. This challenges the tacit assumption in international legislation that prisoners are exploited where they are forced to work. This development raises the question that there are imperialistic overtones in the international movement to harmonise penal systems.

This leads us to Chapter 7. In this chapter and in the concluding chapter that follows, I draw attention to the *politics of penality* in societies in transition. Chapter 7 intends to show how penality in societies in transition is increasingly hard to follow. First, because nation-states become embroiled in attempts to modernise and civilise their criminal justice systems and there might be some transferral of innovations in penal administration from other jurisdictions. Secondly, as the chapter shows, the possible reasons why particular theorisations about imprisonment have emerged in response to transformations in policy convergence are mediated by global political trends. Thirdly, penal systems in societies in transition might produce their own penal knowledge, but how is that knowledge disseminated and is there conflict with imported penal forms and norms?

In Chapter 8 I conclude the book by considering a new parameter within criminology: the notion of failed penal societies. I consider the features of failed penal societies and the consequences of these features not only for penal reform but also for developments in mainstreaming discourses on penal punishment. Within the limits of scale, comparisons are drawn with other jurisdictions where criminal justice transformations are taking place. The chapter draws together the major themes identified in the introductory chapter and offers personal reflections on living in, and surviving, Russian prisons.

Translation and transliteration from Russian into English

The transliteration from Russian into English uses the Library of Congress System (Modified). All quotations from the primary research are translated verbatim, including slang words, from Russian into English.

Notes

1   Oleinik's (2003) book, *Organized Crime, Prison and Post-Soviet Societies*, was written and published originally in French and then in English.
2   Source: General Alexander Illych Zubkov who was the Assistant Deputy Minister of the Russian prison system in 1999. He was responding to a question raised by a campaigner from the Moscow Centre for Prison Reform during a press conference to mark the opening of an exhibition on tuberculosis in Russian prisons at the Russian Parliament in Moscow, April 1999, that I attended.
3   In some parts of the book I refer to prison *labour* and in other parts prison *work*. It should be noted that both terms refer to the same activity and the terms are used interchangeably based on how analysts describe the system in the literature and in the interviews presented in the data chapters.
4   Gulag is an acronym for *Glavnoie Upravlenie Lagerie* (the Central Administration for Camps).
5   In conversation in Moscow, May 2003.
6   I have tried for years to obtain reliable figures on the prison population rate per 100,000 of the population for the Soviet period (see also Conquest 1960, 1986, 1990; Tucker 1992; Applebaum 2003). Nowadays, to coincide with European norms, the rate is calculated according to this format.

Chapter 1

Context of research and methodology

This chapter investigates the process of gathering new knowledge on Russia's penal system and begins by answering the question that I am asked most often: why *Russian* prisons? This is followed by a description of the prison system and the methodology (initial research plan and pilot trip). The chapter concludes by describing the unusual main fieldwork: an intense five-month period of close-up observation that included living in the natural setting of four prison colonies for men, and how the data were analysed.

Initial research interest

The genesis of this book was the realisation after reading Russian novels and poems that many Russian writers such as Mandelshtam and Solzhenitsyn had been imprisoned. I pursued my interest in Russian literature more formally while studying for an MA in criminology where I conducted a historical critique of the Gulag. I then went on to study Russian in an intensive language course before embarking on doctoral research in 1997. I found that while the majority of work conducted in Russian prisons is human rights consultancy, which is intended to improve conditions, reduce numbers and implement minimum standards, it was increasingly the case that throughout the 1990s Western social science was missing out on matters of crucial cultural importance in understanding post-Soviet prisons. Thus, conversing in Russian not only allowed me to dispense with interpreters and collect data but it also permitted a more direct critique (even if questions remained unanswered, this could be interpreted within a broader cultural milieu).

The structure of the Russian prison system

It is not within the exigencies of this book to describe in detail the management structure, size and scope of Russia's penal system. I shall instead confine remarks to descriptions of the penal system as they relate to prison labour.

Russia and the US between them account for about one third of the world's prisoners (Walmsley 2000). Since the first records of the prison system were collected in the 1690s, there have been, and continues to be, conflicting figures on the actual size of the prison population due to the different types of establishment included in figures. The Russian Federation has increased its prison population by 36% over the decade since 1991, but the prison population in England and Wales and in the US far outstripped Russia's growth rate (45% and 61%, respectively) (King and Piacentini 2004). The growth of the prison population has slowed in the US and in England and Wales but it would appear that Russia has been more successful, first in restricting the rate of increases in incarceration in line with increases in crime and, secondly, by effecting a substantial reduction. Russia's penal system reached a peak in June 2000 to 1,091,973 (a rate of 750 per 100,000). By December 2000, amnesties led to a drop of 180,000 (*World Prison Brief* 2003). Amnesties tend to offer only short-term relief and the figure rose again until the beginning of 2002. Since that date, there has been a steady fall to 864,590 at the beginning of 2003 with a rate of 606 per 100,000. According to Kalinin (1995, 1998) this has been achieved partly through amnesties for women and young offenders and partly through legislative changes such as alternatives to custody. The reform of the pre-trial process has also reduced the numbers of prisoners held in remand prisons. It is beyond the scope of this book to tackle the problems of incarceration rates alone as an index of imprisonment (see Pease 1994 on factors that come to have influence over incarceration rates). But some comparisons in Table 1.1 on changes in prison population rates in Russia compared with the US and England and Wales prompt further inquiry. At the time of writing (October 2003) the prison population was 874,300 (611), held in 1,010 establishments of various category type that include remand prisons (*World Prison Brief* 2003). Based on its official capacity, the prison system is running at 96% occupancy level. There are seven types of penal establishment in Russia spread over 69 regions (*oblast*) outlined in Table 1.2.

Table 1.1 Total recorded crime and rates of change[1]

Year	Russia[2]	England and Wales[3]	US[4]
1991	2,173,074	5,276,173	14,872,883
1992	2,760,652	5,591,717	14,438,191
1997	2,397,311	4,545,337	13,194,571
2000	2,952,367	4,535,988	11,608,070
2001	2,968,300	4,846,940	11,849,006
% change 91–01	+37	–8	–20
% change 97–01	+24	+6	–10
% change 00–01	+1	+6	+2

Notes

1 Reprinted from King and Piacentini (2004).

2 Source: Barclay and Tavares (2003: Table 1).

3 Since 1994, criminal statistics have been reported for financial years rather than calendar years. There have been major changes made to recording practices that were introduced in 1998. Consequently, the effect was to increase the number of crimes recorded. The statistics provided in this column have been recalculated for financial years and estimated on the basis of recording procedures in use up until 31 March 1998. The statistics use a formula provided by the Home Office Research and Statistics Directorate.

4 Excludes arson and drugs offences. Source: Barclay and Tavares (2003).

Prison establishments fall into four categories: correctional colonies (general, strict, special and settlement or village colony); educational colonies (sometimes referred to as juvenile colonies for those under 18 years of age); prisons (including remand); and medical correction institutions. Most persons sentenced to custody will serve their sentence in a 'penal colony'. Table 1.3 provides the most recent data on the breakdown of establishments in Russia. The Federal Ministry of Justice administers all places of confinement. The prison service in Russia is known in English as 'The central prison authority for the execution of punishment' (in Russian, *Glavnoie Upravlenie Ispolnitelnie Nakazannie*, commonly referred to as GUIN). All types of colonies are numbered and there may be two types of regime in one region – for example, a general regime number 3 and a general number 4 in one region.[1] For all the types of penal establishment there are male regimes. Women are held in only two types of colony: those with a general regime for first offenders and those with a strict regime for particularly dangerous recidivists. A small number of women are housed in cellular prisons. Where a woman's

Table 1.2 Breakdown of all types of prison establishments in Russia

Penal establishments	Description
Izolator (SIZO)	Remand prisons for all persons awaiting trial
General regime colonies	For first-time offenders who have committed minor crimes, or more serious crimes carrying penalties of up to three years' deprivation of liberty
Strict regime colonies	For recidivists, whatever the nature of their crime, and those prisoners whose death sentence has been commuted into sentence of imprisonment
Special regime colonies	For very dangerous offenders
Educational labour colonies	Colonies for children up to the age of 19
Prisons (*tyrma*)	Cellular prisons for very dangerous offenders. Only 1% of the prison population are held in these prisons. They are considered the most severe sanction the system has to offer. Prisoners can be sent to these prisons as a punishment for misbehaviour
Colony settlements	Open prisons. Prisoners are sent to these establishments having served at least one third of their sentence in either general or strict regimes

Table 1.3 Breakdown of the number of establishments in Russia by type[1]

Total prison establishments	1,010
Colonies	749 (includes colonies for women)
Colonies for women	18–19 (11 have children's units)
Children's colonies	64
Prisons	7
SIZO	190

Note
1 Source: *World Prison Brief*, accessed October 2003.

colony is overcrowded, a juvenile colony may be instructed to provide custody (this measue includes prisoners up to 25 years of age). Since there are so few colonies for women it is sometimes the case that a woman can be sent to a prison colony 2,000 km from her home. Children may not be sentenced to more than ten years' imprisonment.

Initial research plan

The initial plans included a broad comparative hypothesis of Stalin's Gulag by applying a theoretical framework derived from the work of Rusche and Kirchheimer and Foucault. I aspired to a study which would embrace the full sweep of Soviet history and trace the detailed ramifications of the Gulag into many aspects of Soviet, especially Stalinist, society. The methodology was heavily dependent on the archives and material which I hoped, but could not be sure, would be there. Gradually a series of alternative strategies began to emerge which would retain elements of these concerns – foremost was the problem of forced labour – but set them in a context of a post-*perestroika* Russian Federation struggling with its past as it acknowledges the force of international treaties, covenants, opinions and trends. There was no guarantee about what kinds of research methods would be employed. Consequently, while it was not possible to prepare for everything, there was a sense that it was necessary to be prepared for anything by being flexible and opportunistic to get the information from whatever source about the questions in mind (Hobbs and May 1993). I made an initial visit to Moscow in 1998 to conduct a pilot trip at the former Ministry of the Interior Training School at Ryazan (a prison service military barracks that has now been restyled as the Ryazan Institute of Law and Economics). Ryazan was chosen because my PhD supervisors had conducted some previous prison research there.

Pilot trip

The pilot trip involved living in the barracks of the Ryazan institute for six weeks. The trip offered the opportunity of practising my Russian in a supportive environment, while I made myself useful in helping out with the teaching of English.

As Jewkes (2003) also found from her pilot work in prisons in England, the pilot trip yielded a range of emotions regarding what I had discovered and explored. My main concerns were that I would face intellectual struggles in my attempts to understand how Russia's penal system has emerged in the present and whether I could develop a sufficient working relationship with the Russians. During the pilot trip a plan to spend time in all the colonies (seven in total) in the Ryazan region near Moscow was discussed. This would enable a comparison between different types of regimes including their relationship to regional head-quarters. This would have been a microcosm of how the region operated and arguably a snapshot of the system as a whole, although it would have been subject to questions of representativeness.

Although I was not permitted any interviews during a visit to a penal colony for girls, the general observations of Russian culture did allow for a degree of interpretation of how to manage the research project. My experience of Russian bureaucracy, for example, mirrored the experiences of Kneen (2000) who in an authoritative study on Russian corruption, found the bureaucratic culture perplexing, unnecessary and regulatory. This has been explained as a consequence of the ideological constraints of the Soviet regime not yet being replaced by compensatory institutional and legal disciplines. I did not anticipate the unnecessary bureaucracy where I was expected to pass over notes for 'inspection' and where the organisation of basic research such as photocopying took weeks to organise. I developed a viewpoint that the overly bureaucratic system of obtaining materials meant that the exciting prospect of reading Russian language, penological material would have to be reduced. With the passing of time I judged that it would be the voices of prisoners and staff that would shape the direction of the research.

I found the pilot trip personally demanding with lots of hanging around, endless broken promises and also dealing with comments (some derogatory, others paternalistic) about my age, gender and grasp of Russian. There were times when I felt like abandoning the project and returning home particularly as I was locked away in the barracks, hidden from any 'unwanted male attention'. A small cohort of senior male military personnel ensured that if a male cadet even approached me, he was warned away and reprimanded. Instead I would receive visits, often at late hours, from officers in charge of my safety. I judged the dynamic very quickly: there was an element of sexual politics at play where officials would argue, with a warped sense of chivalry, that 'my protection' was paramount. Unlike other research settings, I felt disempowered and stuck at the bottom of a hierarchy where my 'otherness' as a woman and as a Westerner was continually reinforced (see Rawlinson 1997; Jewkes 2003). These feelings were confirmed just about everywhere I went. I left the barracks on only two occasions and spent most weekends in the library or chatting to the female caretaker (*xozeiaka*). As the feelings of being isolated and controlled grew, I became more downcast about the main project.

Before returning back to the UK, it was possible to raise questions and concerns over the feasibility of the proposed Ryazan study with my Russian supervisor. Admittedly, I did not want to return to Ryazan. However, he argued vociferously that the research proposal was feasible within the timescale. He convinced me that I might become more comfortable with Ryazan if I could come to terms with the culture there. Also, Ryazan was close to Moscow should I need to leave Russia urgently. The research proposal of seven colonies seemed relatively simple and straightforward to implement. Colleagues at GUIN were consulted and the proposal was approved in principle. Although I endeavoured to place all the experiences and discoveries as symptoms of the turbulent political culture, I was concerned that as this was a society where the sense of 'normal' changes daily, then the research could be at best remodified and, at worst, collapse.

A turbulent society

Disorder has blighted much of Russia's contemporary development. In the new democratic Russia, individual liberties were to be guaranteed under a new constitution and far-reaching economic reforms that would lead to a market economy were promised by the new president Boris Yeltsin. By 1993, this vision had shattered. The fledging democratic institutions crippled by political and institutional deadlock failed to address the country's problems. Political disillusionment soon seeped in and was compounded by mounting economic hardships – perhaps the major failure of the post-Soviet Yeltsin government – and by growing hostility to economic reforms and privatisation coupled with corruption and rising crime. In the economy, just as in political life, many of the problems encountered after the collapse of Soviet communism (mounting inflation; destitution of pensioners and students; corruption from 'legitimate' wealthy business people and the collapse of public health) were part of the legacy of the Soviet regime. But to make matters worse, foreign specialists at the International Monetary Fund (hereafter IMF) had little or no feel for the economic and social scene in Russia and sought to implement plans that worked in countries like Poland which could not work in Russia (Dallin and Lapidus 1995). The opposite difficulty in Russia was that there were very few good economists with a sound grasp of non-socialist economics. Towards the end of the Yeltsin leadership (in the months following the pilot trip), the economy was so badly damaged that in August 1998, it collapsed following a default on an IMF loan of billions of dollars.

Twelve months had passed between the pilot trip and the main study and the impact of the political and economic crisis on the public institutions was immense. Aside from the worsening economic hardships of that period, Russia resumed its military involvement in Chechnya and NATO began its bombing campaign against Serbia in occupied Kosovo (a campaign that Russia did not support). Diplomatic tensions between the West and Russia escalated leading to a temporary resurgence of Cold War secrecy. When I returned to Russia in 1999, I found that the official who had granted access to the prisons in 1998 had moved to another department and I was left to renegotiate access on my own with officials whom my Russian supervisor knew, but who were not known to my British supervisor. Routine negotiations for the main study in Moscow in 1999 evolved into mini-interrogations over my views on the NATO campaign. The very real feeling was that access to the prison establishments was contingent on my support for the Serbian government. There was heightened awareness of Chechen terrorists following the bombing of apartment blocks in Moscow in 1998 and on-the-spot passport checks, where to look 'European' and 'dark' meant being stopped for looking Chechen. When my passport was examined, being British meant being Western and therefore 'anti-Slavic'. I was accused of being 'another bloody anti-Serbian Westerner' and during access negotiations and during the fieldwork, with a mixture of disdain and humour, staff would joke about not giving an interview to the 'British/Chechen spy'.

Following these developments I was offered a different research locale: a strict and general regime for men in Smolensk in Western Russia, near Belarus, and a strict and general regime for men in Omsk, Siberia. Given the great geographical distances between the two regions (Smolensk and Omsk are 3,000 km apart), it was felt that it would be better to live in the natural setting of each establishment for two weeks at a time. The remainder of the time would be spent in Moscow, briefing officials, interviewing penal reformers and gathering literature from the Central Lenin Library. The new design was radically different from my initial plan of research study and had the potential of adding an interesting dimension in that it provided the prospect for pursuing historical questions on prison labour in Siberia, as well as an analysis on how the current climate of decentralisation is impacting on regional prison management. The new design had none of the carefully constructed support structures in Ryazan: the Russian PhD supervisor was far away in Moscow and the contacts in Ryazan, both professional and social, were to no avail. I was instructed to make a decision within two hours during which time I contacted my PhD supervisor in the UK and we envisaged all possible outcomes. I had my supervisors' support, should I return home, though there would be disappointment that the careful preparation (particularly learning Russian) had been in vain. If I accepted the new research design and stayed in Russia, I would have to organise all the fieldwork as I went along, I would have to travel to Siberia alone and I would have to live in male prisons.

In the end I chose to stay. Moscow was unsafe for Westerners and, moreover, I had the guarantee of GUIN's support. I did, however, feel unhappy that it was my strength of character that was being put to the test rather than concerns over my safety.[2] I quickly came to accept that my status as a Western criminologist, a woman who was relatively young at the time and who spoke Russian, would provoke bemusement and possibly resentment. On an intellectual level the prospect of visiting Siberian penal colonies was tantalising. Russian forced labour is often associated with the steppes of Siberia so to have the opportunity to talk to people closely connected to that environment would help in understanding how prison staff and prisoners view prison labour. During the hastily reconvened meeting I was instructed to return to my accommodation in Moscow, pack my bags and book a flight to leave for Omsk in Siberia within 48 hours.

The strategy for the main phase of the research

I was interested in investigating not only the modes of penality but also the ideas that come to underpin penal punishment, now that it is no longer governed by a dominant ideology, as historically was the case. I aimed to locate the experiences and descriptions of Russian prisons within a culture where identities were shifting and changing continually. Consequently, I took the lead from methodologies that focus on the identity of the researcher and the researched. Two approaches to social research were useful for managing the fieldwork, interpreting the findings and surviving the fieldwork that could not otherwise have been found from criminological methodologies in Western locales. Geertz's (1975) social anthropological approach was useful in locating and interpreting penal practices within a cultural context. Deveraux and Hoddinott's (1992) text on conducting professional research in developing countries provided a reliable approach for participating in fieldwork during exceptionally turbulent periods. In drawing from the cultural anthropological literature, I found that I was able to overcome the ethnocentricity that has become a feature of Western prison research (Metcalf 2000; Wacquant 2002).

Western portraits of prison life

What grabs you immediately about published prison research is that most of it is premised on Western research experiences. The majority of prison research in the UK focuses on developing a social analysis of the allocation and administration of imprisonment. The methodologies are based on being in the field: semi-structured interviews with a sample number of prisoners and staff; observational research; surveys and one-to-one desk interviews.

Accounts of research pitfalls discuss the nature of the access granted, negotiating research and wider political tensions that may arise following changes in penal policy (see Ramwell 1993; King and Wincup 2000). The post-research testimony typically aims to provide a reflective account of the often-daunting business of prison research. Through these accounts we learn not only about the effects and effectiveness of various methodologies, but also the element of mystique in investigating the hidden world of the prison, particularly when it comes to the researcher's identity as the 'outsider', is revealed. Establishing a common identity between the researched and the researcher is seen as essential for rapport building to 'suspend moral judgements' (Jewkes 2003: 78) and to achieve social access (getting on after getting in); a particularly difficult task as it involves engendering co-operation amid restrictions while breaking down barriers to achieve fluent qualitative and quantitative data. The peculiar dynamic of the prison space as divided between 'prisoner' and 'guard' produces conflicting emotions: being seen as odd, as a spy or without position or purpose (see Sparks *et al.* 1996; Jewkes 2003), or feeling that one must take sides and this is made considerably harder for the researcher as he or she navigates a setting that operates in complex webs of interdependence between staff and prisoners. Problems of identity also extend to gender, the consensus being that it is harder for women to engage with the research field even where the research and the researched are the same sex (see Liebling 1992; Jewkes 2003; Carlen 1998, 2004).

But what about prison research in settings where common identities are reduced even further beyond gender and sociodemographic status? It quickly became apparent to me through comparing my field research experience with those elsewhere that the problems, pitfalls and experiences I faced were not *Russian-prison-specific* but were, rather, *Russian-culture-specific*. This brought me to a crucial question: are the competencies and skills that are recognised as practical guides in Western field research in prisons useful and, indeed, relevant in non-Western research settings? It is impossible to go native in any prison research setting, but in conducting prison research in one's 'backyard' (so to speak) it is possible to identify with culture, language, history and contemporary development. The feeling of being an outsider is heightened and the demands are greater for researchers who operate outside familiar cultural spheres. Further difficulties may arise where the unfamiliar culture has been generally under-researched and under-theorised from within the culture (Fitzpatrick and Viola 1990).[3] Consequently, to function with at least a modicum of success in the 'alien' culture, the researcher devises roles, identities and perspectives to gain data but also, in some instances, to survive (see Kommer 1993 and Rahikainen 1995 for comparisons with the Scandinavian countries).

Related is geographical distance from home. The prison, as an unknown and unfelt social institution where social relationships and prison management are patterned to ensure that individuals behave in certain ways can generate an emotional response in the researcher. Yet these effects can be minimised when the researcher leaves the field and returns home to a culture where the dynamics of penal politics operate within relatively stable and familiar environs. Everyday routines like listening to the radio, telephoning a friend or watching your favourite soap opera – re-emerging from the prison into familiar patterns of behaviour – can minimise the feelings of isolation and distance.

How the researcher constructs a formula for observing events, engaging with subjects and gathering data is also mediated by wider political events. While it is often said that changes in imprisonment follow changes in the wider culture (Morgan 1997, 2000), rarely is it the case that prison researchers operate in societies where daily life is disrupted (destroyed even) by political scandal and danger and where to be blind to wider political events can place the researcher in danger. I was well advised to develop a checklist approach and 'keep an eye on everything'. Cultural accounts of Russia often talk about lost geographies and shifts in identifying with culture (Kneen 2000), so the checklist became a reliable way of monitoring events and balancing fresh observations with previous recordings.

Prison research in non-Western cultures offers new challenges to what Wacquant (2002) has referred to as the parochialism of Americanised prison research. For example, researchers must prepare for changes in health and diet, master bureaucracy and politics while conversing in a new language (although even when conversing in one's own language, problems can occur in the use of language), and in some cases radically alter their lifestyle. I found that Western criminological research experiences expose a taken-for-grantedness in the process of 'doing research' that arises because there is a greater level of stability in Western locations (economies are successful, politics is stable and material affluence is unparalleled). Consequently, the criminological conditions are considered within coherent, unwavering and reliable cultural settings. The formal order of Western cultures may lead to a more systemic understanding of social institutions and social behaviour, but this formality can lead to the cultural aspects of criminological findings being played down. For example, the disruption of Russian culture since 1991 where faded symbols of bygone eras appear alongside Western images revealed the tension between past norms and the future state of things. This became an ever-complex world to negotiate because the main dilemma I faced was to decipher whether events were 'real' and therefore 'true' or whether they were a short-term artefact of transience. Indeed, the confused imagery came to throw up transient penal imagery (see also Ragin 1994). It was necessary, in the end, to take a plunge into that cultural chaos and embrace these opposing emblems of everyday life in order to construct a picture that served me well in the field.

A cultural anthropological approach to prison research

A cultural anthropological approach is a way of interpreting a social context by making a break with the mode of life that is familiar or 'opaque'. It led me to reject distance and objectivity in favour of engaging with the cultural imagination of contemporary Russian society. According to Geertz (1975) 'thick descriptions' of the identity of different cultural subjects are essentially stories of how culture is constructed over space and time. I set about 'casting' an identity of Russian imprisonment by examining the formulae that Russians use to define their own culture. Even though Russia is viewed by Western measurements and what we know (or are told) consists of truths, half-truths, embellishments of the truth or reconstructions of the truth, these notions of reality found in propaganda symbols and ideology have given meaning to the lives of millions of citizens. Soviet culture had shaped lives with a degree of stability. Nowadays fear and uncertainty continue, hence, the distorted past ideologies from the Tsarist, Soviet and Western cultural realm.

The problem I faced was how to place my data on prison labour in a *reliable* context and then interpret the meaning. To ensure the reliability of evidence, it was necessary to leave behind, or at least minimise, personal realities from home and to be touched by the changes in the wider culture that is investigated. In other words, I lost contact with the familiar and embraced the instability in order to collect the 'facts'. The approach adopted was not so much about becoming an insider in this institutional setting, but rather to see the world from the perspective of the environment in which it is located and to be sensitive to changes in that world. This involved, in as far as was possible, getting into the mindset of Russians. For instance, there were many late-night discussions with prison staff about how professional and life experiences as prison officers related to changes in cultural sensibilities such as changes in the nature of domestic relationships, employment and education in Russia. I would then pursue questions on how wider cultural shifts might come to impact on prison officers' roles as 'punishers' as opposed to 'political correction officers' (the title of Soviet prison officers). It would later emerge that prison officers found it emotionally difficult to abandon their previous identity as 'defenders of the state ideology' (as one Soviet-trained prison officer put it). Even the breakdown of negotiations was placed within a cultural context of a society in turmoil. The resurgence of Cold War secrecy marked a return to a discourse already familiar where the state acted on behalf of the people. Prison officers often remarked about the need to protect the 'Russian/Slavic soul' and there were many bold defences of nationalist thinking, authoritarian leadership and tradition. Indeed, as Giddens (1994) notes the past became the 'glue' that held people and places together, and in Chapter 3, I describe how the turbulent society of the penal realm has reawakened traditions where custodians tell and retell the stories of the past to create new penal identities.

To sum up, a cultural anthropological approach allowed me to validate my findings as I systemised the respondents' descriptions of Russian culture (on language, education, health and lifestyle changes) into a suitable record of the direction that the prison system might be heading. Contained in the data on prison labour were 'thicker' descriptions on the contemporary social relations of Russia since prison labour was part of the state ideology. I was able to arm myself with these descriptions and test for their presence in the wider society before reclarification in the penal realm. Initially I did not see much mileage in comparing Western and non-Western norms as advocated by Russian social scientists such as Kurasawa (2002). Rather, as time passed, the formal and informal reflexive comparisons were between the prison world in Russia and the non-prison world in Russia. That is, the moments of reflexivity in this study were about making sense of prison life in Russia within the changing cultural conditions. My own cultural sensibilities were placed in the background. It was only when I returned to Russia in 2003 that I set about expanding the comparative dimension further by critiquing how changes in Russian prison labour reveal developments in global penal politics where the Russian penal system is taking on a more 'modern' form.

Main study

The main research sites were strict regime number 7 and general regime number 3 in Smolensk region and strict regime number 6 and general regime number 7 in Omsk region. The two Smolensk regimes were located in rural areas near (respectively) the villages Roslavel and Safonovo. The colonies were reached after driving 200 km over country roads and dirt tracks. The Omsk regimes were located around 10 km from Omsk. Smolensk city is the capital of the region and has a population of around 340,000 inhabitants. An important centre for commerce and trade with Europe, Smolensk is celebrated as the city that defended Russia against Napoleon's French army. Omsk is located on the southern edge of the western Siberian steppes just to the north of Kazakhstan and is the capital of the Omsk and Tyumen regions. The population sits at around 1.3 million. Aside from trade in forestry, agriculture and farming, Omsk had been the home of exiled political dissidents since the nineteenth century until 1991. Dostoevsky, who wrote of prison labour as: 'Punishing and securing society against encroachments on its tranquillity' (1860: 36), was exiled to Omsk's prison fortress and his novel *Memoirs from the House of the Dead* must count as one of the earliest Russian prison memoirs.

Methods and data analysis

I chose a qualitative study because I aimed to explore the social meanings and concepts shaping the contours of imprisonment in Russia, rather than to quantify the mechanisms of imprisonment and also because social research in Russian prisons is thin on the ground. Initial entry into a prison is a crucial moment so to step into that 'alien' culture and distribute questionnaires might have created hazards in terms of building social rapport. I triangulated the methods: semi-structured interviews with staff, prisoners and senior prison officials in each region and observational research. All the interviews in Russia were conducted in Russian. Most in Omsk and around half in Smolensk were tape-recorded. There was a set of key topics in mind and some prompts to structure and guide the interviews. The setting and structure of the interviews varied. In some cases it was possible to sit down face to face to probe all the issues in-depth and to tape-record the whole proceedings. On other occasions, an 'interview' might be conducted over two or three sessions, picking up from the last interview on the basis of the copious notes.

While the majority of interviews generated a good range of observations and data, the recorded interviews did not yield as much information as off-the-record conversations and this reflects the majority of prison research (see the Special Issue of the Journal Ethnography 3(4) (2000) featuring a range of rigorous theoretical and sociological accounts of prison research). I would often abandon my tape-recorder and notes and talk freely with respondents and I would return to my accommodation that night and record my impressions and findings based on memory recall. It was necessary, therefore, to recall gestures and body movements where even a pause seemed to generate meaning in some settings. For example, one prison officer answered 'yes' to every question that was asked while pointing to the ceiling during the entire interview. He later stated that he was afraid because he thought that he was under surveillance. Russians are generally reluctant to express uncomfortable truths in formal settings, having lived under the presence of a bugging system (whether this is real or imagined, the effect is still the same) for most of their lives. I was not certain if the system of surveillance extended to my own accommodation. I constantly checked and rechecked my recording equipment and laptop for any signs of tampering and I did sense that in one colony my room was searched once or twice. The responses were categorised sometimes into rather broad dichotomous variables and in others across a range of response categories. Where it was possible to clarify responses, where there were significant numbers, statistical tests were performed to explore whether there were significant differences between colonies and between regions on the nature of prison principles and practices.[4] Considering the unique nature of the research and the constraints, a sample of 224 prison staff and prisoners were interviewed formally and informally (31 prisoners and 193 staff) from all four colonies, as shown in Table 1.4. Appendix 1 provides details of the senior staff who were interviewed and who are *not* included in the total in Table 1.4.

Table 1.4 Breakdown of the number of respondents interviewed for the main study

Respondents interviewed[1]	Smolensk strict regime	Smolensk general regime	Omsk strict regime	Omsk general regime
Industrial staff	34	26	40	38
Psychology staff	9	21	3	3
Priests	7	7	4	1
Prisoners	7	7	8	9
Total	57	61	55	51

Note
1 Industrial staff include all staff involved in prison labour. In the four colonies visited, the industrial staff comprised industrialists, economists, marketing staff, work managers (*Master*), accountants, product developers, engineers, technologists, work trainers and liaison staff. The types of staff will vary from colony to colony. For example, in some regions where there is less prison labour, there may not be marketing staff or product developers. Psychology staff comprise psychologists, psychology assistants, psychiatrists and arts and crafts teachers.

Theoretical approach

I understood the cultural milieu of contemporary penal developments in Russia as an evolving process that I characterise as 'occasions of penal identification'. The operation of the prison system has progressed through three routes in response to different political and economic conditions. The first occasion is marked by uncertainty in the modes of penality and their points of origin. The second occasion involves custodians and inmates formulating rationales and practices in punishment because the penal system becomes dislodged from direct political patronage. With the onset of globalisation, the penal system enters a third phase whereby the indigenous penal sensibilities become subverted by universal mandates that aim to regulate and harmonise societies in transition and their prison system. Thus, I locate the third stage of substantive transformations in penality in Russia within the universal doctrine of human rights. By framing the changes in prison labour within these transitions, I was able to explore how ideas are diffused on the ground.

Russia's prison landscape and juggling researcher identity

The regimes I visited were different in their history, their location and penal practices. Both the Smolensk colonies were built around 1956 (although the exact date varies). This was the Kruschev era when the Soviet regime dismantled the Stalinist camps. The Smolensk regimes produced manufacturing products such as car parts and commercial vehicles. Each site had a large clothing workshop that employed prisoners to make prison officer uniforms, prisoners' garments, school clothes, hospital garments and industrial work clothes. Prison industries also included gas welding, aluminium sheets and coal mining. Lighter industries included clothing, kitchen goods, woodwork and office furniture which were confined to one massive warehouse. Interestingly, the strict regime number 7 was built on top of a large coal mineshaft. Hundreds of prisoners would be sent down the shaft to mine for coal which was then loaded on to large carriers that sat on tracks built deep into the mine. The carrier vehicles would then be transported out of the shaft and onto a train that sat on the track inside the colony. That track extended through the colony to the entrance gate.

The Omsk colonies were built from the remains of the Gulag, OmskLag, some time in the late 1940s. OmskLag held 20,000 prisoners. The establishments I visited were built in 1953 (strict regime number 6) and 1954 (general regime number 7), on rich arable farmlands because of the abundant natural resources. Prisoners worked in timber and agricultural industries making ploughs, tractors, household goods and combine harvesters. The layout of the colonies was large enough to accommodate production of small country cottages (*dacha*). During the Soviet period as many as 20 lorries would park at the entrance of each Omsk penal colony. The lorries would transport prisoners daily to the gigantic forests to the east and west of the Siberian steppe. Prisoners would load felled trees on to the lorries that transported the goods across Russia.

Nowadays, there is a range of different establishments in each region: nine establishments in Smolensk (three strict regimes for men; three general regimes for men; one strict regime for women; one children's colony; and one remand prison). There are 11 establishments in Omsk: one special regime; three strict regimes for men; two general regimes for men; two general regimes for women; two remand prisons; and one children's colony. In 1999, the prison population of the colonies visited was as follows: 1,560 prisoners (Smolensk strict regime); 1,550 prisoners (Smolensk general regime); 1,648 (Omsk strict regime); and 2,278 (Omsk general regime). In that year, Smolensk general regime number 3 was overcrowded with 400 extra prisoners.

Beyond the call of duty: living 'inside' prisons

For those unfamiliar with Russian prisons, the physical landscape they might conjure up would be of an image of squalor, overcrowding and poor sanitation. This vision is not entirely false. The physical appearance of Russian prison colonies offers a challenging image that has changed little both in the physical conditions and in structure since the dismantling of the Gulag camps in 1956. Appendix 3 provides a layout of a typical penal colony. The map reveals how unlike Western penal systems where the penal architecture is designed around security, risk, isolation and containment. The most striking feature of the physical structure of Russian penal colonies, is how they were designed around the needs of production. Russian prison colonies are divided into two zones: one industry and one accommodation. The post-Stalin planners retained elements of Soviet penal thinking: prisons were the archetype of Soviet identity (a place of work and rest) while demonstrating that the human rights abuses of the Stalin period were over. The physical appearance of the four colonies visited in the main study was similar.

Just from wandering through the colony, it becomes instantly clear that the prisons functioned way beyond crime control in the usual sense. Nowadays, the industrial zone serves as a hollow memory – a penal wasteland – of the past with peeling paint giving way to faded symbols from the Soviet period: 'Work to Live!', 'Mother Russia Needs Our Labour.' Rusted trains with broken windows sat on tracks that descended out from the Smolensk colonies; industrial warehouses were closed; and buildings were crumbling making many areas unsafe to walk. Rubbish, disused machinery and pieces of metal lay strewn in some places while other sectors were kept tidy. Most of the large industrial warehouses, particularly in Smolensk, lay empty. Where work was conducted, prisoners were found huddled together in smaller workshops making what one prisoner described as *melkii veschii* ('trivial goods': footballs, toys and tablecloths). Movement of prisoners between zones is generally restricted by up to four layers of barbed-wire fencing with one foot separating each layer. Surveillance technology was antiquated and sparse when compared with the regular innovations in CCTV and other big brother technologies used in American and Western European prisons. Russian authorities instead rely on many more staff, on heavily armed guards and guard dogs.

The living quarters were self-contained and were separated from the rest of the prison by two layers of barbed-wire fencing. An armed guard patrolled the living area. Prisoners reaching the end of their sentences were offered maintenance work in the staff quarters, although they were not permitted access to the living quarters. It was commonplace to meet prisoners in the stairwell where there was a degree of informality in talking to the prisoners as they worked. The accommodation was basic (bed, desk, toilet and, in one colony, a television), clean and safe. The food that was provided consisted of one cooked meal a day (typically, a fat-saturated soupy stew or fried potatoes as the fieldwork was conducted in winter). The presence of other staff living in the quarters made the whole experience of living in these isolated colonies bearable and also enjoyable as social gatherings and off-the-record comments yielded more interesting data and observations.

To say that the expectations of a novice researcher were certainly stretched to the limit would be an understatement. Indeed, the adjustment to Russian prison culture was a great personal challenge. My physical health deteriorated quickly because of a very poor diet. On some occasions the water supply in my accommodation was cut off because the colony could not afford to pay for water in that building. My gender, coupled with my age (I was 27 at the time), also led to remarks that prisons were an unsuitable research venue for a youngish woman. The passage from an 'outsider' to 'insider' (see Warren 1988), moreover, was made more difficult to navigate because of my status as a 'Westerner' which led many to assume that I was wealthy and powerful. Prisoners were receptive to the research once I had assured them I was not working on behalf of the Russian secret service while staff warmed to me once I had convinced them that I was not there on behalf of the Council of Europe.

It became clear that the range and type of information that I would be given was mediated by whether I would display an engagement with the wider culture. I therefore had to abandon all the types of formality that typically accompanies Western social science research and engage in a range of behaviour. This included attending many social gatherings where I was the guest of honour, socialising with relatives of prison officers and giving gifts that ranged from official university para-phernalia to books of Scottish poetry.[5] In fact, my interest in Russian poetry proved extremely useful for formal introductions with prisoners and staff, as did offering English lessons to prison officers which initially was a form of participant observation and later evolved into a *quid pro quo* for gaining access to prisoners. I was also expected to engage in the occasional bout of vodka drinking and sometimes sing traditional songs with staff after meetings (and some times during interviews!). The fact that I was someone who was genuinely interested in Russian culture and who could speak Russian, coupled with living inside the regimes, reduced the cultural differences which can arise when Westerners engage in non-Western criminal justice environments (Mawby 1999). There was an expectation from prison officers that I seek to understand 'their world' (both the prisonised world and the non-prison world). However, when one senior prison officer remarked, 'You're one of us now', I was assured that I had earned the respect and trust from a community that for nearly 100 years has been closed to the outside world.

These strategies were seen by myself as part and parcel of the approach that I was keen to adopt whereby I performed my Russian mindset to reflect an empathy and understanding of Russian culture. But my attempt to find a place in the prisons on some occasions created an imbalanced dynamic that when fused with sexual politics, led to feelings of being exploited. One interview with a prison governor was granted only after I recited Russian poetry in his office in front of senior personnel. I did not feel that I was exploiting his culture and instead felt exposed and vulnerable, recalling school days where there was the threat of chastisement and possibly public humiliation if I had not 'done my homework'. Despite these strange behaviours, the various identities I adopted did allow for personal survival. Most important was when I became quite ill and required medical attention (I fainted in one colony during an interview and I received a large tick bite on my scalp during a visit to a rural penal colony in the eastern Siberian region of Kemerovo in 2003), I was cared for by prison staff.[6]

Gender

Criminologists often consider whether the process of gathering data and knowledge on imprisonment is mediated by the gender of the researcher. Aside from feminist prison research, where the discussion centres on the construction of various identities as a counter to the predominantly male world of the prison, the discussion of gender remains underexplored. In order to complete prison research success-fully in Russia, I devised a research identity that projected knowledge and appreciation of Russian culture. Gender, consequently, became problematic.

Unlike Jewkes (2003), who was surprised over the level of access to confidential documents detailing the criminal and prisoner histories of the men she interviewed and to areas of the prison usually kept hidden, possibly on account of her gender, I found the opposite to be the case. While I had been guaranteed access to staff and to prisoners, there were no further guarantees over which staff and prisoners would come forward for interview. Certainly, I found that I was 'offered' interviews with a good number of senior prison officers who were unconnected to the research questions. I understood this in several lights. First, that – inexperienced in prison researchers visiting the colonies – the officers who were assigned to my research would introduce me to colleagues simply on the grounds of their status as prison personnel (I recall two very long and quite unnecessary interviews with the heads of food supplies and the prison doctor). Secondly, as tactics to divert me away from questions on prison labour and human rights which might be interpreted as injudicious considering Russia's penal history. Alternatively, it could have been that my status as a female 'foreigner' produced a high level of suspicion. I judged that while officers felt safe in the knowledge that I was a woman, they were distrustful of my status as a *Western* woman. Masculine values routinely dominate prisons but, in Russia, masculine values routinely dominate society and it is very rare for women to conduct prison research, let alone live in the prisons. The protective stance of male prison officers indicated to me that I would have to show some level of conformity to Russia's male world.

The process of conforming (to some degree) did involve what Rawlinson (2000) describes as 'bending gender' – that is, wearing cosmetics and different jewellery depending on whom I was inter-viewing and where I was conducting the interview, adapting social skills to either blend in or stand out. And I was certainly aware of problems arising from gender and sexuality that other female criminologists have experienced, particularly where in some instances, but not all the time, I was expected to amplify my femininity to reflect the patriarchal nature of

Russian society (see Smith and Wincup 2000). On one occasion, before the interview, I was told forcibly to return to my accommodation and wear cosmetics because 'the governor liked that'.

Initially I resisted colluding with such gender constructions that expect women to look their best and behave in a subservient and passive manner (for men). I always dressed casually and comfortably in clothes that I would wear every day. But, in the end, I reconciled the feelings of guilt that others too have expressed when faced with the realisation that utilising their gender may be advantageous to the research and, instead, I embraced the expectation to look youthful and attractive. My view was that while my maturity, deep interest in Russian culture and a fluency of Russian language might have got me into the prisons, I would have remained on the 'outside' if I had not abandoned my preconceptions about the process of social research (Jupp 1989). This would appear to support the experiences of other female prison researchers (see Liebling 1992). Yet, the difference is one of degree. During my research, the situations that involved becoming estranged from one's own culture did create problems in coping especially as the male world constantly had the upper hand both in the prisons and in the wider culture. Unlike the majority of prison researchers who conduct research within their national territory my retreat from prison life to home life while in Russia was remarkable only because of the similarities in the social norms in each setting. I could not escape from the gender constraints in my non-prison world where personal expectations are based less on gender and more on ability, which is not to assume that 'men's settings' do not exist beyond the prison realm in Western cultures (see Kauffman 1998). The point I wish to make is that my choices in how to behave and, importantly, exist outside the fieldwork setting were restricted. In common with other prison research conducted by women, particularly in male settings, any obstacles I faced to do with my gender were likely to reside so long as I resisted the culture investigated. I shaped my fieldwork into an experience where I accepted difficult male behaviour in all social environments (in hotels, in libraries and on the extremely rare occasions of visiting bars and restaurants).

The process of 'giving in' extended also to my relationship with women, who on the whole were suspicious of my status and motives. I judged that being a woman was more of a hindrance in the female relationships I attempted (albeit unsuccessfully) to build. There was very little, if any, common personal and experiential ground with the women I met who would often look on at me with disregard and jealousy that, through our different autobiographies my life had afforded me far greater social, intellectual and financial opportunities to live independently and 'free of men' (as one cynical female prison officer stated). As Lindlof (1995) notes, reduced common boundaries can often become the main focus of inquiry. It was undoubtedly the case that for the females I met in the prison realm, our cultural differences prompted many uncomfortable questions about my personal circumstances, in particular the issue of marriage and family. While the issue of sexual politics was rigorously addressed by the respondents and also by myself on a daily basis, it was my status and identity as a Westerner that influenced how I was perceived.

Westerners in non-Western prisons and becoming 'one of them'

The ethnographic approach was evaluated continually for its usefulness, especially where my desire to be accepted by all those involved (a specific feature of ethnographic research) resulted in becoming overly consumed with the proximate culture. I became burdened with the traumatic personal struggles of prison officers who would frequently disrupt interviews by bringing in other officers or bring relatives to the colonies to 'meet *Shotlandka'* (little Scottish woman).[7] As I became submerged under the personal struggles of the respondents, I engaged less with the research questions. The change in the direction of the interviews was exacerbated further by a tendency for prison officers to overperform during the interviews. I judged this as their way of asserting a moral and intellectual high ground in a world order in which Russia was no longer a superpower. They also needed their stories to be heard. I reflected at length about how I could improve the context, structure and content of the interviews in order that I got the best possible data while maintaining the trust of respondents. As the research progressed I interviewed fewer respondents and opted instead to sit in at meetings and observe social interactions. I would then politely remind staff of the objectives of the research. In addition, I reorganised interview locations away from the main administration buildings where staff moved freely, so as to avoid interruptions. Consequently, as time passed and I felt that I 'owned' enough data and observations to draw meaningful conclusions on post-Soviet imprisonment, I began to decline invitations by personnel to social gatherings.

In changing the format, however, I was in danger of 'becoming one of *them'* (someone from the 'outside' whose role is to catalogue terrible events and to audit and regulate international norms). Also, I could not be assured that, in restricting the range of participants, the respondents I chose were best placed to provide informed opinions about prison labour. Another concern was that the fieldwork would be transformed if

I imposed control and order. As much as this might have made the fieldwork easier to cope with, such control would reflect little of the chaotic cultural context of the research. A more formal arrangement to the fieldwork, perhaps a Western one, was emerging such that prudent localism derived from Western realities (order, stability, restraint and control) rather than a survey of what Elias (1984) defines as the cultural life-world of the researched areas began to surface.

In the end, I reverted back to the chaotic fieldwork arrangements because, ironically, I had plugged myself into the turbulent wider culture. Sharing in prison lives, presenting the findings at seminars in the prisons, favouring social behaviours that were unfamiliar, moving around relatively freely, not knowing who would be available for interviews from one day to the next, pitching in with making tea and coffee and joining the Russian Criminology Society all reflected my strong desire to gain acceptance by the prison establishment. It was not possible to understand fully the cultural sensibility of Russia's prison system. However, the approach I adopted not only sharpened observations about imprisonment in this complex transition phase but also enabled an appreciation of the penal culture that was welcoming me into its remit. While living in the establishments provided opportunities for both humorous and disturbing observations, the uniqueness of the fieldwork did raise problems in reflecting on the research experience in the UK.

Leaving the field and coming home

I judged the research design and methods to be effective on many levels. The design enabled mutual respect and trust to evolve; it produced a wide range of observations over lengthy periods and it allowed for a degree of personal survival. It enabled ongoing evaluation and interpretation that went beyond the research boundaries of the prison leading to a better appreciation of Russian society as it passes through a difficult transition period. As well as acquiring a range of data, the approach I adopted also allowed for progress in other areas – for example, reciprocating generosity; social involvement; good relations with bureaucrats; living with others; and positive professional relations with respondents. As with other ethnographic accounts, genuine interest in culture and language also minimised any feelings that I had exploited situations by feigning interest in culture in order to get data. I had resolved some methodological dilemmas and could attend to the process of developing an analytical framework for understanding prison labour.

There were many mixed emotions on returning to the UK. In particular, I underestimated getting away from the research. It was relatively easy to leave physically, but getting away emotionally and intellectually was more challenging due to the feelings of isolation, reduced networks of support and the great distances from home. The isolation of the fieldwork continued once I had returned home as, for colleagues, friends and family, there was very little that they could relate to in terms of Russian language and culture, let alone the prison world. Also, re-establishing my life necessitated returning to my reality where I resumed my Western identity and returned to more ordered patterns of living. Daily rituals became opportunities to compare with Russia and I often felt guilty over frivolous spending knowing that prison officers struggled on their $50-a-month salaries.

Putting the anxieties of returning home to one side, my observations of the dominance of Westernised worldviews on prison research paved the way for pursuing new knowledge on penal systems generally as they undergo transition in a global context. I felt certain that I had left the field having ensured that I had 'done my time' and 'left the site as clean as possible', to borrow two of King's nostrums for effective prison research (2000: 304–8). Put simply, I felt confident that I had engaged with Russian prison culture and survived.

A note on Kemerovo region

In 2003, I returned to Russia for four weeks to assess the operationalisation of the findings four years on from the original 1999 study. This time, I negotiated access directly with the Ministry of Justice in Moscow. In addition to returning to the two Omsk colonies, I also visited a remand prison and a strict regime for men in Omsk. I was also given the opportunity to visit prison colonies in Kemerovo region which is a further 1,000 km east of Omsk in eastern Siberia, tucked in front of the Altai Mountains which form a natural border with Mongolia. I visited five prison establishments in Kemerovo. I stayed in hotels and was picked up by a driver to visit the colonies. I conducted semi-structured interviews with regional prison officials and senior prison officers. In total, 32 interviews were conducted: 14 senior prison personnel in Kemerovo and 11 senior prison personnel in Omsk. I also interviewed the generals who manage each region, the Director of the Moscow Centre for Prison Reform, a Russian politician who campaigns for penal reform, a junior prisons minister and two officials who work at the Delegation of the European Commission in Moscow under the European Initiative for

Democracy and Human Rights. On this trip, prisoners were not interviewed.

The second trip was more successful than I had anticipated. In the 1999 study, I faced problems in obtaining interviews due to wider events. I met very little resistance second time round having obtained a stronger foothold in the system following the success of the main study. I was free to choose interviewees and I was less dependent on staff to facilitate the research. I did experience some obstacles arising from my status as a woman, but fewer problems from my status as a Westerner. This is because I found the prison system in 2003 to be more stable and this reflects the generally less turbulent economic and political conditions, and a more Westernised Russian society under the orthodox President, Vladimir Putin. There has been increased regulation of all spheres of Russian society (particularly the promotion of legitimate politics and greater accountability and centralisation). Above all, the 2003 trip was useful in helping me to feed the findings into a wider discussion of global penal politics. The book continues with a review and critique of the literature on prison labour. In Chapters 3 and 4, I present and analyse the findings from the 1999 and 2003 research trips.

Notes

1   Colonies are given numerical titles and are referred to as 'Colony number X'. Some establishments are given proper names such as Beli Lebed (The White Swan) in Perm, and Butirka in Moscow.

2   The official jokingly remarked 'So you want to see a Russian prison do you, let's see how you survive a prison in Siberia'.

3   Today's generation offers a fresh approach to academic scholarship that is considered by many Western academics to be less biased than Soviet accounts of their own history. More needs to be done to ensure that criminological research remains rigorous and testable, and it will be some time before there is a steady stream of critical empirical and theoretical research into Russian prisons.

4   See Appendix 2 for details of the research questions and how responses were analysed. The statistical tests used were the Kolmogorov–Smirnoff test and the chi-square test.

5   The alterations and improvisations that researchers make to their methodological approach are not limited to research in non-Western societies.

6   But I remained concerned over my health and also how, if at all, I would be cared for should I become ill. So, I carried my passport with me at all times

along with access letters from GUIN, my entry visa, documentation on immunisations, a small dictionary, some medication for headaches, some dried fruit in case I would not get the chance to eat that day, gifts for research participants and also photographs from home to show prison officers.

7   This was one of the more affectionate names that I was given.

Chapter 2

Prison labour, reform and economics: a review of the literature

In this chapter, I introduce readers to a penal system that most will be unfamiliar with by discussing the history of Russian prison labour and its contemporary context. I argue that although prison labour can be characterised as offering inmates an opportunity for reform (as a channel to pass time, learn skills and gain employment experience), evidence also shows that prison labour can be politically and economically exploitative where private contractors administer some prison functions. This paradox is revealed clearly in a diverse range of literature that will be brought together in this chapter. For example, in the better known historical literature (the theoretical tradition that extends from Rusche and Kircheimmer (1939)) and in the very recent work (Davis 1999; Parenti 1999; Wacquant 2002) prison labour is discussed as having some explanatory value where its reformative capacity aims to produce individuals adjusted to the norms of capitalist political economies. An examination of Soviet prison labour, or indeed Soviet imprisonment generally, could be framed quite comfortably within a discussion of this tension between reform and exploitation because prison labour in that country functioned in relation to existing social relations to develop the communist political economy. Reform was measured against political control and economic outputs. Before I critique the literature within this paradox, it is first necessary to outline the Soviet penal system. To do this, I will abandon an analytical framework in favour of a chronological description of Soviet penality for two reasons. First, as I have already mentioned, most readers will be unfamiliar with Soviet imprisonment. Secondly, the falsification of information during the USSR has made calculations of the nature and scope of the Soviet penal system a matter of guesswork so it is best to avoid a detailed analysis.

This chapter is divided into two parts. The first part discusses Soviet prison labour and employs the historical, theoretical literature to explain its emergence and continuance for nearly 100 years. In the second part, I discuss contemporary prison labour more generally and critique practices in light of international law.

Soviet prison labour and the greedy consumption of prisoners by the state

It is not within the exigencies of this book, nor is it its aim, to present a historical analysis of the entire Soviet prison system. The history of imprisonment in Russia is major both in scope and size and has been tackled most recently by Anne Applebaum (2003) in her important book: *GULAG: A History of the Soviet Camps*. Instead, my intention here is to offer a snapshot of how Soviet prisons encapsulated Melossi and Pavarini's notion of the prison as the factory, and much more besides. That is, throughout the USSR, the use of prison labour created a country within a country.

Subversion of penal ideology

The Russian author and former prison camp survivor, Alexander Solzhenitsyn, wrote that vast numbers of Soviet citizens were 'greedily consumed' by the state because labour was to contribute to the sustainability of the Soviet infrastructure (1986: 214). In making this comment, Solzhenitsyn has exposed how the state, and therefore its citizens, would benefit from the existence of a very high prison population. This observation may seem unremarkable in light of ever-increasing prison populations (particularly in the US) where the massive enterprise of prison building and associated sentencing policies that are often determined along the lines of race, class and risk, are inexorably linked to the fortunes of political parties. Even in the UK, anti-social behaviour orders have been critiqued as manufactured, leading to the criminalisation of visible young people (Waterhouse *et al.* 2004). The difference, however, is one of degree. In most jurisdictions while, on the one hand, there has been a generalised shift towards more punitive measures, there has also been a continued investment and experimentation in community-based initiatives. In the Soviet Union, the incongruity of Marxist/Leninist penal ideology did not permit alternative discourses to exist alongside the aggressive expansion of the prison system.

It would be a mistake to assume that in Russia forced prison labour was re-invented by the successive cohort of Marxist/Leninist dictators and leaders. This profound deprivation has been widespread since the birth of the prison and cannot be attributed to any one culture or society (Christianson 1998). In Tsarist, pre-Soviet Russia, forced prison labour was a staple of the penal realm, where the prison day was organised around hard bed, hard labour and hard prayer (Bunyan 1967; Dugin 1990; Asanaliev 1993; Depov 1994; Detkov 1994; Adams 1996; Hughes 1998). In twentieth-century Russia, however, the creation of the vast penal empire first involved reinventing Marxist criminological theory; a process that took approximately 17 years from the Russian Revolution in 1917 to the establishment of the Gulag prison agency in 1934. Almost as soon as Lenin seized power in 1917, crime was reconceptualised as transitional social excess and later under Stalin as deviant behaviour, at war with communism. Stalin's view of crime was initially faithful to Marxist/Leninist theory: crime does not exist in sustained socialist societies (Medvedev 1971). Yet, this version came to be eclipsed by an even more extreme view that *all* crime was anti-Soviet and therefore sympathetic to capitalist ideology (Connor 1972). Subsequently, if hooliganism was punishable then it was because it was capitalist.

The principal aim of penal policy under Stalin was to control anti-Soviet elements by way of criminalising wreckers of the Soviet cause. There were many ways in which this was achieved but several relate to prison labour and its constructed links to the political economy. First, propaganda was utilised to control citizens through the relentless pursuit of agitators in need of political re-correction and to convey the message that 'enemies' were in all walks of life. Secondly, once society had submitted to the twin process of surveillance and propaganda, the Soviet machine could begin the process of recruiting its prisoner workforce. Finally, the individual body was reduced to a social and economic function, constituted as part of a 'multi-segmentary machine' (Foucault 1979: 164) which aimed to correct offenders politically into perfect citizens, loyal to the USSR.

Changes in the economy and the recruitment of prison workers

The corruption of criminal justice was part of a wider process of ring-fencing all the institutions and administrative departments of the USSR into small-scale reproductions of Soviet political theory. Under Stalin it was the economic role of imprisonment that was to reflect the most extreme application of the new justice models. Some background to these developments is necessary here. In 1925, Stalin abolished Lenin's New Economic Policy (NEP) because the industrialisation programme of the rural and manufacturing economies failed to materialise quickly enough. Stalin's replacement 'Five-Year Plans' aimed: 'To leave behind the age-old Russian backwardness' (Stalin cited in Tucker 1992: 92) through forced collectivisation and industrialisation. One solution was to introduce a series of resettlement programmes that offered tens of thousands of engineers, doctors and scientists attractive housing and job packages for relocating to less populated areas of the USSR in order to build up the economic infrastructure. As Tucker (1992) and Bacon (1994) separately note, the plans were at best ambitious, and at worst wholly unachievable and depended on a vast non-existent labour force. Thus, the stage was now set for the second phase in the creation of the penal system.

The Gulag: a penal empire; a country within a country

As a function of economic policy, imprisonment exploded in the USSR and cannot, therefore, be said to be determined by offending behaviour. The Gulag Prison Agency was created in 1934, as a solution to the problems the regime faced in proceeding with industrialisation by providing additional labour to meet the economic plans. The condition of the Soviet labour market affected the characteristics of imprisonment, such that the prison population increased where demand for work exceeded supply. The 1933 Penal Code enabled the widespread use of prison labour, first by forcing individuals who would not be convicted but who would be accused of posing a potential threat to the USSR to take up new jobs in new cities. Secondly, the legislation was used to arrest and send into exile the intelligentsia and those party members who were high on Stalin's target list. By 1940 the stability of the command economy and political structure was dependent on the vast prison workforce.

Incarceration had important policy effects for the Soviet regime. The Gulag Prison Agency was a prototype of the centralised management and organisation of labour in both prison and in non-prison life. The agency managed most prison camps known also as Gulags[1] and comprised several specialised agencies that were created to administer different types of industrial projects. Industries that included metallurgical industries, railway construction, road construction, timber and forestry work were developed by scores of prisoners as well as engineers, scientists, workers and managers and so on. The smaller Gulag administrations fulfilled many of the requirements that the government of a nation-state would have to make. Security, health care, education, provision of food, political indoctrination and surveillance – all these roles exercised by the Soviet government in national life had their Gulag equivalent in prison life. On the one hand, the prison encapsulated the Soviet dream of society as a: 'primal model for the reconstruction of the social body' (Foucault 1979: 169). On the other hand, the giant Gulag was an exaggerated microcosm of the bureaucracy and social control of the Soviet regime and reinforced a central position of the prison in relation to the labour market.

How many prisoners?

The precise number of prisoners held in Soviet concentration camps has become a matter of guesswork. Figures vary depending on inclinations for support or dislike for the Soviet Union (see Carter 1977) and also on sources (see Bunyan 1969; Bucholz *et al.* 1974). Otto-Pohl (1998), Amis (2002) and Applebaum (2003) separately note that the left indulged in Soviet communism while being obtuse in its denunciation of forced prison labour. Former victims tend to present higher figures. For the whole of the Stalin period (1926–52) it is claimed that 20 million citizens were imprisoned (Mora and Zwierniak cited in Bacon 1994). Lower estimates (between 4 and 9 million) have been gathered from methodologies based on the size of the Soviet economy (Jasny 1951); census figures (Wheatcroft 1985); mortality rates and arrests from the Soviet police (Rosefielde 1987); and also from historians who disliked the American role in the Cold War (Applebaum 2003). The figures do not reflect the enormous movement of people in and out of the Gulag camps (some left, some escaped or died, others were promoted to administrative duties while others joined the Red Army). Bacon (1992, 1994) and Applebaum (2003), in addition, have also found from recent excavation of the archives that the extreme variations in the prison population numbers are also down to the interpretation of the term 'forced labour'. The regime's commitment to utilising labour led to a massive expansion not only of the prison population but also of forced labour workers generally. Not every person condemned to forced labour served his or her custody in work camps run by the Gulag administration. Whether a person was sentenced to penal confinement or forced labour without incarceration depended on his or her perceived 'social danger' (that is, moving a bust of Stalin without permission could lead to a prison sentence), but this person was not a criminal in any normal sense of the word (Penal Work Codes 1926, 1933, 1977; Chao 1970).

There were also special colonies for prisoners of war and for special exiles (revolutionaries), and there were colonies for the rich peasants (*Kulaks*) who were exiled to forced labour colonies. Applebaum (2003) reaches a figure of 28.7 million forced labour workers in the USSR between 1926 and 1952 by including all categories of workers and of camps (penal and non-penal). I am interested in the numbers sent into custody. The answer is complicated because of the problematic classification system, but Bacon's figure of a total 12 million prisoners for the years 1934–47 is widely accepted as accurate because the figure is based on actual numbers imprisoned and not on numbers 'repressed'. The figure also takes into account the different types of camps (forced settlers were not classified as 'prisoners').

Prison labour and exclusion

Soviet propaganda promulgated the myth that prisoners were living and working under the self-image of Soviet society, the outcome of which would be rehabilitation and honour. The wall-newspapers of the camps and colonies showed Soviet dictators as quasi-religious leaders whose messages hung from giant banners across hundreds of acres of camp and whose words were broadcast through loud-speakers. Prisoners were expected to be able to recite Marxist/Leninist theory wherever they happened to be and at any time. Witness accounts expose the paradox between reform and exploitation where citizens were procured for the latter: 'During interrogation we were rigorously "assessed" about our loyalty to the Soviet regime. But when we got to the Gulag, the most important question on the Gulag registration card was trade or profession' (Solzhenitsyn 1986: 589).

The strong bonds between incarceration and the labour market certainly did lead to career employment for some prisoners, and imprisonment did not interrupt the transition to stable career employment for everyone. Since the Soviet regime was the sole employer and the primary labour market was the development of the national infrastructure, ex-prisoners could be ensured of some job continuity. But imprisonment had other punctuating effects that made entry into society a stigmatising experience. While it is now commonly accepted that imprisonment in the West can undermine the acquisition of skills and social capital leading to marginalisation, in the USSR, the barriers facing former prisoners were linked to their loyalty to the Soviet cause. Former camp survivors describe how prisoners were profaned in the eyes of Soviet society. Poor health, social exclusion, a fanatical obsession with former prisoners as enemies of the state, together with continued surveillance post-release, meant that personal and social rehabilitation was a struggle (Rossi 1989). The level and nature of exclusion of prisoners are surprising given the huge numbers moving in and out of the prison in the 1950s, 1960s and 1970s and it must have been the case that exclusion affected not only employment opportunities and resettlement but also it must have put to test the loyalty of former prisoners to the regime.[2] While there is some evidence of former prisoners restating their belief in the Soviet Union and the collective ideology it espoused (see Applebaum 2003: 465 for examples), few believed that they became more loyal to the Soviet cause as a result of forced labour and education: 'We started working as soon as we stepped off the trains, in the clothes that we were arrested in. Some were in nightclothes.'[3]

The end of the Gulag

The Gulag was disbanded in 1956 and millions of prisoners were released as part of the process of Kruschev's 'de-Stalinisation'. The integration of prison labour into the centralised command economy and the imprisonment of anti-Soviet criminals continued under successive leaders. Despite some distance between nominal aims and material practices (the efficiency of the camps continues to ignite debate) during Stalinism and after, the prison system remained an industrial monolith that reflected a body of knowledge that prisons conform to a centralised penal ideology or *penal identity*. Historians and former prisoners are universally agreed that production was *de facto* the main goal of the Soviet penal system masked by the thinly veiled goal of political re-correction. For the best part of a century prisons were presented as mechanisms that benefited the political economy, but there is little doubt that they also blurred the boundaries of civil society.

Where does the preceding discussion of Soviet prison labour leave us? At the very least, we can make tentative connections between Soviet prison labour and the theoretical work on imprisonment.

Theorising Soviet prison labour

That the USSR displaced any form of abstract, *illusory* notion that the individual is at the centre of the prison system should by now be apparent. The conditions of modernity have shaped modes of imprisonment in Russia and given rise to an identity that was constructed by synthesising subverted versions of ideology with economic conditions.

Changes to the consumption of capital; the articulation of state power through the penal realm; the need for harsh methods and productive practices; the swelling of the labour workforce; productive prison labour that was 'turned into' capital, were the causal forces that led to the swelling of imprisonment. Quite simply, prisons and prison labour functioned in response to the push towards industrialisation. In this respect, Rusche and Kirchheimer's thesis on how prisons were major cogs in burgeoning political economies has great explanatory power in the Russian context.

On the emergence of prison labour in Western Europe during the industrial period, Rusche and Kirchheimer posited the view that the social institution of the prison operated in relation to capitalism. To coincide with the growing global market of the nineteenth century that necessitated more labour than was available, legislation was introduced that targeted certain individuals viewed as docile and poorly trained to create a penal aesthetic, so to speak, that combined elements of old-fashioned work houses (comprising mainly of persons from the lower classes) with poor houses (targeting the lower classes). Vagrancy laws such as the Vagrancy Act 1530 and the New Poor Law Act 1834 targeted the recalcitrant classes and forced peasants into workhouses. Those writing in the Marxist tradition argue that social policies and legislation were designed to *turn* beggars and vagabonds into criminals because their lifestyle was contrary to the standards of propriety set by the powerful forces in society. So the poor got prison, which aimed at controlling deviant classes and converting the idle through forced labour into workers, imbued with a capitalist work ethic. Once incarcerated, prison labour adjusted to the needs of the economy. Generally speaking, in times of shortage – and therefore high value – of labour, punishments become more lenient and prisoners are put to more useful work because of demand. Whereas in times of excess – and therefore low value – of labour punishments become harsher and less constructive because the state is supplied with a 'free labour' force that it can put to useful work. It follows then that in times of labour shortage more prisoners are put to work and in times of labour abundance prisoners will work less. In order that prison labour become: 'integral to the whole social system' (Rusche and Kirchheimer 1939: 207) all aspects of the prisoners' personal life were integrated into the economy of the prison where they would 'surrender' reform to: 'every crisis in the market' (Rusche and Kirchheimer 1939: 151). Thus, prisoners were trained in how to work with an unconditional submission to authority so that they would submit willingly to their fate as a lower class. By making the regime of labour sufficiently unpleasant to deter the lowest social classes from committing crime and to construct penal policy around a discourse wherein convicted prisoners were less morally deserving than the least well-off persons who were enjoying freedom in society, inmates were not allowed to enjoy a lifestyle superior to those outside prisons and workhouses (see Rusche 1978; Melossi 1985).

How can we understand these developments in the West in a Soviet penal context? I estimate that the process and policies that led to the creation of forced labour across Western societies generally, first through legislation and later through economic policy, was a trend that was also emerging in state socialist societies. On a micro sociological level, crime predicaments took back-stage and forced labour was tolerated where it was utilised to advance nation-states and technologies. On a macro sociological level, the prison came to reflect class relations: one was capitalism, the other was communism and the prison was designed to produce not only labour products but also perfect proletarians (this was its reforming potential). Witness testimonies of former prison camp victims reveal this paradox between reform and exploitation vividly. The symbolic images of the political regime displayed the message that prisoners were the builders of Soviet communism who were no less heroic than soldiers, teachers or engineers. The path towards industrialisation in Russia did not, however, follow the route outlined by Rusche and Kirchheimer where they note that prisons and punishment are used less when economic conditions allow for non-carceral labour to be utilised. Even when prison labour was used less in the 1950s, 1960s and 1970s, the punitive mentality of the regime was limitless and clandestine trials and imprisonment of dissidents all continued.

Melossi and Pavarini's theory of prison labour is more integrative than Rusche and Kirchheimer's thesis in that they extend the analysis of the social relations of capitalism (labour, products and workers) into a thicker account of how imprisonment turns prisoners into *reformed* citizens, fit for capitalist society. It should by now be apparent that, once prison labour was woven into the power relations of Soviet communism, this gave rise to an imprisonment binge. A penal society was created where the boundaries between penal space and non-penal space were blurred especially with regard to the relationship between employer and employee. In the factory, contractual discipline is depended upon, whereas in the prison coerced discipline is imposed. The factory utilises the disciplined citizen, whereas the prison produces the disciplined citizen. Finally: 'for the worker the factory is like the prison' (loss of liberty and subordination); 'for the inmate, the prison is like the factory' (work and discipline) (Melossi and Pavarini 1981: 188). Melossi and Pavarini's thesis that prison becomes the ideal model of society is not limited to the West and its application in the context of Soviet penal ideology is certainly seductive.

Ideal models of prisons and prisoners as workers are also the central tenet of Foucault's thesis on prison labour which, it must be noted, occupies a very small part of his sprawling social history of imprisonment (see Foucault 1979: 239–48). While Melossi and Pavarini see prison labour as reflective of class relations, Foucault sees the principle that he identifies as being characteristic of modern imprisonment – of which prison labour and training are fundamental – as being social control. There is limited scope in considering a Foucauldian theory of prison labour in the context of Russia as, for Foucault, prison labour is part of a broader goal to transform bodies through time-keeping, rhythm, treatment, training, regulation and inspection so that nothing remains idle. The prisoner, argues Foucault, gives him or herself over to his or her own conscience. Prison propaganda in Russia, aimed not only at higher production figures but also at educating prisoners on the best examples of socialist life where isolation and individuality were offences punishable by death or increased sentences. Although there was a surveillance principle to imprisonment and the goal was to correct rather than to punish, the mechanisation and rationalisation of prison life as outlined by Foucault are not echoed in the historical material on Soviet imprisonment. Instead, witness testimonies reveal a system of chaos marked by shirking by staff, random increases in targets, breakdown of machinery, prisoners ignoring orders by staff and absconding regularly and poor management.

Where we can make links between Foucault's work on imprisonment with Soviet penality is in the ways that he traces the development of the prison as the central feature of how daily life, *modern life*, is organised. For Foucault, the disciplinary social models that are external to the prison come to 'penetrate' modern penal forms. In the USSR, economic and political models came to determine the path of penal development (the discipline came later). Hence, the Soviet system was not evolutionary in the classic Foucauldian sense. Rather, it was a two-way process with the penal system and the political and economic milieus becoming inextricably linked feeding off each other's own subverted goals and dreams.

The Soviet penal system was unique and cannot be readily compared with other penal systems of similar size or physical feature. The centralisation of penal ideology led to a neutralisation of alternative discourses of crime and punishment. So too is it the case that the Soviet prison system did have an extraordinary capacity for violence through the arbitrary use of criminal justice legislation, through the use of confinement as a 'technology of power' and through the climate of fear and later obedience that was perpetuated through surveillance policies that permeated all sections of society.

Soviet prisons, moreover, transcended any notion of imposing a panoptic order. Foucault shows us, as does Goffman (1961), that the prison has absolute control over itself and operates outside the exterior world. The interior prison world and the exterior world mediate and create spaces for norms to fill. Soviet prisons evolved as an extension of the exterior world; they offer the reader a lens through which it is possible to evaluate the organisation of Soviet life. The Soviet penal system was an extreme example of an overpopulated and over-powerful institution that came to be understood as a reduced reproduction of the wider society.

That the interior and exterior world met and merged suggests that the Russian prison system has been deprived of a portion of its modernity that was occurring in the prisons in Western Europe. For example, modernisation implies the process of transforming less developed or 'simple' societies where civic, industrial, scientific, artistic, domestic and political systems are separated and function with a degree of autonomy. The market is separated from other spheres, free of social, political and community influence. From what I have stated so far, there was symbiosis in the USSR between the state and the party such that political, economic and administrative functions were mixed and this was far removed from the political economies that were evolving in Western Europe and in the USA. Where systems are autonomous, individuals are able to live relatively autonomously in a private world freely chosen, giving rise to the rights of the individual. The social construction of Soviet society, however, excluded the separation of the public from the private. As Oleinik (2003: 14) notes, 'Totalitarian institutions, including the prison, also serve to illustrate the lack of differentiation in the extreme since private life there is annihilated'. Hence the order of prison life and the state are mutually dependent. Punishment, economy and politics are not, therefore, mutually exclusive categories. Oleinik adds: 'The State, deprived of a mechanism for mediation and social representation cannot allow the ordinary people to stray outside the reproduction of the prison model' (2003: 5).

Prison labour around the world

As the different theoretical traditions and the Soviet system revealed, prison labour is contradictory, complex and dynamic. It has functioned within various agendas: as an expression of state power; a statement about redemption or reform; a vehicle for social control; a set of symbols that display a cultural ethos; a mechanism that reaffirms ideology; and an economic subsystem that transforms labour into capital. Recently, there have been arguments that prison labour, properly managed, can be profitable and defray the costs of confinement.

Generally speaking, prison labour remains under-researched and under-theorised and occupies a section or, at best, a chapter in studies of imprisonment (although in 1999, van Zyl Smit and Dünkel edited an international collection on prison labour in light of international law). One reason why prison labour has escaped criminological attention could be attributed to its overall decline across Europe such that it has become more or less voluntary. Another reason has been presented by Simon (1999) who argues that prison labour is viewed as one of the success stories of modern imprisonment and it, therefore, does not grab headlines. But what kind of success? Is it the case that prison labour is successful when it is measured against reoffending (that is, the rehabilitation of offenders as a maximum benefit of prison labour is quantified partly in terms of whether work in prison can reduce reoffending), or is it a success when it operates within the context of penal confinement where the perspectives of staff, prisoners, work trainers and educators assist reform for those who 'live' in the prisons? Prison labour practices across countries reveal how societies come to import historical practices, cultural sensibilities, localised knowledge, global ideas and an absolute faith that 'work' minimises insecurity, creates mobility, promotes equality and improves standards of living (see Baumann and Bales (1991) on the reinvention of socialism in Nicaraguan prisons and Smartt (1996) on community punishments extending from nineteenth-century penal attitudes in Scandinavian countries). Although most contemporary prison systems aim to provide the foundations for what could widely be called social rehabilitation, recent studies raise questions about how the prevalence of punitive attitudes results in exploitative prison labour practices. This is a moral and political conundrum for prison systems everywhere, particularly if two recent trends, the decline of prison labour and greater private sector involvement, are taken into account.

The decline of prison labour

In a 1995 United Nations survey of 75 countries, less than one third stated that they could provide all prisoners with work of a useful nature to keep them engaged for a full working day (Henriksson and Krech 1999). Analysts cite three factors that have led to the decline of prison labour around the world: shortage of resources, a rise in unemployment generally outside the prisons and increases in prison populations (Ruggiero *et al.* 1995; Harding 1997; Simon 1999).

As the overall number of prisoners working in prison has declined, so too has the quality of prison labour. Ever since the 1960s studies have shown that the nature and type of prison labour were a significant factor in whether prisoners reoffended following custody (Empey and Rabow 1961; Simon and Corbett 1992). In a valuable study of prison labour, Simon (1999: 184) found that prison industries do not support *prisoners* needs and instead focus on the needs of the *prison*:

> The primary purpose of labour in prisons should be to prepare and help prisoners – those who want to – and most do – to get worthwhile work when they leave. This need not preclude other purposes but the most important aim should be to provide labour and skills to enhance prospects of employment after release.

Indeed, evidence shows that those who have access to work and training (the lucky ones, according to Reuss 1999) do value these activities as they provide for a sense of personal achievement and self-respect. In light of reduced work opportunities, prison labour is often played down and personal growth talked up as providing prisoners with a range of inter-personal abilities. Where training programmes are in place, they have come under fire for disconnecting prisoners from the rhythms of work – that is, its ability to create an environment where prisoners synthesise their work experiences with their own previous personal experience and cultural sensibilities so that prisoners can 'own' rehabilitation.[4] In the absence of empowering, reflective prison labour, there is a possibility that prisoners will face obstacles transferring the different social and personal experiences that prison life throws up (from seeking employ-ment to maintaining social and personal contacts and relationships).

Overall increases in worldwide unemployment are also affecting prison labour. In Belarus and Latvia, for example, weak national economies have led to a market decline and not enough work is available for prisoners (Henriksson and Krech 1999). The dramatic increase in the world's prison populations has also impacted on provisions for prison labour. Between 1989 and 1999, Australia's prison population rose by

63%; America's population by 73%; Ireland's by 38%; England and Wales by 35%; Scotland by 21%; Italy by 68%; and Russia's by 52% (Walmsley 2000). Population increases have been aggravated further by reduced government expenditure on resources and increased expenditure on security that controls the movement of inmates. Flow control of inmates restricts their movements and reduces opportunities for travelling to workshops inside regimes.

We can infer from these points that prison labour is beset with problems in facilitation. Many workshops face a continual threat of closure and programmes are abandoned before they are given the chance to be assimilated into the prison.

Prison labour and the private sector

The inertia of debates on prison labour is ever baffling, particularly since the exploitation of inmates finds its greatest expression in the debates on privatisation and imprisonment. There has been some involvement of the private sector to create prison industries since the nineteenth century (Ignatieff 1978) and these can be broadly situated in Western anglophone countries through contracting out services such as escorting prisoners to court, or providing food services so as to relieve prison officers of a non-custodial task and to enable them to concentrate on core prison duties. The private sector can also take the form of market testing a whole prison by inviting bids for its management from private bodies and from existing staff particularly where there is scope for improvement and where there is the least evidence of progress. The private sector may also manage and, in some cases, design, build and finance a new prison from the outset (this is more common in the US). Private sector involvement is intended to lead to, among other things, more economical and efficient prisons generally, and better work and training of prisoners specifically. These claims have been critiqued mainly on the grounds of historical arguments that private prisons have been abandoned (some say with good reason, see Sparks 1994) so long ago that it is now accepted that the management of the prisons and services is the intrinsic function of the state.

According to Radzinowicz (1988) modes of punishment are a matter exclusively for the state: 'In a democracy grounded on the rule of law and public accountability, the enforcement of penal legislation should be the undiluted responsibility of the state' (cited in Shaw 1992). Christie (1996: 104) puts the same philosophy more explicitly where he sees the matter as one of communitarian responsibility (the community owns the public institutions) and democratic participation: 'The communal character of punishments evaporates in the proposals for private prisons'. This is a strong argument that states explicitly that the state has the moral authority to govern behind bars and that when the private sector becomes involved, that moral authority is eroded. The key question thus becomes whether the contractor is effectively accountable to the state and whether in turn the state is effectively accountable to its citizens. Christie's arguments are commanding, yet they weaken somewhat when considered in the context of Soviet penality. For most of the twentieth century the state was the only consumer of the varied economic functions of the prisons. This did not mean that the prisoners were not exploited simply because the state administered imprisonment. As has been shown, the state in the USSR was far from being a publicly accountable body of institutions, which was what Radzinowicz and Christie believed a penal system should aspire to be. Rather, the moral authority of the state in the penal realm was to implement procedures that exploited prisoners *for the sake of the state*. Not only that, but the evidence from the Soviet Gulag shows that prisoners did not 'own' the prison experience as Christie suggests they might when the state is responsible for supervising imprisonment.

Prison labour and exploitation

The UK provides a particularly interesting example of how the function of prison labour has been confused over the last 45 years. The confusion I refer to is perhaps better described as a 'tension' over whether prisoners should work for penological goals (building character/keeping prisoners active) or for economic purposes (introducing enterprise into prisons was a response to labour shortage in the 1940s and 1950s). The Prindus Affair in the 1980s sparked controversy because of corruption, poor management and inefficiency in contracting out prison labour. Then in the 1990s penal ideology came to encompass a wide range of different narratives that reflected the Conservative Party's rhetoric of efficient public services. New terminology reflected a new penal language: 'efficiency', 'privatisation', 'cutbacks', 'decentralised management' and 'market testing'. Business plans and performance indicators measuring the goal of 'positive regimes' were to be measured partly by the average number of hours per week prisoners spent in purposeful activity, including work. The strategy to contract out prison labour services reflected the political and economic rationality of the Conservative government (and the subsequent New Labour government) to drive down the costs of imprisonment and to introduce competitiveness into the public sector.

41

The transition into new efficiency-conscious penal forms has been most dramatic in the American penal system. In the US two decades of punitive legal reform and a law enforcement crackdown have created what Christie (1996; 2000) terms a giant Gulag. American imprisonment has recently been constructed within a political discourse that links the political rationality of neoliberal societies to the economic restructuring of capitalism from the 1970s onwards (Parenti 1999). Top-down decisions that have led to the rise of incarceration to 'cope' with the surplus labour supply that followed the economic crisis of the 1980s; zero tolerance; the 'war on drugs'; and 'three-strikes laws' are just some of the recent crime policies that are located in capitalist phenomena. While rates of incarceration have increased across Western Europe from 1985 to 1995, the rate of growth has been far slower than the American system where the prison population has risen by 92% from 1985 to 1995 because, argues Parenti: 'Politicians use the canard of crime and punishment to get elected while masking their all-important pro-business agenda' (1999: 169). Parenti, writing in the same radical spirit as Melossi and Pavarini, argues that the prison serves to insulate society from a surplus population, dispossessed by the economic policies of neoliberals. The prison, therefore, plays its part in building and maintaining a political consensus. How prison labour is linked to this development has been documented by Hogan (1997), Lippke (1998) and Davis (1999) who argue that American criminologists on the right support the involvement of the private sector in prisons because fiscal savings can be made if prisons are privatised.[5]

It is striking how much of Rusche's notion of less eligibility, and the Soviet penal system for that matter, resonates in the American literature on prison labour. According to Burger (1982), Borna (1986) and Logan (1990) prison labour represents a prison subeconomy utopia that can operate more effectively if enterprise is allowed to dominate. Not only can prisons cease to be a drain on public taxes but also prison labour can produce a new generation of workers. Writing in more recent times, Fleisher and Rison (1999) emphatically deny prison labour's exploitative potential and instead argue that contracting out prison labour can create factory discipline or what Flanagan and Maguire (1993) earlier describe as converted work communities where work conditions for a group of people for whom employment may not have been included in the normal course of life events, are normalised. Opponents of this position argue that the political and economic culture in the US has given rise to a form of forced prison labour capitalism that is notable for the autonomous operation of prison labour from the rest of the penal realm. Moreover, prison labour has become part of the political estate because it is in the interest of business to have large prison populations:

> Private prisons have multiplied at four times the rate of expansion of public prisons. It is now estimated that by the twenty-first century, there will be three times as many private facilities and that their revenues will be more than one billion dollars. In arrangements reminiscent of the convict lease system, federal, state and county governments pay private companies a fee for each inmate, which means that private companies have a stake in retaining prisoners as long as possible (Davis 1999: 153).

Consider the following. The Sentencing Project in Washington has investigated the links between prison labour and corporate business. The Corrections Corporation of America (hereafter CCA) contributes significantly to the American Legislative Exchange Council (hereafter ALEC) which is a Washington-based public policy organisation that supports conservative legislators. Over 40% of ALEC's members are the state legislators who constitute a significant force in state politics. One of the main goals of the ALEC organisation is to promote legislation that supports conservative principles (privatisation is one of them). ALEC receives funding from CCA. Thus, by funding this policy group, the CCA has a direct influence on penal policy. Corporations also offer financial lobbying support to judges who favour tough law-and-order policies and high prison populations. In return, elected political figures guarantee the promise of new prisons, new bed spaces and a new labour force. Hogan (1997) believes that these political and economic conditions assure the prison commercial complex of continued growth. Prisons, he argues, have become businesses designed for the exploitation of the poor whose labour may not in itself make prisons self-sufficient, but who provide a cheap labour source that operates unmonitored by the political economy they seek to serve.

Is prison labour, therefore, devoid of justice and instead aimed at providing a natural resource? Davis (1999) predicts that prison labourers will become the New American Workers who, far from owning their rehabilitation, as advocated by Davies (1974) and Reuss (1999), are a group of individuals who possess basic workers' rights and no legal rights to control their labour. The utilisation of prison labour to generate profits is further guaranteed because the location of some American prisons in remote areas circumvents the requirements that the prevailing wage in the industry be paid to prisoners (Mauer 1999). This allows the system to 'enslave' prisoners (Davis 1999: 154):

'Prisoners' in some American prisons work 18 hours a day earning up to $5 an hour picking pineapples and producing products consumed on a daily basis. Companies have learned that prison labour can be as profitable as Third World Labour. Some of the clients that use prison labour are IBM, Compaq, Microsoft and Motorola, and Boeing. Prison labour includes inspecting glass bottles and jars used by Revlon, computerised telephone messaging, dental apparatus, computer data entry, plastic parts fabrication, oak furniture and the production of stainless steel tanks (Davis 1999: 149).

Prison labour use is also mediated by community attitudes and by race (Hochstellar and Shover 1997). In the US, the general public supports the use of prison labour in periods of economic stability when demand for labour is generally high, but there is an overall ambivalence to prison labour (Flanagan 1989). Hawkins (1985), Buck (1994), Amnesty International (1995) and Parenti (1999) found that private business favours the labour of white prisoners and subjugates the work of black prisoners who are viewed as having fewer useful skills. While these studies do not consider that for some prisoners any type of labour is meaningful because it takes them out of their cell and engaged in activity, they do tell us something about cultural attitudes. For example, of the ten legislative priorities of the American Correctional Association, promoting correctional industries is ranked second whereas rehabilitation is fifth, followed by a balanced approach to sentencing (the ninth priority). The prison industrial sector does not operate to make profit for the institutions to any comparable level in Western Europe as it does in the US. Yet, all too quickly what happens in America (electronic tagging, private prisons, tough law-and-order policies, for example) happens in the UK, in Western Europe and beyond (policing models used in Thailand, for example, are based on UK models; see Brogden 2003).

Where does contemporary Russia feature in current penological debates? The introduction of the private sector into the penal realm may have implications for the management of the contemporary Russian prison system. For example, in order to alleviate state funding of the prison system, authorities may move towards contracting out prison labour to private industries. This will be of utmost political significance for the direction of Russia's prison system as the farming out of prisoners' work to private industries does raise questions with regard to forced labour – though this may be offset by agreements about wages and conditions. In the section following, a discussion of international norms that seek to promote reformative prison labour, and prohibit forced labour, is intended to offer insight into the international prison context within which Russia has been propelled. I will conclude the chapter with recent developments in the management of Russia's penal system.

Prison labour and international law: soft or hard protection?

The chapter has thus far shown us that the exploitation of prisoners' work increases in breadth when it is used to develop economic infrastructures and sustain political cultures. And while there is a shortage of work for prisoners in most jurisdictions, it does not necessarily follow that prison regimes are incapable of exploiting the captive population. Given the outrage that the issue of forced prison labour has ignited following its use in wartime Germany and Japan, one would expect international legislation to set out clearly various prohibitions against prisoner exploitation. Yet, Fenwick (forthcoming) argues that this is a topic on which international law is not highly developed due to three reasons. First, the state has long compelled prisoners to work. Secondly, prisoners work for private profit is not a particularly new or novel development. Thirdly, international law preserves state power, albeit subject to qualification. I shall confine remarks here to the third development.

The most important international human rights legislation protecting prisoners who work are the International Labour Convention's *Forced Labour Convention 1930* (hereafter ILO); the *United Nations Standard Minimum Rules for the Treatment of Prisoners, 1955* (hereafter UNSMR); and the revised European version, the *European Prison Rules 1987* (hereafter EPR). Each of these sets of rules contains a detailed breakdown of the conditions where prisoners' rights might be violated and each affords prisoners some protection. The spirit behind these norms is that they are intended to serve as 'guides' and 'recommendations'. The UNSMR and EPR are not binding in law but they are accepted almost without reservation because they do not impose burdens that are viewed as unacceptable to governments which are constrained by resource considerations and by political priorities.

There is a general prohibition of forced or compulsory labour in any form in the ILO Convention 29. Where compulsory labour is not prohibited is when it is used as a consequence of conviction in a court of law; where it is carried out under the supervision and control of a public authority; or when it is used at the disposal of private individuals, companies and associations. Article 2(2) ILO Convention 29 does not prevent private benefit from voluntary prison labour. As to what constitutes 'voluntary' is a matter of debate. Formal consent is necessary, although national guidelines stipulate that all prisoners are 'expected' to work; the condition of work must also approximate a free employment relationship in order that an objective assessment of consent can be made.

The lack of a compelling rationale against forced prison labour in prisons must constitute one of the gravest oversights of these international norms. For example, that the ILO Convention did not allow for delegation of supervision of prisoners and control to a private business must have had enormous appeal to the Soviet bureaucrats. Indeed, even as evidence emerged in the 1970s of forced labour in China and in the USSR that was so grave in nature that it threatened the fundamental rights of prisoners, the ILO excused the practice because it was utilised for civic benefits that could conceivably be argued as contributing to prisoner rehabilitation (Alcock 1971). Besides, the Soviet regime denounced ILO Convention 29 on the grounds that it was capitalist.

These days, as with other jurisdictions, it is the UNSMR and the EPR which are the main reference points for prison management in Russia (King and Piacentini 2004). Rules 71–76 in both the UNSMR and the EPR deal with prisoners' work. The EPR prioritise the right to work and vocational training at the prisoner's choosing (Rule 71, part 6). While the inclusion of 'choice' into the EPR was intended to prioritise the right to control which training would be undertaken as a 'human right' it is a misleading inclusion into the rules that is beset with caveats. First, where a prisoner decides to refuse work or training, then this may give rise to a punishment. Secondly, the right to choose work and where to work is provided within the requirement of the institutional administration which effectively means that prisoners' rights may be subordinated to the needs of the prison should institutional requirements necessitate a specific kind of labour.

In addition, both sets of rules contain no provision for prohibiting forced prison labour which is surprising when one considers that the UNSMR were created to instil better human rights across Europe following the atrocities in Nazi Germany that included forced labour. There is a vague statement about forced labour in Rule 71, part 1 that states that prison labour should be a *positive element* of custody. Forced labour reappears (again, indirectly) in Rule 72, part 2 where it is stated that prisoners under sentence are 'required' to work. Accordingly it is up to national penitentiary laws or penal codes to determine how 'requirements' and 'expectations' are to be determined. It is preferable, state the EPR, that the state or public administration, and not contractors, should supervise personnel, administer punishments and manage the prisons generally. And where the private sector is involved the EPR do not offer guidance on the extent of this involvement, on how wages are to be paid and the conditions of work and how prisoners can be protected. Thus, national jurisdictions that have absorbed these norms may justify harsh prison labour practices where a case can be presented that the regime will benefit. What, therefore, actually constitutes 'afflictive' prison labour? The EPR are vague in this regard. Rule 72, part 2 states that utilising prison labour for financial profit can be: 'invaluable in raising standards and improving the quality and relevance of training' and that the treatment of prisoners should not be subordinated to training (see also United Nations 1995).

Alongside the doctrinal inconsistencies that weaken the rights of working prisoners, there are also additional problems in overseeing private sector involvement in prisons and this creates problems in calculating who is responsible for the prisoner and his or her labour. Prisons change in a myriad of ways and it is extremely difficult to monitor private sector involvement in prisons particularly in the current global climate where the penetration of the private sector into public institutions has become almost unavoidable. But a more telling issue is the environment to which these norms apply. The problems of deficiency in clarification and application may not feature as a significant problem for jurisdictions that operate democratic and accountable criminal justice systems that are reforming and updating national guidelines to reflect recent changes in international legislation. Yet, for countries where ideologies have been abandoned without discovering new goals, and where there is transition towards democratic prison management, the vagueness in meaning and the paradoxes within rules will become problematic. How will new emerging nations face sanctions if they can justify forced prison labour because economic and social conditions necessitate it? Also will there be political reprisals following accusations of violating norms even where there are inconsistencies in doctrine and principle? The answers to these questions are difficult to calculate. We can, however, begin that process by examining how Russia's contemporary penal system might be utilising prison labour and the questions over reform and exploitation that may emerge from its usage.

Russian prisons after the USSR: turmoil and the penal system

In Chapter 1, I referred to the turmoil and crisis that enveloped Russian society following the collapse of the Soviet monolith. The demise of the

Soviet Union in 1991 triggered the collapse of Soviet penal identity and its connection to the larger structures of ideology and political economy. With the exception of contemporary China where some features of Stalinist orientation and function have been maintained (thought reform through labour), the centrally managed system with its integrated ideology and command economy has fragmented in all the former Soviet satellites (Mosher 1992; Wu 1992, 1994).

In June 1992, the first post-Soviet penal code was signed following three draft versions that either did not go far enough to reduce the human rights abuses (the first version) or were too radical in vision (the second version), or raised expectations too quickly (the third version led to riots in September 1991 in several penal colonies and riot police were sent in). The 1992 code led to improvements in entitlement visits and the practice of feeding prisoners on punishment a reduced diet was abolished along with the practice of keeping punished prisoners in cold cells without bedding. Prisoners were now entitled to food parcels and the right to use a telephone.

In 1991, the prison system was found to be massively overcrowded, particularly the pre-trial prisons. King (1994) notes that remand cells intended for 20–25 persons slept 60 with less than one square metre of space each. Penal reformers often talk about how in Russian prisons one has to queue to obtain a bed to sleep. Kalinin (the then Director of the prison system) when he gave parliamentary evidence in a hearing in October 1995 noted that deaths in custody: 'due to a lack of oxygen took place in almost all large pre-trial detention centres in Russia' (cited repeatedly in The Moscow Centre for Prison Reform 1993a, 1993b, 1998a, 1998b, 1998c). Up to 8,000 prisoners could languish in the pre-trial prisons for many months, sometimes for years, before they heard of the outcome of their cases. Consequently, with worldwide attention focused on these violations it is not surprising to find that improving human rights has emerged as a forceful impetus for directing reform.

Conditions in the colonies were marginally better. I have already described the dilapidated industrial zones. The living zones fared no better. Posters of Western rock bands from the 1980s held up peeling paint and meeting rooms would be furnished by old pieces of school furniture, donated by local schools through a barter exchange (see Chapter 4). Large dormitories housed up to 100 prisoners whose bunk-beds were separated by less than 1 foot of space. A very unhealthy prison system, marked by disease and poverty – the inevitable consequences of overcrowding and poor medical provision – was recorded by human rights campaigners (see Stern 1998). Critics have argued that TB in the early 1990s was 17 times higher in Russian prisons than in wider society.[6]

Torture was widespread and the violation of human rights was the norm. Prison officials argued that the insufficient funds from Moscow (60% of a colony's needs were allocated between 1991 and 1996) coupled with an antiquated system and a massive population were leaving the prison in a scandalous state. When funds were allocated the amount was insufficient even to meet the costs of staff wages. Many staff, therefore, worked without pay at various periods until as recently as 2001.

While it was not clear what direction the prison system would take in terms of ideology, alternatives to political correction did emerge in the form of evangelical literature and an embryonic psychology service. I describe these developments in more detail in the chapter following. Suffice to say that the enormous captive population was facing what could be construed as an imperialistic invasion from Western ideologies. For example, it is somewhat ironic that religion, once described by Marx as the opiate of the masses, was flooding in to fill the void left by the collapse of Soviet communism.

Forced labour

The 1992 code did not resolve the issue of forced labour and officials were unclear and nervous over whether prisoners were required to work. But there were some assurances. First, there was reassurance from King (1994) that as prison labour had become more or less voluntary around the world due to an overall decline in work, so prisoners would readily volunteer, as is the case in Western prisons. Secondly, it must also have come as a small comfort that not only is it a disciplinary offence to refuse work in Western prisons, but also, that the punitive mentality of compulsory labour was not in breach of international norms and that international norms prohibiting the practice are vague and contradictory, leaving considerable latitude for debate as to whether prisoners had any rights in this regard. I believe that these debates highlight something interesting that I explore later on in the book about why officials attended so swiftly to the business of ensuring that Western penal norms (that were flagrantly ignored for nearly 100 years) were met, whereas the US, has until very recently, resisted recognising the UNSMR as a body of principles that penal institutions must be aware of.

Changes in management structure

Following the new code of 1992, a concept paper was produced: *A Concept Paper for the Reorganisation of the Penal System of the Ministry of the Interior of Russia*. The paper envisaged how places of custody would administer criminal justice in their own territory. It mapped out how a

49

devolved prison system might operate and the paper set out plans for a more individuated prison service where psychological and social programmes would concentrate work on pedagogical diagnosis. Russia joined the Council of Europe in 1996 which necessitated further change in how the prison system was to be managed. In 1997, Yeltsin announced that there was to be a moratorium on the death penalty. In order to ensure that the prison system could perform effectively within an international context, the following reforms were outlined: independent and well remunerated judges who presided over independent courts; the establishment of legal representation for defendants; speedy trials and the utilisation of bail over custody; and many more amendments (Bowring 2002).

Although a regional system was created with each of the regions being affiliated to the central prison authority in Moscow, the impact of the reform was minimal as the majority of the penal colonies were located in the north and to the east while the majority of the population lived in the west. The reforms were disabled further because the prison system remained under the jurisdiction of the Ministry of the Interior, which represents one of the last vestiges of the Soviet Union. Its uniform continues to bring benefits and allowances. But there was often talk of corruption among high-ranking officials and it was this reputation, coupled with the fact that, under the ministry, the vast penal Gulag was created, that led to calls for a transfer of management of the penal system to a European-friendly, justice-oriented framework. The transfer took place in August 1998. The nostalgia for the past, coupled with frustration that the movement to reform the prison system was *external*, led some senior officials to reject the move. The transfer also led to further problems. Kalinin (2002) notes that in the immediate three months following the transfer (late 1998 and into 1999), no funds were made available for the prison system and with only 60% of the total budget coming from central funds anyway, the system was in an acute crisis. Since that crisis, the Federal Budget to the prisons has increased to four times the level of funding under the Ministry of the Interior so that the ministry can get on with the much-needed business of maintaining the dilapidated prison system.

International treaties

It is undoubtedly the case that the main impetus for reform came from Russia's accession into the Council of Europe in February 1996. Russia ratified a number of conventions including *The European Convention for the Prevention of Torture and Inhuman or Degrading Treatment or Punishment, The Convention on the Protection of Human Rights and Basic*

Freedoms and several others. There have been over 2,000 legislative Acts or amendments in the years since accession. It is worth mentioning the recently created Federal Law of 9 March 2001 No. 25-FZ which aimed to restrict the use of custody for those convicted of more serious offences, and which tried to ensure that those guilty of lesser offences would only be imprisoned in exceptional circumstances. This law created the provision for yet another new criminal procedure code that was introduced in 2002 which brings much of Russian criminal procedure broadly into line with other countries of the Council of Europe. A new Human Rights Department was established in 2002 at central and regional levels that is overseen by Russia's first Prison Ombudsman. An Assistant for Human Rights was established in each prison region in 2002. The assistant has the power to visit each institution, report to the regional offices and liaise with bodies to ensure better human rights practice.

In many respects the movement to reform the prison system into one that is based on human rights highlights some of the reasons why we expect modern prisons to be more humane. Institutional practices do vary from society to society, and there remains a vigorous debate about what prisons 'do' in terms of their own work (at the most basic level, prison is about ensuring that prisons work both as punitive sanctions and mechanisms that can rehabilitate). We know more, however, about what prisons should 'not do', that is, perform additional punishment that subjugates the rights of inmates. Anyone who is familiar with the process of reforming criminal justice understands that instituting reform in a particular society is not solely about having the structures in place. It is also about locating change within a wider sensibility and cultural context. I will argue that we have to remain cautious over our attempts to side-step penal sensibilities in favour of importing 'democratic institutions' especially when it is considered that in societies around the world one type of political order is giving way to more democratic movements governed by international norms.

It would be foolish to pretend that what follows in the next two chapters is indicative of the entire Russian prison system. My intention, instead, is to show how some prisons are responding to the dynamic of change.

Notes

1 There also existed camps and colonies that were managed by the NKVD (the Ministry for Internal Affairs) which was responsible for policing. Some camps were semi-independent. Bacon (1994) argues that these camps would

have been few in number and that administering ideology and co-ordination of the types of industry conducted would have been controlled centrally.

2 Statistics on the reconviction rates of former prisoners who returned to the Gulag and post-Gulag prison colonies are difficult to find. Gulag survivors revealed to me how prison sentences would be increased during custody and this often coincided with increases in production targets. Prisoners were not given access to any judicial defence.

3 Former Gulag camp survivor during a personal communication in 1999.

4 Reuss (1999) focuses on prison education (as opposed to prisoner education). 'People' in prison, argues Reuss, 'weave' learning based on the many cultural elements of their previous lives and their prison lives and this can form part of the rehabilitative process.

5 The Sentencing Project in Washington, quoting the Bureau of Justice Assistance, has found no evidence that the quality of services had improved greatly under private contract despite the claim that private companies operate services of higher quality compared with the state.

6 Although the official response was that the TB figures were higher because cases which had gone unreported were diagnosed while the person was in custody.

Chapter 3

Filling the void: Russia's new 'penal identities'

In view of the fact that the state is no longer primarily concerned with utilising prison labour to support the economic and political infra-structures, the present-day Russian government is facing major dif-ficulties in determining precisely what prisoners should do and what prisons should be for. Three developments were found to have taken place: first, alternative rationales to justify prison labour have had to be found. In the 12 years since the collapse of the USSR in 1991, re-habilitation is the most widely claimed task of imprisonment but practices carried out in its name vary widely. Secondly, alternative ways of filling time have had to be developed. Thirdly, the prison colonies are turning to alternative means to provide essential resources. These developments vary across the different colonies, reflecting something other than a 'dominant ideology' as historically was the case.

In this chapter, Smolensk prison region is presented first followed by Omsk prison region. How staff and prisoners perceive the goal of imprisonment and the function of prison labour is discussed. The chapter includes descriptions and illustrations of the ways in which prisoners and staff relate the goal of imprisonment, to levels and perceptions of criminality, as in most jurisdictions discussions about imprisonment take place alongside a critique about the levels of crime even where the two are not seen to be causally related (see Pease 1994; King and Piacentini 2004). Any alternative strategies aimed at filling prisoners' time are then described in detail and the role that the wider and local community plays in meeting these objectives is also described. While this chapter outlines penal practices, it locates these within changes in penal *ideology*. In Chapter 4, the use of barter as an alternative means of providing resources is discussed as a development in the penal *economy*. Following the discussion of changes in Russian penal ideology and in the penal economy, the final chapters of the book offer a critique of how these developments in Russia translate internationally. Under current political conditions, national propensities to punish are being reconfigured to address universal interests of human rights and it might be interesting to assess how attempts to establish an 'indigenous' penal sensibility evolve alongside the standardisation of penal systems according to human rights.

The new penal identities in Smolensk and Omsk

There are conceptual differences between regions in the way that prison staff and prisoners comprehend imprisonment arising from varied ways of conceiving the individual.[1] Alternative penal vocabularies have had to be found which I call the 'new penal identities': 'Character Reform' (Smolensk prison region) and 'Social Reform' (Omsk prison region). The new penal identities are distinct and operate outside of direct political patronage and hence have become the hallmarks of the penal culture of two geographically disparate regions. The new identities, moreover, operate as a way of seeing and understanding imprisonment in an otherwise vacuous, loosely coupled and turbulent system. These identities, illustrate how the local cultures are following a different set of values and cultural expectations from those previously provided by the state in its (centralised) frame of reference.

Most of the respondents I interviewed did not think consciously that they were seeking to use this sanction or that method in order to pursue these individualised penal identities. From piecing together the words, experiences and observations of prison officers and prisoners, it has been possible to construct a picture of how the respondents assemble these linguistic constructions so as to articulate a habitus or a general idea in a society where imprisonment has become perplexing and mystifying. Bourdieu (1994) notes that language becomes legitimately produced and reproduced when it operates beyond its value as an object of contemplation and is instead viewed as an instrument of action or power. This is how I came to understand and categorise Russian penal forms – as 'vocabularies of motive' (Melossi 1985) that provide for penal ideology (bodies of knowledge that can shape and guide the contours of imprisonment) and which ultimately give imprisonment meaning and legitimacy thus preserving its effects.

These identities are not merely speculative or contemplative nor should they be viewed as *total*. They are wrapped around 'real' events: the nature and amount of prison work; the repertoire of different methods used to promote rehabilitation and how these are linked to the location of the prison colony, the political situation and the economic conditions; and also on re-embedding historical narratives on punishment. I came to understand these identities as temporary junctures of identification marked by incomplete and unfinished changes in penal principle and penal policy.

Imprisonment in Smolensk prison region

Prisoners and staff were asked about the goal of imprisonment as it was felt that it would be interesting to investigate if and how the language of punishment had changed since the collapse of Soviet penal identity. Overall, respondents argued that the goal of imprisonment aimed to achieve rehabilitation, although the sample of prisoners is very small and any discussion in statistical terms should proceed with caution (see Table 3.1). There were no significant differences between staff and prisoners in relation to the goals of imprisonment, and further comparisons of prisoners and staff within the regimes reveal no significant differences for the goals of imprisonment, as shown in Table 3.2.

What is immediately clear from these data presented in Table 3.2 is that the prisoners (72% and 86%) and the staff (88% and 93%) in the strict and general regimes respectively believed the goal of imprisonment to

Table 3.1 Goals of imprisonment as presented by all respondents in Smolensk[1]

	Prisoners $n = 14$ (%)	Staff $n = 104$ (%)
Rehabilitation	11 *(79)*	94 *(90)*
Punishment	3 *(21)*	10 *(10)*

Notes
1   The *n* total is the number of respondents. The number in parenthesis is the percentage. If the counts do not match those in the *n* total this is due to missing data (i.e. someone not answering the question). Subsequent tables present the counts followed by percentages in brackets.
2   $\chi^2 = 1.756, p = 0.185$; d.f. $= 1$

Table 3.2 Goals of imprisonment according to the regime in Smolensk

	Prisoners		Staff	
	Strict $n = 7$	General $n = 7$	Strict $n = 50$	General $n = 54$
Rehabilitation	5 (72)	6 (86)	44 (88)	50 (93)
Punishment	2 (28)	1 (14)	4 (12)	4 (7)

Notes
1   χ^2 prisoners = 0.424; p = 0.500; d.f. = 1; χ^2 staff = 0.630; p = 0.322; d.f. = 1. Assumptions of chi-square test violated since 50% of cells have frequencies of < 5.

be rehabilitation. The following quotations from the interviews illustrate these results: 'The prisoner learns that he must mend his ways in order to return to society healthy' (chief psychologist, Smolensk strict regime); 'For me, the goal of imprisonment will always be about rehabilitation' (prisoner, Smolensk general regime). While Soviet penology constructed an image of the criminal as a wrecker of the cultural capital of Marxism/Leninism, nowadays, in Smolensk, the prisoner was viewed as a person possessing a psychological malaise and innate propensity to crime. Thus, correcting the psychological temperament and moral character formed the basis of penal interventions: 'My job is to counsel prisoners and help them understand why they commit crime. I focus on their psychological temperament' (senior prison officer, Smolensk strict regime).

The data gathered from the interviews show that in contemporary Russia prison officers and prisoners are basing their views on more concrete models of individual behaviour. This reflects a marked shift in penal ideology. For almost an entire century the various definitions that criminologists refer to when attempting to construct an image of, and explanation for, crime were subverted, reduced to a generic explanation: all crime was labelled as anti-Soviet. Consequently, questions such as 'what causes crime today' were important to ask, not only because of the constructed links between imprisonment and attitudes to crime but also because, as Cavadino and Dignan (1992) and Carlen (2004) argue, attitudes to crime expose mainstream values inherent in the political culture and could therefore provide indications of the new directions in criminal justice policy.

All the prisoners and staff were asked for their views on crime in order to explore the sources of knowledge and assess how this knowledge was constructed in a society that is increasingly governed by democratic principles. Two types of explanation for crime, one that located the causes of crime in individual differences (inborn or acquired) and one which located the causes in social or environmental factors, were presented to respondents.[2] For both strict and general regimes there was a perception that crime is a problem residing in the individual and prison officers viewed their job as one that involved 'curing' criminality: 'The criminal's mind is fascinating because it is very different from normal people. I believe that they are different. They need to be cured' (prison officer, Smolensk general regime). The majority of staff stated that it is the individual who is responsible for personal conduct and that the breakdown of society is not a factor leading to crime: 'There is something not right with criminals, they are backward' (psychologist, Smolensk general regime). One prison officer stated: 'I think that it is too easy to say that crime is a result of social decline. We are all suffering but we don't all choose to hurt or kill people. I think that crime is complex, something isn't right inside' (prisoner industries officer, Smolensk strict regime). While others argued forcibly that: 'Crime is caused by increasing numbers of young men who have grown up disregarding the civilising institution of marriage and without moral awareness brought about through family responsibilities' (governor, Smolensk general regime).

These views were common among prison officers in Smolensk and they reflect one strand of contemporary (conservative) Russian criminology (Kovalev *et al.* 1997; Ushatikov *et al.* 1997; Gilinskii 1998; Zubkov *et al.* 1998). There were some contradictions among prisoners on the causes of criminality which indicated that prisoners were confused or undecided as to whether their crimes were motivated by personal factors or wider social or economic factors. For example, some prisoners justified their behaviour in terms of character traits: 'I am addicted to alcohol. I committed the crime because I am ill' (prisoner, Smolensk general regime). Others, however, were undecided about the distinction between inborn traits and causes of criminality that are a consequence of the wider social and economy instability: 'I want a good job, some money and a family, but I feel completely lost in myself' (prisoner, Smolensk general regime).

It made sense for prisoners and staff in Smolensk to talk of penality as relating to their 'selves' because it provided them with an identity, an embodied point of view, in an otherwise loosely coupled prison system. The new penal identity of character reform operated through the interplay between similarity and difference. This is not entirely distinct from, or in contradiction to, Soviet penology where there was a substantive differentiation between the identity of the criminal as 'politically imperfect' (inadequate) and the non-criminal who was the 'perfect proletarian' (not requiring the brand of penal remedy unique to the Soviet Union). Yet that particular identity, character reform, does represent a shift in the conception of the individual whose primary identity is not as an actor in a shared consciousness but as someone who has become privatised from the wider cultural sphere.

Prison officers and regional managers have implemented various models that reflect this new language of the 'penal self'. Each is considered in the following section. The models are constructed in terms of the offenders' perceived difference in character from non-offenders and they reflect the new solutions that have emerged in the wake of the decline of Soviet political culture.

Styles and approaches for rehabilitation in Smolensk

Regrettably, there is insufficient government material to allow for a full account of prison labour in all the prison colonies in Russia. Zubkov (1974) argues (without providing empirical data) that during the Soviet period and allowing for changes in the wider economy, the prison system operated a full to capacity 100% prisoner workforce. Smolensk region was allocated contracts for mining, aluminium production, manufacturing and production of agricultural machinery. In Smolensk, rail tracks extended directly from the penal colony and joined other rail tracks that transported goods throughout Russia.

Prison labour and vocational training

In Smolensk until 1994 all but a handful of prisoners worked (elderly prisoners and prisoners with physical disabilities). Since 1994, Smolensk region has struggled to provide prison labour. The overall percentage of prisoners who are allocated work has dropped significantly to between 30 and 50% of persons working at any one time in each establishment. In Smolensk prison region in 1999, the average prison working population for all the colonies in the region had reduced by one third from around 80% in 1994 to 51% in 1999. The two regimes visited had a lower than average workforce. The population engaged in work in the general regime has reduced by one third from 80% in 1994 to 51% in 1999 and has reduced by nearly two fifths in Smolensk strict regime from 71% in 1994 to 47% in 1999.[3] The following two quotations from interviews illustrate how working in the prison has become, for many, unsafe, or a source of embarrassment, since the physical spaces now resemble industrial wastelands:

> When you walk around the industrial zone, God it is depressing here. There is nothing to show you [laughs]. Em, I think we can look here at where we keep aluminium wire. See there! We have some

prisoners working. That is all we have here. We have closed so much, so much has gone (prisoner master responsible for supervising work, Smolensk general regime).

While another prisoner warned: 'It is not safe to walk here. Be careful! Everything is crumbling away. I've been here for ten years, these big warehouses were absolutely full with workers in 1989. It was so noisy. It had a buzz, you know' (prisoner, Smolensk strict regime).

The main prison industry in the two Smolensk prison colonies was light assembly or 'Goods for Civil Society' (hereafter, GCS) as it is formally known in Russian prison jargon.[4] In both regimes, there were up to 30 different types of GCS products that included garden materials, kitchen furniture, funeral paraphernalia, rakes, parts for combine harvesters and ploughs, water coolers and car parts. Although different aspects of the agriculture and manufacturing industries were provided for and within these industries more kinds of labour, most production was concentrated in GCS. More than 75% of the prisoners who were offered work produced GCS. Prison officers did not refer to GCS as purposeful activity. This was surprising as not only was a high level of practical skill essential in building, for example, bedroom furniture, but also there is an element of creative skill that is required to produce ornate funeral headstones. As the research into prison work in the UK by Reuss (1999) and Simon (1999) illustrates, purposeful activity should be measured according to whether prisoners take pride in their work. It seemed to me that a lot of time, effort and pleasure had gone into producing the lavishly ornate goods for civil society. Could light prison industry in Russia produce feelings of personal satisfaction? One senior prison officer answered with a hint of shame: 'Well it's not real industry. I mean it's not real labour … not like the kinds of work we used to do'. This comment was understood in a historical context. Nowadays, prison officers were self-conscious that the once-monolithic prison industrial sector was now producing hundreds of furry gorilla toys, footballs and dishcloths.

Though there was a steady flow of work (for those who were allocated it but not for all prisoners), the majority of prisoners interviewed resented the limited opportunity to learn new skills: 'All I do is make cloths. Nikolai here makes dolls. This is not real work, it's a waste of time' (prisoner, Smolensk general regime). These responses about how the quality of the prison labour determines purposefulness mark a notable departure from Soviet penal discourse when all prison labour regardless of type, quality and quantity was vitally important for economic development. However, as the fieldwork progressed, and more data and observations were collected, these broad dichotomous categories of purposeful and non-purposeful activity would feature less. For example, although there were complaints that the quality of work was poor, there were some oblique references about how every kind of work undertaken was contributing some resources to the prisons: 'All labour is purposeful because we can use the products to get extra resources and supplement our income' (prison officer, Smolensk strict regime). As Chapter 4 shows, developments in the penal economy impact directly on how prisons function in Russia and importantly on the expectations of prisoners.

Relatedly in Smolensk, there were problems in providing training to prisoners. Between 1955 and 1993 training was provided to around 60% of the total prison population. In 1999, less than 2% of the total prison population at any one time underwent any form of work or vocational training. In the UK for example, Simon (1999) has found that in the six prisons that participated in her study, some training was available for up to 60% of the prison population. In my study, only one workshop out of 15 was found to be in operation in only one of the colonies. The workshops providing manufacturing and agricultural skills training had closed in both colonies in 1997. The decline in prison labour and training was reflected in staff attitudes as to why prison labour might be perceived as useful. Table 3.3 sets out reasons for prison labour as indicated by prison officers from a predetermined list.[5] What Table 3.3 appears to show is that there was a very significant difference in the reasons given by staff, with 36% favouring 'to build character', followed by 24% choosing the response, 'habit of responsibility'. Almost no staff in

Table 3.3 Reasons for providing labour as presented by staff

	Smolensk staff $n = 104$
To give the prisoners time to think about why they committed crime rather than be idle	17 (16)
To build the prisoners' character	38 (36)
To keep the prison running	1 (1)
Because work is punishment	1 (1)
To keep prisoners busy	12 (12)
As a commercial enterprise	0
To inculcate a habit of work	10 (10)
To inculcate a habit of responsibility	25 (24)

Note
1   K-S: $z = 3.122$; $p = 0.000$.

Smolensk believed that commercial reasons for work were important (that is, 'commercial enterprise' and 'keep prison running', rated 0 or 1). The utilisation of work as punishment was not perceived as particularly important with a rating of 1.

All the reasons cited as important relate to the personal benefits of prison labour (building character, personal responsibility and keeping prisoners busy) and indicate that prison labour targeted the psycho-logical well-being of prisoners. The interviews illustrate further how staff in Smolensk define the role of prison labour: 'Prison labour is effective if prisoners reflect on their crimes, but it is not the only means for reflection' (governor, Smolensk strict regime). A prison psychologist added: 'The prisoner needs to repent and think about why he has chosen to commit a sinful act. I mean we all live in poverty here, but I don't react by committing crime so how can that be the main cause?'

There were common features in the responses gathered from Smolensk that reveal a movement towards Western penal discourses where the focus is on the character of the offender. First, the terminology used suggests that introspection was an important aspect of achieving reform. Secondly, the responses revert to causality, which was perceived by prison officers to be 'innate'. Thirdly, staff discussed 'remedying' criminals (*Lekarstvo protiv prestuplennii*), 'treating' crime (*Lechit' prestuplennii*) and 'assessing' (*Operedelyat'*) motivations for crime. The language of psychology was also evident: staff referred to 'risk factors', 'paths' and 'inner development'. This points to an ideology that seeks to reform prisoners into fit citizens through teaching and helping, and not solely through physical labour, which undoubtedly can also be useful in keeping the prisoners' mind and body fit. Labour, it was argued, assists prisoners in 'seeing the error of their ways' (governor, Smolensk strict regime), but it is psychology and religion that were perceived to provide a sort of therapeutic magic.

Psychological 'treatment'

Prison officers in Smolensk region focused on alternatives to prison work. Psychology and religious doctrine identify the causes of crime and isolate different approaches and traditions that aim to 'cure' criminality. These methods mark a significant shift towards positivistic assumptions that are derived from American criminal psychology. Consequently, they capture a new mood that is distinctively non-Soviet.

Psychology is used to identify the inherent (not the social or political) causes of crime by establishing which types of personality commit crime. Smolensk region has implemented a strategy, 'Paths to Reform' (*Put k Reformu*) in all the colonies whereby psychological programmes were used to re-condition behaviour while religion targeted the individual's moral character. Prison labour is included in the overall strategic objective of the document, but the wording of the literature places emphasis on the reforming qualities of psychology and religion in the following ways. First, identifying the personality traits of the offender. Secondly, the document 'guarantees' that some psychological and social reform will take place during the period of custody; thirdly, training of staff in ascertaining a personality profile. The Russian version of Eysenck's Personality Inventory devised by Russian psychologist Alexander Ushatikov in 1995 was utilised in all the penal colonies in Smolensk region. The model shown in Figure 3.1 replicates Eysenck's model in that it isolates certain personality traits (introversion, extroversion and psychoticism) that may lead to criminality. The terminology in this model bears a strong resemblance to the models discussed in the work of Krone and Reddon (1995).

All prisoners were labelled according to this model during the first two months of arrival to the colony. Prison staff first isolated specific features of extroverted and introverted personalities perceived to be at

Figure 3.1 The personality circle (*Krug Lichnosti*)

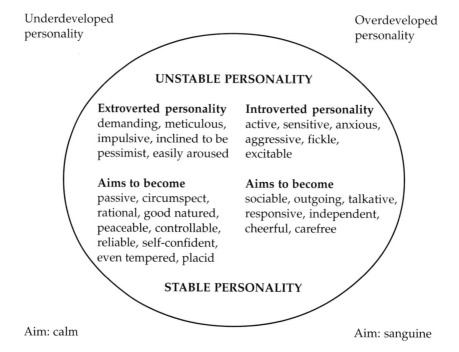

Underdeveloped personality

Overdeveloped personality

UNSTABLE PERSONALITY

Extroverted personality
demanding, meticulous, impulsive, inclined to be pessimist, easily aroused

Introverted personality
active, sensitive, anxious, aggressive, fickle, excitable

Aims to become
passive, circumspect, rational, good natured, peaceable, controllable, reliable, self-confident, even tempered, placid

Aims to become
sociable, outgoing, talkative, responsive, independent, cheerful, carefree

STABLE PERSONALITY

Aim: calm

Aim: sanguine

the root of crime: introverts become neurotic and extroverts psychopathic. After the prisoner's personality traits are established, 'diagnostic tests' are undertaken that aim at altering 'extreme' behaviour. Prisoners are asked to describe any personal problems or any anger. These problems are then grouped according to the traits that make up what was predetermined as either an extroverted or introverted personality. The director of psychology services at Smolensk region explained: 'The personality circle allows us to make scientific investigations to understanding the interaction between genetics and the environment that may lead to crime.'

Prison staff conducted tests in a 'psychology booth' which was one large furnished room for each accommodation block. Each booth was lavish when compared with the rest of the accommodation buildings, with padded walls for soundproofing (in one colony the walls were bright red) and floor-to-ceiling photographic landscapes. Pamphlets and books were readily available in the audio-booths where prisoners could also listen to ambient music: running streams and birds singing. In some colonies soft music was transmitted over the prison Tannoy at nights accompanied by soothing words about the staff. These somewhat old-fashioned ideas about prisoner reformation were shaped into a 'Four-step Programme for Diagnosis of Criminality and Ways in Re-habilitation' which aimed to reform the character of a prisoner from a 'deviant and morally bereft individual' into a 'fulfilled and civilised human being' (Ushatikov *et al.* 1997). The prison psychologists use a variety of visual images and psychological tests, from memorising facial features to animal visualisation, in order to discover any *kind* of explanation for crime. That the collapse of the USSR threw up the problem of how to identify new causes of crime and punishment was evident from the way in which ideas had been readily imported. This grab-bag approach to understanding criminality seemed chaotic and lacked rigour. Nor did these programmes necessarily reflect the kinds of local conditions that can lead to criminality, for example, if prisoners were employed prior to custody, their domestic relations and their housing arrangements.

Religion

There was evidence of religious indoctrination in Smolensk, channelled into the colonies via Russian Orthodox priests who delivered exhortatory meetings for prisoners and staff. Religion was everywhere in the Smolensk colonies, from the classrooms (the colonies could not afford to pay for a full education curriculum so priests were used 'for free' instead), to the staff dining-rooms (pamphlets and books were littered about). Whereas once upon a time it was the sociological insights of Marx and Lenin that inspired prisoner reform, nowadays it is religion that directs much of the rehabilitative process. In a bold break with Marxist/ Leninist penal ideology, the director of prison industries who had trained under the Soviet system and who, not so long ago in 1987, had been awarded for his loyalty to 'Red Industries', stated: 'Religion is about inner peace, personal reflection, the morals of prisoners and it's about family values'. One prisoner who had received a socialist education as a civil engineer added: 'If I had the choice between working in the light assembly we offer or religious education, I would choose religion as I can reflect and think about my crimes.' This comment was illustrative of a commonly-held view that prison staff and prisoners no longer defended prison labour as providing purposeful activity and this was reflected in staff and prisoners' specific views on religion, as shown in Table 3.4. The different views between prisoners and staff on the role of religion were not found to be significant.[6] None the less, it is immediately clear from Table 3.4 that the predominant view is that religion plays a fundamental role in prisoner reform (100% of prisoners and 71% of staff). According to the Head of the Orthodox Church for Smolensk region: 'As an institution, the Church sets standards on morality. We must teach prisoners how to be "whole" again in order that they live obedient lives.'

Interestingly, a view was also expressed among prisoners and prison officers that post-Soviet imprisonment lacked what one prison officer described as 'a moral core'. In an effort to create a core and fill the penal void, Smolensk region had established a strategy titled 'Paths to

Table 3.4 The importance of religion in achieving the goal of imprisonment for all Smolensk respondents

	Prisoners $n = 14$	Staff $n = 104$
Important	14 (*100*)	74 (*71*)
Not important (including 'no opinion')[1]	0	30 (*29*)

Notes

1 The logic for combining the reason 'not important' with 'no opinion' is that if respondents do not have an opinion on the role of religion, it can be safely said that it is not important. Chapter 1 outlines the procedure for analysing the statistical data and the tests used.

2 $\chi^2 = 5.415; p = 0.020;$ d.f. $= 1.$

Spiritual Reform' (*Put k Duxovnuyu Reformu*) that was designed and implemented by religious leaders and prison officials with the central prison authority's approval. The programme included meditation classes; step-by-step programmes; 'libraries of religion' and family fellowships which were based on American models of religious prison education such as the American Christian Evangelical organisation, the Prison Fellowship (McAlister 1999). Smolensk region employed up to 12 priests who were seconded to work on the penal colonies on a weekly basis. Despite deriving from different branches of knowledge, religion and psychology together secured a penal identity for the prison sites as socially relevant institutions by providing a conceptual vehicle – a dominant penal ideology – that prisoners and staff could identify with: 'This programme gives us direction' (governor, Smolensk strict regime).

Post-custody character reform in Smolensk

The process of rehabilitation in Smolensk was designed to concentrate the minds of prisoners during custody into reflecting and 'see the error of their ways'. With little else to offer prisoners by way of prison labour, vocational training, music or artistic programmes, the character reform programmes made sense. Prisoners, moreover, become fit for society through reformation of their spiritual and psychological character both during and post-custody. In 1998 Smolensk region had introduced a pilot scheme with assistance from the Smolensk branch of the Russian Orthodox Church. Based on a similar commune-type scheme set up in Tver, the Smolensk version involves employing former prisoners to work for their keep in a 'Family Fellowship' that is managed by priests. Prison staff had to guarantee that prisoners sent to the fellowship were sufficiently reformed, but not fully reformed as further rehabilitation takes place in the commune. During the period of residence in the fellowship, participants must make the commitment to stay actively involved in the church. Although when compared to the American Prison Fellowship, the Smolensk scheme does not generate a profitable cash revenue, there are interesting parallels, particularly in how church leaders are now at the forefront of debates on Russian society's 'moral decay'. Also, religion has enormous appeal because it was described to me as a 'free' resource for measuring reform. It is not difficult to see how this has instant appeal in a penal system searching for solutions and which operates with massive debt and reduced state investment.

Looking at all the evidence from Smolensk and before I address imprisonment in Siberia, several points are worth mentioning. The rapid changes in the past decade, together with Soviet penal discourse, should be taken into consideration when evaluating current conditions. The opening up of the decentralised economy to global markets has meant that the prison industries sector must compete with the import of cheaper goods from the Far East and the inner Asian realm. Moreover, in the absence of a dominant ideology in whose name statements about the purpose of prison labour – or any other intervention for that matter – are issued, the prison regions have been left to fend for themselves in how penal punishment is administered. The utilisation of psychology and religion in Smolensk marks a major deviation from Soviet penality wherein the focus has shifted from the social self to the psychological self. The surfacing of these disciplines from the rubble of the collapse of the Soviet penitentiary system is notable also for how we come to view centralised penal ideology in exceptional societies. Nowadays there is greater separation of the state from society. As mentioned in Chapter 2, the absence of ideology renders vacant the space usually occupied by the state which it requires for articulating and mediating its power. The prisons, therefore, have become vacated of an ideology. To function with some measure of success, the prisons have imported and consumed alternative rationales. Psychology has an obvious attraction as a body of scientised knowledge. Following almost a century of brainwashing on the benefits of imprisonment to the state and society, the version of psychology – as that taken up in the extraordinary rooms with easy chairs, murals and soft music – does seem ready made. Religious doctrine, so long suppressed as the opiate of the masses, now flows in to fill the void left by Marxism/Leninism.

A simplistic evaluation of post-Soviet imprisonment would attribute these developments in Smolensk solely to the collapse of the USSR with its loose boundaries and penal voids. Yet something else is happening that is connected to policy transfer and some of the features of globalisation that lends to Smolensk the salient features of psychology and religion and their character-reforming prospects. In conducting a comparative analysis of how the demise of the Soviet penal system has impacted on another prison region, a more robust explanation can be found as to the nature of the phenomena that are steering imprisonment in Russia's transition period.

Imprisonment in Omsk prison region

Researching post-Soviet penal phenomena involved travelling to Omsk region which is located approximately 3,000 km east of Moscow in the Siberian steppes. Consistent with the findings from Smolensk region I found that the goal of imprisonment for prison officers in the Siberian colonies was rehabilitation, but for prisoners the goal of imprisonment was punishment. Whereas the penal identity in Smolensk, 'character reform', revealed a new assumption about imprisonment that, mainly, there has been no hangover from the Soviet period in that region and the order of prison life is not fixed on prison work as it was in Soviet times, so in Omsk, rehabilitation was shaped by a penal identity that aimed at 'social reform'. Table 3.5 presents the findings on the goal of imprisonment in Omsk. The data presented in Table 3.5 show clearly that, in the Omsk sample, the differences between all staff and prisoners concerning the goal of imprisonment were very highly significant with the majority of prisoners viewing imprisonment as punishment (70%) and the majority of staff as rehabilitation (90%). Comparisons of prisoners and staff within the regimes are shown in Table 3.6. The predominant view among staff is that the goal of imprisonment is rehabilitation (85% and 96% of staff in the strict and general regimes respectively believed this to be the case). There were no significant differences within regimes for prisoners or staff as to the goal of imprisonment. Among prisoners, 62%

Table 3.5 Goals of imprisonment as presented by all respondents in Omsk

	Prisoners $n = 17$ (%)	Staff $n = 89$ (%)
Rehabilitation	5 (30)	80 (90)
Punishment	12 (70)	9 (10)

Note
$\chi^2 = 32.860; p = < 0.001;$ d.f. $= 1$.

Table 3.6 Goals of imprisonment according to the regime in Omsk

	Prisoners		Staff	
	Strict $n = 8$	General $n = 9$	Strict $n = 47$	General $n = 42$
Rehabilitation	3 (38)	2 (22)	40 (85)	40 (96)
Punishment	5 (62)	7 (78)	7 (15)	2 (4)

Note
1   χ^2 prisoners $= 0.476; p = 0.490; \chi^2$ staff $= 2.505; p = 0.108;$ d.f. $= 1$. Assumptions of chi-square test violated since 37.5% of cells have frequencies of < 5 (see Diamantopoulos and Schlegelmilch 1997: 156).

and 78% believed the goal to be punishment, although the sample was so small that any discussion of prisoners' responses should take this into account. The interviews confirm the contrasting views on the goals of imprisonment: 'We aim for rehabilitation' (governor, Omsk general regime). A prisoner from the general regime stated: 'I am locked up in an overcrowded room that smells and is dirty. I have to work hard for a few measly kopecks.'

The views of prison officers in Omsk reflected elements of Soviet penal discourse that prisons should aim to preserve the principle of 'community' to reduce social exclusion: 'Since *perestroika*, we have lost our collective spirit, you know, looking out for each other. That is what I think about when I think about prisons' (prison officer, Omsk strict regime). But for prisoners, it was the harsh living conditions and not the idea that prisons are designed to enact some kind of revenge, punishment, incapacitation or rehabilitation that shaped their views on imprisonment: 'Well it certainly feels punitive here. We have to work really hard, just to get an extra slice of bread or some new clothes' (prisoner, Omsk strict regime).

All the respondents were asked a series of questions about crime, crime causation and crime prevention. The respondents' views on crime echoed research findings from Western jurisdictions where crime is understood not as a single event, but as behaviour that arises from a multitude of different historical, social, political, economic and inter-personal elements (see Bottoms and Wiles 1998). Prison officers and prisoners were especially concerned about how the continuing social and economic decline in Russia is leading some individuals into crime: 'Well, we never had crimes like rape, burglary and so on before. Now everyone is much poorer and life is generally more unstable. This has created a crime wave' (governor, Omsk strict regime). A prisoner from Omsk strict regime added: 'I was a civil engineer in a factory. It closed after the USSR collapsed. I lost my job, then my home and my family. I ended up a drunk. I was poor and destitute.'

In searching for the causes of crime, the respondents in Omsk continually returned to the events of 1991 which, they argued, marked the end of a world that they had grown familiar with. That world of control, curtailed freedoms, censorship, surveillance, fear and, of course, the Gulag, was also a world where prices were relatively fixed, where employment was guaranteed and where public bodies and institutions received full state funding. As one respondent put it: 'Back then, everything was normal. Even the price of bread was the same day in day out.' The stability that had shaped the lives of those who were interviewed has now given way to economic turmoil, public institutions that do not come up to scratch, social insecurity, political ineptitude[7] and an increase in social problems such as homelessness, alcohol and drug abuse, child poverty, prostitution and money laundering. The arguments posited by the Omsk respondents were not that the Soviet Union was an idyllic paradise devoid of human suffering and acts of harm. Rather, the collective unity that was intrinsic to the survival of the Soviet ethos had been shattered and that the rise of individualism had created what one prison governor described repeatedly as: 'a selfish society where we have stopped to take care of each other. That is the way I was brought up. We don't have that sense of mutual responsibility anymore' (governor, Omsk strict regime).

Given the turbulent environment of the last 13 years, it was hardly surprising to find prison officers and prisoners referring to Russia's recent past because reaching into the past also provided the answers and therefore the solution to Russia's 'crime problem'. The overall view was that the prison realm was one of the last vestiges of promoting social cohesiveness. Aided by the layout of the colony which served as a microcosm of a Soviet lifestyle where there was a forceful interplay – a dualism – of work and rest, it was the prison space where the capacity to restore collectivity, even if this meant restoring past ideas about (harsh) penal punishment, could be found.

Styles and approaches for rehabilitation in Omsk

In the survivors' folklore, forced prison labour will for ever be remembered as concentrated in the northern regions of Russia and in Siberia. Prisoners worked to cultivate these rich and vast lands of their natural resources. They broke the ground for rail and road networks to be established in this 'virgin wilderness' (Applebaum 2003: 87) Omsk was no exception. Omsk prison region came under the jurisdiction of OmskLag. Even today, OmskLag continues to have a somewhat ghostly presence in the few crumbling buildings that lie in the rural areas and also in the mindset of some of those who have trained under the Soviet system and who are employed as prison officers. And while in political and literary debates it is common to hear Russians describe *nash mentalitet* ('our way of thinking') in the penal realm, this way of thinking and seeing was bound up in historical narratives, and for some, nostalgia about forced prison labour.

Prison labour and vocational training

Outlined in Chapter 1 was a historical description of the quality and quantity of prison labour in Omsk region. Work was varied to reflect the range of economic activity in the USSR. Custodial sentences also varied to reflect the different work assignments of the centralised economic policy and the different professional backgrounds of prisoners. The history of prison labour in Omsk is particularly interesting because the giant OmskLag is a reminder of that despotic form of slavery associated with Stalinist criminal justice, whereby a perception that prison labour could be profitable was fused with a form of 'megalomaniacal madness' in the crime control industry (Applebaum 2003: 69). Omsk encapsulates what historians have amply demonstrated as Russia's two-pronged penal miasma: extreme brutality coupled with functionality.

Throughout the Soviet period, the majority of prisoners held in the Omsk penal establishments worked. All kinds of manufacturing, from building lorries to machine-gun manufacture, were produced in Omsk. Arms production became a profitable prison industry after Omsk become officially 'closed' to Westerners during the Cold War. Since 1991, prison labour has been in decline but, interestingly, the collapse of prison industries has not been as marked as in Smolensk. Compared with some prison regions where the prison working population was found to be between 30% and 40%, the number of prisoners working in the Omsk colonies has only steadily declined from 83% in 1994 to 67% in 1999 in the strict regime and from 76% in 1994 to 60% in 1999 in the general regime. The percentage of prisoners working in Omsk was similar to the numbers employed in prisons in England and Wales (although the numbers engaged in work can be as high as 89%, as in Maidstone prison in England; see Simon 1999).

Since the numbers of prisoners working in Omsk is quite high when compared to other areas in Russia, the region has operated a varied industrial sector offering a good range of prison labour. In 1999 and 2003, I found that over 170 different types of merchandise are produced in prison industries in both colonies. The largest industrial sector in Omsk region is the agricultural sector followed by manufacturing. Prison industries include farming ploughs, household goods, manufacturing parts, police boxes, children's playground furniture, aluminium, tin, steel, all parts for buses and large goods vehicles, radiators, fridges, dachas and 'merry-go-rounds' (children's carousels).[8] Omsk prison region produces tractors and combine harvesters but production has slowed considerably compared with 1990 (the annual production of tractors was 50 in 1990 compared with 10 in 1999). The GCS sector is not categorised as a major industry, but the range of merchandise produced shows that it is an important industrial sector, none the less (10% of prisoners who were allocated employment worked in this sub-sector). Prison officers in Omsk apply an interesting work philosophy to the GCS sector where it is viewed as providing prisoners with a sense of the world beyond the prison. The Head of Educational Training explained: 'It is about providing prisoners with a window to the outside world. These goods can be found in the home. I think that prisoners need to be reminded of home when they are here, to minimise any future problems to do with adjustment.'

In adopting the approach – that all prison labour is significant – prison personnel minimised the commonly-held view that GCS was a tedious, non-purposeful form of prison labour. This approach appeared to be successful, as prisoners felt that their work was 'appreciated' because the institutional survival of the prison was heavily dependent on prison work. This will be explored in more detail in the chapter that follows.

Prison officers were asked to rank the reasons for providing prison labour. Staff were asked to choose incentives for utilising labour from a predetermined list. The responses are given in Table 3.7. Percentages are presented in brackets. It is clear from Table 3.7 that there were very significant differences between prison officers in the reasons given for providing work. The most-cited reasons for prison labour were 'inculcating a habit of work' (31%), followed by the response 'to inculcate a habit of responsibility' (17%). Commercial reasons for work were also cited as important with 12% of staff citing 'keeping the prison running' and 7% of staff stating 'commercial enterprise'. The utilisation of work for punishment was perceived as more important than using work for building character (ratings of 10 and 6). Compared to Smolensk, where

Table 3.7 Reasons for providing labour as presented by staff

	Omsk staff $n = 89$
To give the prisoners time to think about why they committed crime rather than be idle	7 (8)
To build the prisoner's character	5 (6)
To keep the prison running	11 (12)
Because work is punishment	9 (10)
To keep prisoners busy	8 (9)
As a commercial enterprise	6 (7)
To inculcate a habit of work	28 (31)
To inculcate a habit of responsibility	15 (17)

Note
1   K-S: $z = 2.461$; $p = 0.000$.

36% of staff favoured 'to build character' (see Table 3.3), the Omsk responses were more disparate. Diverse rationales such as 'to keep prisoners busy' and 'work as punishment' were similarly dispersed (rated 9 and 10 respectively). This suggests that the goals of imprisonment and the reasons for specific methods for rehabilitation in Omsk were not clear cut, based sometimes on reform and other times on punishment. The interviews also revealed clearly that most staff favoured prison labour that aims at rehabilitation: 'Above all else, work has to reform the man' (governor, Omsk general regime). Other staff offered responses that suggest that labour can rehabilitate offenders if it combines punishment with education: 'Labour is only useful if the prisoner is punished. He will be accepted in the community if s/he can communicate to society: "I have been punished, and I have also learned some skills" ' (director of prison industries, Omsk strict regime). Others believed that institutional survival is achieved through prisoners' work: 'The prison and the community benefit. He learns skills, so that he can find a job. He also produces goods to keep the place operating' (prison education officer, general regime).

The work that was available, while being appreciated by prisoners in terms of its time-passing qualities, was viewed less favourably in terms of its usefulness and how it was approached and implemented by staff, particularly in the strict regime, which raises questions as to whether Omsk region was meeting the guidelines of the 1997 Corrective Labour Code in providing 'meaningful and humane labour'. One prisoner said to me: 'It is just like the old days. We work really hard' (prisoner, strict regime). Work epitomised 'hard labour' that involved long hours and difficult work conditions where not all prisoners were skilled for the heavier types of work: 'I am really exhausted. Not all of us are working, but those of us who work do really difficult work that is bloody hard. Then again, it's is better than not working' (prisoner, strict regime).

In Omsk the overall impression was that prison labour was viewed as achieving different goals (punishment, education or paying society a debt). Staff consistently placed emphasis on work as providing for rehabilitation *and* punishment. Only through labour and education could prisoners receive the kinds of reform that combine the goal of paying a debt back to society with useful education. This suggests an absolute faith that prison labour (the types of work and the ways that it resembles work outside) can prepare for a socially useful life after release. Moreover, while staff argued that all prison industry was useful for social reform, and this was reflected in the diverse range of prison labour, it was heavy industry in particular that was cited as the most 'reformative': 'no one ever suffered from a hard day's prison work' (governor, strict regime).

Vocational training was utilised throughout the Soviet period on an arbitrary basis and did not conform to a rigid set of procedures (Jakobson 1993). Most prisoners were insufficiently skilled for handling machinery and were often forced to work in dangerous, life-threatening situations. Nowadays, vocational training is receiving more serious attention. Unlike Smolensk region, Omsk region was able to provide a better range of training for prisoners. Between 1955 and 1993, Omsk region provided up to 70% of prisoners with some form of training and this is higher than in Smolensk (around 60% of prisoners for that period). When the unstable wider economy is taken into account, the range of training programmes offered to inmates wherein all courses, regardless of level and length, underwent formal accreditation through the institutes and universities in Omsk city, is impressive. Figures for 1999 show that up to 50% of the prison population at each site was engaged in training at any one time (which is striking compared with the figure for Smolensk which was 2% in 1999). Every effort was made to supplement each prisoner's work skills with additional training. Training was allocated a high priority, and for some senior staff it was viewed as more important than prison labour: 'Training is at the heart of the work ethic' (governor, strict regime); 'Without training, work is meaningless' (governor, general regime).

Omsk region had instituted a regional penal policy that involved collaboration with local businesses. 'Training and Work: Preparation for Life after Prison' (*Podgatovka i Rabota: Prigotovlenie posle Govora*) aimed to match investment in training with investment in prison labour. A further aim was to set up a Department of Social Education in each colony that would oversee Community Liaison Partnerships which were established between the penal colonies and community networks. According to the director of prison industries in Omsk strict regime: 'The private sector is immensely important, from monitoring the quality of our goods, to offering advice on how to improve training and industry. In turn we help them.'

That the order of prison life has been disrupted since 1991 to such a degree that the entire ethos and ideology of imprisonment were being overhauled was apparent at all the sites visited. And while there was a strong desire to offer individuals in prison something more than prison work there was equally a sense that the step forward in the transition period was to innovate the concepts from Russia's recent past into a penal policy that was not alien to Russians. Moreover, such a reformed version of Soviet penality would not be unfamiliar to Western analysts or to the international bodies who would be scrutinising the contemporary system. This was particularly evident in the Community Liaison Partnerships which were being piloted in 1999.

Community Liaison Partnerships

The Community Liaison Partnerships (hereafter CLPs) came about following the establishment of a new department at Omsk region's prison headquarters titled the Department of Social Education. The department was referred to 'as a network of local people from the surrounding villages and towns; business people; community leaders; religious leaders and Omsk City Council representatives' who would meet at Omsk headquarters once a month to discuss various 'socially inclusive solutions'. The broad aim of the network was 'collective responsibility for offenders and their rehabilitation' and the objectives were to design and oversee three new programmes: 'Social Re-habilitation after Prison' (*Sotsialnaya Riabilitatsiya posle Govora*), 'Sustaining Work after Release' (*Biderzhavaya Rabotu posle Govora*) and 'Care for the Community after Release' (*Uvazhenie na Obshchestva*). Regional prison officials had set a recruitment target for prison officers wherein 40% of the Omsk prison officers would be employed from academia, secondary education and from the financial, economic and marketing sectors.

Given the severe economic crisis in Russia in the late 1990s, these programmes were ambitious. The CLPs relied on sponsorship from the private sector. Prison officials told me that this was not the most difficult obstacle to overcome for the regional managers as the complex system of barter (see Chapter 4) meant that the private sector was already involved in resource provision. Local farms, Omsk City Council and the company Electrovest were the main sponsors of the CLPs. Prisoners would be supervised by a prison officer on a day-release scheme that involved 'shadowing' work staff in a range of industrial sectors (factories, farming and metal plants, for example).

The programme 'Care for the Community after Release' was par-ticularly interesting because the programme emphasised care *for* the community. Prison labour under this scheme included road maintenance jobs, cleaning public buildings and service employment. This com-munity programme appeared to operate on a number of levels. First, the economic crisis in Russia has seen the unemployment rate soar and so the likelihood of prisoners gaining employment other than that found in low maintenance work was minute. For senior prison managers it was vitally important to persevere with training prisoners: 'Listen, have you seen some of these factories and farms? They are massive. Just because it's maintenance, or road sweeping, it is still a job and with that comes responsibility and dignity' (director of prison industries, Omsk region).

Secondly, the CLP 'Care for the Community' can be interpreted as having two layers: a punitive element and a rehabilitative element. If a placement that involved tending the cleaning of machines at a factory leads to future employment then this might minimise the risk of reoffending by providing former prisoners with an income and, importantly, a connection to the social world they are released into. This is supported by research findings from the UK (see Reuss 1999; Simon 1999).

Thirdly, road-sweeping, cleaning work and employment at ticket-vending machines are low skilled and poorly paid in Russia as they are in many Western countries. Directing prisoners into these types of employment may appeal to the more conservative members of the public, some of whom were members of the prison work committees and who may resent skilled work being offered to former offenders. The interviews with prison officers supported the view that hard labour while punitive in its conditions (wages, career development, hours of work, nature of work) can also be reforming in that it instils a rigorous habit of work: 'Hard labour is very difficult? Yes I accept that but we must ensure that work is prioritised here. Prisoners need to pay a debt back to society and hard work, difficult work, is the best way' (senior prison industries officer, Omsk strict regime); 'In the old days it was work that helped us to reform prisoners. It also held us together. I still believe that whatever the work is that prisoners undertake, it must be hard so that it can reform' (governor, Omsk strict regime).

The majority of prisoners did not share this view. Some were grateful of any work opportunity offered to them because employment relieved boredom: 'God I will do anything in here. I would even lick envelopes. Anything to stop me looking at the clock' (prisoner, Omsk strict regime). Others, however, argued that current work provisions could only sustain post-custody rehabilitation in the short term: 'Cleaning streets will not make me less likely to commit crime. Maybe for a month or two. But if I am in a job like that for more then three months, and the pay is so low, then how am I to ensure that I do not pick up old habits?' (prisoner, Omsk general regime); 'It's dull work. I was an engineer before I arrived here. I will probably end up raking grass or something. It is un-dignifying' (prisoner, Omsk strict regime).

What was interesting was that amid the turbulent conditions and dislodging of the penal system from its point of origin, Omsk prison region was able to formulate a penal policy that involved local groups and organisations, that reflected the local cultural milieu. Prison officers welcomed the quasi-autonomous status of the region. Prison officers also appeared unconcerned that the increased involvement of the private sector may lead to the marginalisation of the central authority: 'Who is here to help us with funding? Certainly not Moscow so why should they complain when private business offers resources?' (director of prison industries, Omsk strict regime). Moreover, there was also very little debate over who was the main resource provider and whether this might impact on rehabilitation. Given that the private sector was involved in providing essential resources to the colonies, and that the survival of these programmes very much depended on funding, there is a danger that the utilisation of prison labour as a reforming mechanism may become ancillary to keeping the colonies operational. This is explored in detail in Chapter 6.

One striking feature of the community programmes was that they did not take into account the possibility that some prisoners might not want to work, or work in the community for that matter. Omsk region did not offer the kinds of person-oriented reform initiatives available in other regions. Psychological services were reserved for persons who had been diagnosed with mental health problems and while religion was available, this was only to the degree that it has been accepted as a democratic right to practise a faith. As for 'testing and analysis', these focused on personal ability and commitment to work. Table 3.8 illustrates the views of prison officers and prisoners as to the role of religious doctrine in the process of rehabilitation. There was a highly significant difference between prisoners and staff in their views of religion as a mechanism that can enhance the process of rehabilitation. The majority view among prisoners was that religion is important (76%) whereas for staff religion was viewed on the whole as not important (74%). The interviews

Table 3.8 The importance of religion in achieving the goal of imprisonment for all Omsk respondents

	Prisoners $n = 17$	Staff $n = 89$
Important	13 (76)	23 (26)
Not important (including 'no opinion')	4 (24)	66 (74)

Note
1   $\chi^2 = 16.313$; $p = 0.000$; d.f. = 1. One cell had a frequency of less than five, violating the chi-square assumption.

support the differences between staff and prisoners: 'Work is much more important than religion, because it can provide the prisoner with an opportunity to obtain work and then survive in society' (prison industries officer, Omsk strict regime); 'I think religion is important. Work, skills, training and asking God for forgiveness are all that is needed here' (prisoner, Omsk strict regime). Among staff, there was a sense that prisoners wanted to be seen to be repenting for their crimes. Among prisoners, religion was favoured over work because the work undertaken was seen to be punitive, and not rehabilitative, with little or no remuneration. Attending mass and engaging in religious doctrine, prisoners argued, provided individuals with an opportunity to reflect on why they were in prison.

From the discussion so far, it can be inferred that in Omsk region, the rehabilitation programmes in place focused attention on how the reforming capabilities of prison labour must aim to restore the social harm caused by crime, namely, social exclusion. This was further evidenced in how Omsk region facilitated post-custody supervision and rehabilitation.

Post-custody social reform in Omsk

Although a follow-up study of former prisoners to assess the level of reoffending was not possible, staff did offer views about whether the policies described in this book as aiming to bring about 'social reform' could be sustained after release. The main issue for consideration relevant to the Omsk prisons was the kinds of action being taken to ensure that prisoners find employment once released so that they do not reoffend. While the programmes were at the pilot phase, it was possible to explore how staff might perceive their effectiveness and their general views on how current provisions might reduce the risk of reoffending: 'I believe in useful hard work that can be supported by training' (governor, Omsk general regime); 'The official view is that these initiatives offer new ways of thinking about reform that are based on the best of the past, but which also look to the future' (chief, Omsk region). A minority view was that hard punitive labour is the only means to repentance: 'I am not ashamed to say it, but our goals incorporate a forced or hard labour element. We know from history that prisoners benefit from forced labour by being suitably punished while learning a skill' (director of prison industries, Omsk strict regime).

Prisoners had a different view. Staff, they argued, were indifferent about work conditions and were ignorant of the many other ways that reform could be achieved: 'I cannot see myself building country houses and producing car parts when I get out and yet we are still forced to work' (prisoner, Omsk general regime). Prisoners also cited inconsistencies in what staff aspired to achieve (social reform, training and work experience) and the reality facing prisoners in terms of the kinds of employment available, which is predominantly low skilled: 'It is hard to imagine how I can sustain a law-abiding crime-free life if wages for this kind of work are well below the national average, which is about $40 [US] a month' (prisoner, Omsk general regime).

As has already been shown, the problem in providing prisoners with meaningful work experiences that can minimise social exclusion following release from prison is not unique to Russia. Yet, the overall decline of the Russian economy and the failure of marketisation have exacerbated the situation in that country. Omsk region has avoided much of the economic decline that has blighted Russia's contemporary development due to the stability of agriculture in Western Siberia and the cheap rents companies pay to locate further out from Moscow. Particularly in actual content (products and processes) many kinds of prison labour in Omsk were becoming like their counterparts outside and the investment of quality control managers from the private sector mean that their quality was also comparable. However, the comments from the prisoners above about the low level of skills attained should not be underestimated and should be a matter of concern for the future management of prison labour. Beyond the prison, success of these programmes will depend on better state funding and state funding is dependent on the stability of Russia's economy. The CLPs could enable the region to calculate which types of crime feature in reoffending statistics, the geographical locations of crime, the demographic background of offenders and track records on obtaining employment. In effect the CLPs, could be fashioned into a probation-type service.

To conclude the findings from Omsk region, the new penal identity of social reform was, in part, reminiscent of the Soviet period. Prison officers clearly articulated nostalgic yearnings towards the Soviet penal system and referred openly to Marxist/Leninist criminology when explaining the importance of restoring a homogeneous, united community in reforming prisoners: 'The prisoner will reform if s/he knows that society benefits from their work' (governor, Omsk general regime).

Indeed, the governor of the strict regime stated that the working practices in the Omsk colonies reflected a moderated version of the bureaucratised, centralised and authoritarian approach to imprisonment that characterised the Soviet penal system. In his aspirations to lead the development of a new penality, this governor was promoting the region above the state as the principal administrator of imprisonment. He also expressed views that indicated that he supported the Omsk Gulag: 'Once a Gulag, always a Gulag. The name may have changed but we are still a prison whereby we emphasise work.'

Prisoners, as I have shown, did not conceptualise their prison experience by adopting a mindset from the Soviet period. When it came to the gruelling work schedules and poor conditions staff they argued, were non-responsive to their needs and were ignorant of the many other ways that reform could be achieved. Clearly, there were many mixed messages about the nature of imprisonment based on an amalgamation of Western prison practices and Soviet penal histories that rendered the new identity complex and at times confusing. When prison officers harked back to the bygone era of forest zones when production was contingent on prisoners' work, they conveyed a sense that a shared consciousness and a connection to the process of production linked the prison population to the institution. This came to be understood in two lights. First, as a hangover from the Soviet period which remains because Omsk is located over 3,000 km east of Moscow and is not as readily exposed to Western ideas. Although prison managers were not found to be adopting extreme versions of Soviet thinking about crime, there was some evidence that compulsory work was still perceived as a useful mode of punishment by regular references to 'hard labour'. Soviet prison propaganda posters in the industrial zone and the casual references to the 'Red Industry Sector' indicated that Omsk region had not broken free entirely from its Soviet past. The continuities from Marxism/Leninism were particularly evident in the ways in which the colonies united around an ideology that connected the prisoner with the environment into a shared collective conscience that, for staff, allowed for a degree of legitimisation of penal policy in an otherwise transient phase.

Secondly, social reform in Omsk was reminiscent also of Western approaches, particularly in the ways in which character reform is incorporated into social reform as the vocational skills and opportunities that prisoners carry with them after custody assist them in leading a law-abiding life. The decline of work generally across prisons in Western Europe has meant that new alternative treatment programmes have had to be found. At times, the penal phenomena in Omsk appeared to mimic, parody even, Western penal phenomena, particularly the CLPs, which were found to be similar to programmes that focus on employment as a critical factor in reducing offending (for example, I am thinking here of the work inside and outside prisons undertaken by the APEX Trust in the UK). Most prison systems experience problems in ensuring that skills and training initiatives are comparable with skills and training in the community and this was a significant concern for prison officers in

Omsk. If the CLPs do prove to be effective in both reducing offending and enabling resettlement in the community, then the often-cited problems of obtaining employment and social inclusion could be reduced.

Comparisons between Smolensk and Omsk

The overarching aim of imprisonment in Smolensk departs from Soviet penal ideology in that the region has implemented positivistic models to promote the goal of character reform. Omsk, on the other hand, has retained much of the Soviet prison rhetoric. Smolensk region offers prisoners far less prison labour (both in quality and quantity) and vocational training compared with Omsk and instead relies more on religion and psychological treatment models in pursing its individuated penal policy. Omsk has been more successful in its prison labour with up to 76% of prisoners being offered work compared with a maximum of 51% in Smolensk. In the absence of a centralised agenda, the prison regions oscillate in the policies and practices they pursue. The different emphases on the innate characteristics (Smolensk) and prisoners as social actors (Omsk) were reflected in the numbers of staff employed in each region. Table 3.9 presents the patterns of employment in each region.

While the numbers of staff employed in specific sectors were similar within regions, the regional differences in the total numbers of staff employed are very striking. Each Omsk colony employed more than double the amount of industrial staff than each Smolensk colony (85 and 248 in the Smolensk strict and Omsk strict regimes respectively, and 63 and 199 in Smolensk general and Omsk general regimes respectively). Smolensk strict regime employed over four times the psychology staff than Omsk strict regime (42 and 9 respectively) and Smolensk general regime employed over twelve times the psychology staff than Omsk general regime (37 and 3 respectively). In both Omsk colonies, industrial staff made up around half the total staff workforce. This is markedly different from Smolensk where the strict regime's industrial staff made up around one quarter of the total number of staff and, in the general regime, around one fifth of all staff. Nearly four times as many priests can be employed at any one time in Smolensk strict regime than Omsk strict regime (19 and 5 respectively). Similar comparisons between the general regimes across regions can be made with five times more priests working in Smolensk general regime compared with Omsk general regime (10 and 2 respectively).

Table 3.9 Staff breakdown in each colony in each region[1]

	Smolensk strict	Smolensk general	Omsk strict	Omsk general
Industrial staff				
Industrialists	44	34	90	57
Economists	1	1	3	2
Marketing managers	2	0	5	5
Marketing assistants	0	0	7	4
Work managers (*Master*)	25	21	67	60
Accountants	2	1	6	3
Product developers	0	1	2	3
Engineers	2	1	7	5
Technologists	1	0	4	1
Trainers	7	4	32	39
Community liaison staff	1	0	25	20
Total	*85*	*63*	*248*	*199*
Psychology staff				
Psychology staff[2]	42	37	9	3
Psychiatrists	3	3	1	0
Arts and crafts specialists	0	1	2	4
Total	*45*	*41*	*12*	*7*
Priests (employed at any one time)	19	10	5	2
All other staff	330	300	400	370

Note

1   In most of the prison regions in Russia staff are divided into two categories: 'industry staff' and 'other staff'. Industry staff implement prison labour, training, management and industrial contracts. Psychology staff comprise psychologists, priests and trainers who all provide alternatives to work activities for prisoners. The staff numbers are totals from the four colonies in each region and are not the total number of staff in *all* colonies in each region.

2   Social work staff are included here.

The diagnosis of the problem of crime in Omsk was seen as less to do with the individual and more to do with the relationship between the individual and society. Therefore the aim was to inculcate 'work habits' that would be useful after the period of custody. There were a token number of priests but not enough to prioritise this as a method for bringing about reform. Psychology clearly had a role in Omsk, but it was much lower key than in Smolensk. By contrast Omsk had huge numbers (compared with Smolensk) of vocational trainers and community liaison staff. Both Omsk regimes employed around three times the amount of work managers whose job is to supervise production than the Smolensk regimes.

There were also regional differences in the background of staff employed. The majority of prison officers (around 75%) in the Smolensk region were recruited from Prison Service Training Academies and the remaining staff had backgrounds in education (former schoolteachers and academics). In Omsk the staff quota was roughly equal between officers trained at prison service training academies and staff recruited from education. In Smolensk the professional background of staff was not considered a factor in providing the best environment for re-habilitation to occur. For example, staff involved in psychological analysis in Smolensk were not required by the region to be qualified psychologists and could instead be employed as a 'prison psychologist' if they completed one or two classes as part of their prison service training. The governor of Smolensk strict regime remarked: 'There is no generally accepted model of training used for psychologists or industrialists. It seems to me that the only important knowledge an officer needs is, first, how to keep prisoners locked up, and then how to control them.' Omsk region organised recruitment around the regional penal policies. According to the director of prison industries for Omsk region: 'There is no point in employing psychiatrists when I need help to sort out targets and budgets.' Omsk region had continued with the Soviet tradition of recruiting economists and industrialists who could provide for reform by instilling work habits, whereas Smolensk region looked to priests and psychologists to achieve character reform.

It seemed to me that the kaleidoscope of penal identities that shape the contours of imprisonment in contemporary Russia reflects a com-petition between altered images from the Tsarist and Soviet periods, and how these appear alongside distorted images of Western culture. In explaining the differences in the nature of the identities adopted, three areas are worth looking at. First, the ideological vacuum that followed the collapse of the connection between prisons and the wider political and cultural universe of Marxism/Leninism. Secondly, how the identities of the prison are determined by the spatial dispersal of prisons from the centre. Thirdly, the permeability of the prison system to ideas from elsewhere and patterns of consumption. I explore these areas in more detail in Chapter 5 where I discuss the analytical framework for understanding the development of penal policy in transition.

In conclusion, the collapse of Soviet centralist orthodoxy has led to scope for variety in the new formations in the prison system. The ongoing sustainability of prison labour, the geographical distance from the centre and the weaker connection to the state have led Omsk region to revive Soviet penological ideas. Whereas in Smolensk, the region is importing knowledge from the West which is running parallel to another Western trend: the decline in prison labour.

What was striking was how the prospect for change raised new and imaginative possibilities for how the prison system comes to define itself. The prison officers I interviewed talked enthusiastically about 'their versions' of imprisonment. That this was an exciting time for knowledge sharing was evident in the ways in which traditional social norms were revived in some areas and in the localised knowledge of demand and supply for prison goods in other areas and, also, in the ideas that were coming to have some influence on prison regions located near Western Europe. Certainly, the ideas were uneven, but the tools in place (work, training and religion), the visual displays (psychology booths) and discussions of imprisonment were remarkable because punishment was calibrated on the seriousness of the offence and on new ways of conceiving of the individual. Programmes, moreover, while indi-viduated from the centre, were constructed around welfare principles.

The transient state of imprisonment in Russia and the theoretically improvised modes of punishment opened up new lines of inquiry about how Russia is positioned in a world where penal politics are constantly evolving both in practice and governance. My research, moreover, uncovered something else that I found to be complex and extremely interesting. Prisoners worked for personal survival. Current conditions necessitate that prisoners must work to produce goods that can be exchanged with the local communities, local businesses and commercial companies through a system of barter. These transactions provide the prison establishments with essential resources and provisions. In the following chapter I describe how barter is contributing to the sustainability of the prisons with the assistance of prisoners' work.

Notes

1 I would like to add the caveat that it would be irresponsible to assume these findings were typical given the scale and scope of the penal system.
2 The terms 'inborn' and 'social' were chosen because they were easily identifiable to respondents (see Ushatikov et al. 1997). The term 'social' relates to causes connected to the wider environment. The term 'inborn' describes all behaviours that are 'habitual', 'inherent', 'personality induced' and 'psychopathic'.
3 Source: Department of Prison Information, Smolensk Prison Region Headquarters, Smolensk.

4 The Russian title for 'Goods for Civil Society' is *Tovarii na Narod*.

5 The list of responses was taken from the prison service publication *Penitentsiarnie Uchrezhdennie v Sisteme Ministerstvo Yustitsii Rossi* (*Penitentiaries under the Ministry of Justice*). In the publication, the Deputy Minister of the prison service, Yuri Igorovich Kalinnin, outlines reasons for providing prison work (see Zubkov *et al.* 1998).

6 Although this finding is inconclusive since there was a 0 frequency in one of the cells (that is, assumptions of chi-square are violated).

7 Between autumn 1997 and spring 1999, five prime ministers sat in office in Russia.

8 Other products include farming equipment, agricultural repairs, industrial machinery for collective farms, industrial springs, tin wiring, household goods, bayonets, barbed wire, knives, swings for children, furniture, kitchenware, garage repairs, coffins for people and animals, garden furniture for children, shopping bags and headstones.

Chapter 4

Barter: Russia's 'penal micro-economy'

Ideas about penal punishment come in all shapes and sizes. The new penal identities addressed in Chapter 3 – where prison staff and prisoners impose an identification on concepts and norms in the prison realm that are detached from centralised orthodoxy and where the social organisation of the penal world is loosely coupled and borderless – should be viewed as a consequence of the state of penal volatility in that country. In precise terms, transition has resulted in changes in the rationales underpinning imprisonment. Under the present system people are sent to prison as a punishment in response to a crime committed and not for political reasons. The utilisation of Marxist/Leninist symbols in prison establishments continues to some degree in the regions that are geographically distant from Western Russia (Omsk). Western models of treatment that focus on cognitive behavioural therapy delivered by psychotherapists, social workers and psychologists coupled with religion have punctured the porous boundaries in Western Russia (Smolensk). In Chapter 3, I introduced some of the causal factors that can be attributed to shaping the identities of these polarised adaptations: the spatial dispersal of the prison regions; their individualised histories and social geography; exposure to Western norms and their ability to offer prison labour.

I made two observations about Soviet penality. One observation placed modes of imprisonment within an ideological discourse. The other observation within the 'economic science' of imprisonment, the special characteristics of which were that politics joined with economy, making possible a punitive state designed to sustain Soviet identity (carceral and non-carceral). I would now like to turn attention to how the collapse of the economic science – the prison labour – affects today's prison system and how the unravelling of the state structures impacts on prison management. The most direct observation I could make about imprisonment in Russia today is that as well as changes to penal ideology where there are varied rationales underpinning the organisation of prison labour and the use of alternatives, there have also been changes to the economy of prisons. Prisoners now have to work in order to live and not for the sake of the economy. The regions are allocated a budget from the central prison authority in Moscow that is intended to cover all maintenance costs and personnel costs. However, the economic instability from 1995 onwards has adversely affected prison budgets. The central government is currently unable to provide the necessary costs for running the prisons and so it has been left to the regional managers and prison governors to manage the budgets and implement policies and initiatives accordingly. When the centre allocates its scarce resources it does so precisely on the basis of what the prison colonies can do for themselves (bearing in mind their access to raw materials and markets). The remaining essential resources are provided through a system of barter. Ostensibly, therefore, prison labour is not just a mechanism for achieving the reform of prisoners. It has become the very means of survival for the colonies. The different ways that barter is providing for the economic sustainability of the prison establishments are explored in this chapter. In Chapter 6 I critique Russia's penal micro-economy.

Central government funding of the prison regions

The Soviet penal system was funded entirely by the central government. The prison system was grand in its design because it was a microcosm of Soviet society where the normative structures of penal life and non-penal life were fused together (see Appendix 3). Historians amply show how the Soviet regime aspired to a fully workable socialist economy through ambitious building projects and the regime funded all the workforce costs (Bacon 1994). Forced to comply with the impossible requirements of successive economic plans, the penal system pursued unattainable goals and officials sought to use forced labour manpower to *fund the economy* in order to expand their bureaucracies and meet these un-realistic goals. The penal system has gone through different cycles: repressive penal punishment under Stalin in the 1930s and 1940s, which was the era of slave prison labour and Gulag camps that were organised around economic efficiency; the 1950s and 1960s when the fusion of political correction and economic forced labour was somewhat diluted; recently, the 1990s, when the doors of the penal system opened and when political dissidents were increasingly brazen in their efforts to expose atrocities in the penal system.

There has been considerable debate over the industrial feats of prison labour and whether the plans to utilise prisoners' work were as carefully designed as the state propaganda suggested (see Jakobson 1993; Bacon 1994; Applebaum 2003).[1] Certainly, the links between efficiency and output have been shown time and again from the prisoners' testimonies, to be tenuous. Solzhenitsyn (1986) describes a chaotic camp structure where targets were set on an arbitrary basis and where guards had little expertise in managing the prison subeconomy. Putting anomalies over penal efficiency to one side, the management of the penal system, the allocation of funds, the leadership of the system and the organisation of administrative departments were managed under the authority of the Soviet regime who promoted a single-concept theory of a Marxist/ Leninist political and economic penal system.

Prisons were not viewed as a state burden as the physical survival of the regime was dependent on the millions of prisoners. Whatever the state allocated for the management of prisons (transport to and from establishments, personnel, prison industries and political correction) was usually, but not always, released in the full amount to the prison establishments. Budget allocations have been debated by historians in the West and the general consensus is that while the state invested in the public institutions (for instance, the regime would fund the prison system from the industrialisation of manufacturing, transport and agriculture sectors), the national budget was deeply in deficit and has been for years. Dallin and Nicolaevsky (1947), Jasny (1951) and Ahkmadiev (1993) depict an enormously wasteful planning system, declining rates of growth and living standards decades behind the West's. The impact on the prison system is that while the regime's declaration that the fully funded prisons were efficient, economic and effective, both in industrial outputs and penological ends (without prisoners the communist utopia would cease), the regime could not commit to funding the system fully. And as Soviet political ideology did not permit contracting out of prison services to the private sector, which might have helped defray some of the state costs, by 1991, the over-populated and over-powerful penal system was in a much worse state than previously realised. For the purposes of this book, of keynote here is that the state administered all funds to the hundreds of prison camps and colonies. Moreover, while on the one hand, there was a degree of order and stability of daily life in the USSR, on the other hand the prison system was working over-time to meet targets and produce industries that could be exported in order that Soviet society became modernised.

Since 1991 it has been argued that economic disorder has plunged Russia into the kinds of underdeveloped social conditions the Soviet regime was so desperate to abolish (Abramkin and Chesnokova 1995). Gorbachev's failed marketisation programme (*glasnost*) and Yeltsin's attempt to secure democratic institutions through *perestroika* were disastrous and failed to address the country's problems. The legacy of the Soviet system was underestimated and the poor handling of the economic and political scene in the ensuing transition period sent that country into swift decline.

The major obstacles of dealing with the past injustices of the penal system while attending to the high prison population, the absence of minimum standards and human rights are, however, being addressed. The state has been absolutely determined to leave behind these legacies of the Soviet Gulag with a reduction of up to 20% of the prison population and reforms that have been targeted at introducing alternatives to custody. But addressing the bigger normative questions on penal ideology has been less of a feature of penal reform. As I show in the chapters that follow, the very serious human rights issues dominate the penal agenda such that the penal identities arising from localised knowledge and conditions that I have described in Chapter 3 are being submerged under global movements to regulate and harmonise penal systems.

According to Vincentz (2000), the economy of Russia has not been able to develop a functioning financial system over a decade of economic transformation. It is the lack of 'rule of law' that is cited as the main factor in the failure to establish a stable financial sector (Lynch and Thompson 1996). There is little transparency in the economic system: there is a weak banking system; a high level of lending arrears from public and private sectors; ineffective competition arising from poor trade relations; overdue government payments for wages, pensions and so on and a high level of international borrowing (Lynch and Thompson 1996). There are many costs of this financial crisis, but two are directly relevant to the operation of prison establishments. First is the outright use of barter as a second-best solution to the non-cash economy. Secondly there is corruption, as low government wages, paid often with long delays, are forcing employees to make money through corruption. While regional prison managers and prison officers consider the barter practices as entirely normal and acceptable since so much of non-prison life is reliant on barter, the barter practices utilised can become corrupted when staff do not record transactions and withhold goods for personal use.

Central government funding of Smolensk and Omsk prison regions

Trying to explore the costs of maintaining prisons uncovers one of the last mysteries of the Soviet period. According to Tatiana Illyana, a senior researcher at the British Council in Moscow, obtaining data in the first instance is extremely difficult as there are no figures that are readily available such as the Prison Service *annual reports* for England and Wales (see, for example, Her Majesty's Chief Inspector of Prisons' *Annual Report and Accounts for April 1999 to March 2000;* Home Office and Employment Department 1992; Home Office 1993). Any data that *can* be obtained are not presented in a clear or systematic way and vary depending on the organisation that is gathering the figures. In instances where figures that are gathered match, it is almost impossible to guarantee that the figure is accurate as the dollar–rouble rate fluctuated wildly in the decade or so since the collapse of the USSR. So figures should be treated with caution.

In 1999, I found variations in the level of state funds sent to the prison regions and then released to the prison establishments that participated in this study. Following the severe economic crisis in Russia in the period 1995–8 which led to the collapse of the Russian economy, the state, despite its good intentions, was unable to send the regions the full funds necessary to administer places of confinement. In 1998, Smolensk region received approximately 70% of the necessary central funds. Omsk region received a far lower figure of 30% of the funds. There are two explanations for the differences in funds provided. First, Smolensk region receives more because its prison industrial sector is concentrated predominantly in light assembly, which does not generate a sufficient income. Smolensk is heavily dependent on the state for extra subsidy. Omsk region, however, is viewed as better able to exploit the vast natural resources (timber and agriculture) in Western Siberia for the prison industries sector. Second, is the independence that the prisons have from the central prison authority. The regions that are located near Moscow are under greater surveillance from the Moscow government and also from international observers and human rights groups. Hence, it is important to ensure that essential funds are provided to the colonies and are regularly scrutinised to ensure that Russia is meeting its obligation to meet minimum standards.[2] As the chief of Smolensk prison region stated: 'We really cannot manage without Moscow's help. We are under a lot of scrutiny from Moscow so we need to make sure that any funds that are sent are well spent.' Another senior prison officer continues: 'There isn't much of a forum for debating funds. There is quite a bit of control.' In the sections that follow I describe and illustrate the diverse and in some instances innovative ways that extra essential resources are provided for.

Bartering for survival in non-prison and in prison life

Barter is commonly associated with less developed countries where economies can hover between collapse and stability on a daily basis (although in America, organised barter through exchanges is a regular and growing practice not only among individuals but also corporations, regardless of their size; see Williams 1996). Russia is no exception and barter is used as a resource provider between families, at the market, in hospitals and now in prison colonies. There is little question that barter transactions reduce some of the basic problems (the inefficiencies) to do with the poor state subsidy of the prison system and as will be shown, in some settings it is an innovative enterprise. However, barter is notoriously inefficient and outmoded because it depends on a coincidence of needs (Marvasti and Smyth 1998, 1999). While the regular and growing practice of barter is an inevitable development in the current economic and social transition in Russia, in the context of prisons, barter is symbolic. The blurring of the boundary between the 'inside' world of the prison and the 'outside' world has, to some degree, been maintained in the post-Soviet period where the economic conditions necessitate a symbiotic relationship between the prison and the community because the local communities thrive off prisoners' work. Barter, therefore, offers much more than the means for survival and has become massively important for maintaining the social welfare of prisoners and staff for without it, the prisons might destabilise. The local community also benefits from barter as it contributes to the sustainability of local economies such as farming, retail and light industry.

Basic prison barter

Different barter arrangements were operating in all the prison colonies visited. The most basic system was called *Tovarii na Tovarii* (goods for goods). Figure 4.1 shows how this arrangement operates. In this type of exchange the customer, illustrated here as 'a local farmer', would make an appointment to meet the director of prison industries in the reception area of the colony and the goods that the farmer offers would be assessed for quality and usefulness. Russia's conjugal visit programme, whereby the married partners of inmates to spend up to five days in the colony in specially designed accommodation, provided families with the best opportunity to barter. The local farmer in this example brought

Figure 4.1   Basic prison barter or 'goods for goods exchange' (*Tovarii na Tovarii*)

Prison colony

Arrows indicate the direction in which the goods are exchanged

Example 1: prison colony offers furniture and metal goods (aluminium fences, barbed-wire fences). Farmer offers meat and dairy products

Example 2: prison colony offers repairs to agricultural machinery and some expertise on machinery maintenance. Wife of prisoner offers bedding, blankets and other foodstuffs

Example 1: Local farmer
Example 2: Wife of prisoner

foodstuffs (meat, bread and dairy goods) and other products (bedding, soap and furniture), and exchanged them for furniture and metal goods. Alternative examples include the following: on regular occasions, the wife of one prisoner brought eggs and potatoes from the family farm and exchanged these goods for agricultural machinery parts. In a more formal arrangement, the wife of a prisoner operated a business trading in preserves and marmalades in exchange for repairs to farming equipment. In the latter example, staff also purchased the woman's home baking and would trade in products that they had prepared at home (knitting winter jumpers and sewing dishcloths, for example).

Where both parties reached an agreement an 'exchange contract' was established. Every type of product (combine harvesters, tractors, police boxes, farming equipment, prisoner training and children's toys, for example) was exchanged using this type of barter transaction. Barter was used to manage a whole range of relationships, both legal and illegal, and between all kinds of customers (mainly the local community but local businesses and commercial businesses were also involved) and the prison colony. In the more formal processes – the legal exchanges – a cash value was calculated and then exchanged for goods to the value of the amount determined by the director. The director, who submits the amounts exchanged into a logbook that is audited by regional head-quarters, records the transaction. Good community relations were fostered as a result; local traders came to know who the key staff were whom they could rely on to wheel and deal an exchange. I witnessed barter negotiations that were informal, unregulated and certainly not scrutinised or audited. None of the prison-produced goods was taxed and the majority of goods that were traded between the prisons and the communities were well targeted. I judged that the utilisation of prison barter resembles a small and thriving market economy.

The majority of the exchanges that were observed during the period of study were officially recorded. Other exchanges observed were weekly exchanges of 20 dozen eggs from a farm for repairs on dairy farming equipment (Omsk strict regime), the purchase of meat from local farmers in exchange for holiday cottages (*dacha*)[3] (Smolensk general regime) and the more macabre example of the exchange of mattresses from local hospitals for prison-produced coffins (Omsk general regime). In 1997, Omsk general regime opened a shop selling funeral paraphernalia and products (ornate headstones, artificial flower arrangements) that could be purchased using barter. When I returned to Omsk general regime in 2003, the shop was still trading.

A first-hand experience of a barter exchange brings to light how the successful utilisation of barter depends as much on the drive and quick-witted thinking of staff as it did on matching colony needs with consumer wants. A travelling circus that had broken down near one colony had received repairs to its small fleet of lorries in exchange for a circus performance, after a prison officer noticed the breakdown of the lorry fleet on his way to work. The prison officer involved had negotiated, at the lay-by where the fleet of three large trucks had been stranded, a barter contract to provide entertainment for staff and prisoners. This exchange was recorded as a 'primary exchange' because it met one of the requirements of the articles contained in the 1997 Corrective Labour Code (CLC) 'To provide cultural activities for prisoners' (*Ugolovnie Ispolnitelnie Prava* 1997). The role of the prison officer in this situation is a somewhat mutated version of what Ledeneva (1998) describes as the *blatmeister*, a person who administers exchange networks and arranges barter between friends and acquaintances. Rather than having to locate the elusive someone who could produce the good or service needed by the friend (of a friend), the prison officer can have the prisoner make the goods.

There were unrecorded barter transactions that were used to provide certain prisoners with privileges. Senior officials overlooked these exchanges, regarding them as 'entirely normal'; they also stood to benefit from the illegal exchanges by keeping goods for personal use. One such exchange that I observed involved a *mafiya* gang bartering an agreement that one of its members receive privileges during custody in exchange for televisions provided by the *mafiya*. The director of prison industries for that colony told me: 'Where else are we to purchase goods? The region certainly does not have the funds, so we negotiate with prisoners.'

Barter was used at the most basic level, but it none the less provided the colonies with essential items ranging from pork to cleaning materials. In each colony I visited, approximately 70% of all barter exchanges were between the colony and the local community and the majority of products were light-assembly goods. With prices 25% cheaper compared with retail prices it is hardly surprising that local people purchased prison-produced goods. The chief of Smolensk prison region commented: 'Most of our customers are from the villages surrounding the colonies. They exchange eggs, cheese, bread, anything really, for items like kitchen furniture and chopping boards.' Despite providing for a proportion of essential resources, barter did not compensate fully for the shortfall of funds.

Innovative prison barter

The 'goods for goods exchange' was in operation in all four colonies. In Omsk region three additional methods were used to provide resources: cash, barter between the client and the central government on the colony's behalf and Community Liaison Partnerships (CLPs). All the types of transaction in Omsk could be used concurrently.

Omsk regional managers used cash (or 'real money' as it was humorously referred to) to pay staff and for purchasing specialist or heavy machinery. This type of transaction was called a 'colony to bank transfer' (*Peredacha Cherez Bank*) because it was supervised by a regional bank and it involved each party paying a deposit to the bank to protect the sale against collapse. The arrangement was used the least often because many banks have become unstable after the collapse of the Russian economy in 1998.

The second alternative method is non-monetary and involved the client paying some of the colony's debts or land taxes directly to the Moscow government. This arrangement has arisen because sometimes there are situations where the colony offers products for exchange but does not need the products being offered in return. This agreement is called 'customer–Moscow exchange' (*Zachiot k Moskvu ot Klienta*) and it is illustrated in Figure 4.2. The use of this method was restricted to exchanges with large companies such as Omsk Gas, a multinational gas company providing gas services throughout Siberia.[4] The contract for transactions between the prison establishments and the sponsor was presented to the parties in the form of a flow-chart that outlined how goods, services and costs are transferred from three different groups.

As Figure 4.2 reveals, in the first instance Omsk strict regime provided some labour and gas piping equipment. However, the colony did not

Figure 4.2 Innovative barter techniques or 'customer–Moscow exchange' (*Zachiot k Moskvu ot Klienta*)

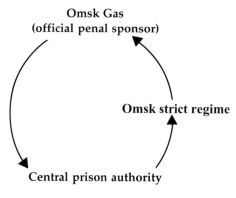

Omsk Gas (official penal sponsor)

Omsk strict regime

Central prison authority

Arrows indicate the direction in which the services are exchanged. Omsk Gas requests gas piping and labour from Omsk strict regime. Omsk strict regime gives goods to Omsk Gas and negotiates a deal for Omsk Gas to pay off accumulated land tax and debt to the central prison authority in Moscow. Omsk Gas agrees to act as the colony's official penal sponsor and pays finances to Moscow

specify goods in return even though goods were very much needed. Instead, the colony governor would negotiate with Omsk Gas and requested that it pay some of the colony's overdue land tax to the central prison authority in Moscow. In this instance Omsk Gas acted as the colony's 'Official Penal Sponsor'[5] by liaising directly with the central prison authority. The outcome was that the central prison authority received the tax it was owed, the client received gas piping and manual labour, and the colony was relieved of some of the debt that it had accumulated – everyone was happy.

Figure 4.2 is interesting because it reveals a process of reciprocal penal trade that does not follow the typical 'two-way relationship' or quid pro quo that characterises most barter agreements (see Marvasti and Smyth 1999 for barter comparisons). Instead services or goods were exchanged through a process of transferring the product (or a virtual product) from one group to another. While none of the groups involved had exchanged a service or product with the group from whom they received a service, the arrangement was accepted by Moscow officials because all parties received some kind of payment. The arrangement was popular with the director of prison industries for Omsk region who stated: 'I favour extending this method of providing goods and services. We could get involved with other companies in agriculture, manufacturing and commerce based in the Western Siberian region.' The arrangement also ensured that a federal connection between the colonies and the Moscow government was maintained, although this was somewhat questionable by the involvement of the private sector as the colonies' 'Official Penal Sponsor'.

A third non-monetary method that was used to provide resources was the exchange of prisoner training and prison merchandise from the colony for the secondment of experts (training managers, industrial staff, engineers and business experts) into the colony CLPs. This was a new initiative at the pilot stage until 2002 and I discussed these partnerships in detail in Chapter 3. Rather than confine prisoners to incarceration until the release date, the regional managers in Omsk instead selected a group of prisoners who were approaching the end of their sentence and who might have qualifications in a range of employment to participate in programmes part-funded by the private sector. Prisoners would not be paid additional wages for work training as it was part of the barter exchange that they gain 'voluntary work experience'. It was common in Omsk to hear about the private sector's involvement in the prison realm as something that was 'innovative' because it enabled the prisoners to gain some work experience – to see the outside world, up close. The prison colonies benefited because the private sector provided essential resources to the colony. A related point is that the public–private partnerships in Omsk's prisons were intended to lead to increased awareness of the benefits of employment that can also lead to improved levels of behaviour during custody as well as rehabilitation in the community. The sources of knowledge of these through-care-type programmes – where the ideas came from – were never made clear to me, although one Omsk manager did state that the region no longer sought to 'insulate itself against' new forms of information and instead opted to modify Soviet practices into a more coherent approach that reflected the employment situation outside and the 'local mood' (as he called it). Accordingly, these through-care programmes were seen as a reworked version of Soviet penal ideology rather than as an outcome of Russia's movement towards European integration whereby the institutions are embracing Western ideas:

> We implement procedures because we know what will work for us. I believe in forced labour. It's not a popular view to you maybe, but I do. So my solution is to temper my thinking about forced labour. But the prisoners know the score, they know they must work to get fed. Yes, I too believe in human rights (chief of Omsk prison region).

This comment serves well as an illustration of the confused and muddled thinking of prison officers as to the modernisation of the prison system, and also is an indication of how prison officers view the movement to humanise the prison system. This is an important conclusion because it tells us something about how European or international values are being understood in Russia prisons, particularly in remote areas.

There were remnants of Soviet penal thinking that have been retained in the prison colonies in Omsk through the economic uses of prison labour, yet none of the resource provisions outlined above is stemming the shortfall in funds entirely and this was confirmed on the trip to Russia in 2003. The chief of Omsk region stated to me in an interview in 2003:

> Things are much better now and the state funds have improved. However, we still rely on barter. I really can't see how we can live without it. We use it everywhere so to have it in the colonies seemed perfectly natural. I will always support barter because we need it to survive. Things are far from being stable in Russia. Will the state resume full funding? I think not.

This view was common. Barter is supported widely among prison officers and senior officials whose view overall was that in order to survive, supplement incomes and provide for the odd 'extra' for prisoners, alternative means of purchasing goods would be utilised. At all the prisons I visited in Smolensk, Omsk and in Kemerovo in eastern Siberia, barter was providing between 50 and 70% of the absent funds. Where barter could not make up the shortfall, staff worked without pay for up to eight months at a time. Meanwhile, conditions would continue to deteriorate, workshops close down, treatment programmes start and end within months and prisoners continue to face degrading prison conditions.

The central government continues to provide different levels of support to the regions based on information about prison industries. Yet to suppose a correlation between better industries and self-sufficiency, as is assumed about Omsk region, is a falsehood because all sorts of factors affect the successful functioning of a prison (the local and wider market; unemployment; sentencing; staff; expertise and numbers, to name a few). It is also incorrect to assume that a wide range of industries can produce a good many types of merchandise, or that this necessarily guarantees that the prison colonies will cope in the absence of state funds. For example, the CLPs were very unstable because they depended largely on the stability of the various private industries involved.

Branding prison barter

The desperate financial situation in the prisons and the pressure that prison staff were under to provide goods and services were reflected in the ways that prison goods were marketed in local media and in local communities. Where barter was relied on less, as in Smolensk, the organisation of it and marketing of goods were poor and staff attitudes conveyed a casual approach. Advertising was restricted to the local villages surrounding the prison colonies, even though there was a potentially rich array of clientele in numerous villages and enclaves in the Moscow area, close to where the colonies were located and where it was inexpensive to advertise.

The professional background of staff did not help matters. The two staff members who were responsible for the delivery of barter trans-actions in Smolensk region worked without additional support. They had trained under the Soviet system. Thus neither individual had the skills or the creative imagination that were vital to operate prison systems in the current economic and political climate. The data also show that in the region where fewer funds were available, Omsk region, and where more innovative techniques for providing resources were in place, the marketing of goods was methodical and formal. In each colony a Department of Marketing devised advertisements in the prison service magazines *Prigovor* (*Sentence*) and *Chelovek: Prestuplennie i Nakazannie* (*Man: Crime and Punishment*). There were quality control of goods, pro-duct development and product control (switching products on demand). Up to 30 senior officers had responsibility for setting up barter contracts. Staff who trained under the Soviet system worked alongside graduates of the post-Soviet university system who had studied business law, international marketing and economics. Such diversity in professional expertise meant that the director of prison industries could draw on a range of expertise and experience.

Of keynote is that prison officers had abandoned the Russian term for marketing, *Xodkii Tovarii*, in favour of the English language word 'marketing': 'We use English because we think like capitalists now. "Marketing" is an international business word that everyone identifies with.' Another officer remarked: 'We are free to look at marketing books. I am keen on branding. Creating a prison-brand would be good.' This comment was judged as further evidence of how structural problems and the absence of a reformed social concept of imprisonment combined to give prison officers a range of mixed categorisations (often diametrically opposite) that enabled legitimisation of imprisonment as a viable and functional institution.

In so far as integrating Western business speak, Omsk prison officers were more likely to parody the jargon of the West rather than consciously make a statement about the direction that penal policy is heading (see Christie 1996 (revised 2000); Hogan 1997; Davis 1998, 1999 and Jacob 1999 for American comparisons). Omsk prison region advertised barter in businesses throughout Russia as well as in council offices, in schools, and in higher education establishments in Omsk city.

Views on barter

The inconsistent support given to the devolved prison regions impacted on how staff and prisoners perceived the use and organisation of barter and attitudes towards the Moscow government. While the majority of prisoners and staff interviewed did not favour having to rely on the local community and private businesses for resources, prison staff in Omsk took full advantage of the distance from the Moscow government to devise their own strategies for managing the funding crisis. To be precise, there was evidence that the colonies in Siberia were becoming self-governing.

The social relations of the prison functioned independently of political patronage (see Piacentini 2004b). Criminal justice officials visit the Omsk colonies on rare occasions, so any changes in the management of the prison and the provision of resources are not likely to be noticed as quickly by the Moscow government. While this is not particularly alarming, and makes sense in the transition period of post-Soviet political and economic devolution, it should be kept in mind that Omsk region is located 3,000 km east of Moscow. There is currently no criminal justice legislation in place to monitor barter and control the nature and scope of barter arrangements. International legislation such as the Forced Labour Conventions do not prohibit forced labour where it is used as part of a custodial sentence. The potential to abuse barter thus becomes greater. Clearly, then, an immediate concern is whether prison labour is exploitative as the ways in which it currently operates disrupts the orderliness of prison life as personal survival becomes a primary goal over and above imprisonment's reformative or punitive capabilities.

Unsurprisingly, I found that prisoners reported different opinions from staff about barter. According to some prisoners, barter ensures their personal survival: 'I know exactly why I work. It is not for my reform, it is to produce goods so that we get heating, staff wages and food' (prisoner, Smolensk general regime). Another prisoner from Smolensk strict regime remarked: 'If we did not work, then the colony would not operate. I work in order that I get food. I work to live.' Other prisoners stated that the pressure to make the prisons efficient and effective, both for prisoners and staff, could be alleviated if the former knew exactly why they worked: 'I do not find that the work really changes the way I think. So I have no idea really why I work in that it is meaningless for my reform. I am aware that the colony needs the prison labour, however' (prisoner, Smolensk general regime).

The evidence gathered from the prisoner interviews in Omsk also reveals mixed views on barter: 'I cannot impress upon you how much we depend on barter. Without it we would close down. From the small exchanges of eggs for car parts with locals, to exchanging thousands of dollars of machinery for equipment that we can train prisoners on. Good God, it's all dead important' (prisoner, Omsk general regime). Other prisoners, while acknowledging the importance of barter, were dismayed that it is private enterprise that is now sustaining the penal colonies: 'It is shit. Moscow officials are indifferent that companies pay our bills. The government receives taxes. That is all that seems to count' (director of education, Omsk general regime). Some prisoners tended to view barter as a minor concern: 'Of course barter is useful but it is not the main thing we worry about' (prison education officer, Omsk strict regime). While other prisoners, and some staff, were overly confident that barter could keep the colonies operational: 'We don't need Moscow. We do fine just using barter. We know the products and the market inside out' (prisoner, Omsk general regime).

Adjusting to new penal pains

Looking at the responses from all those involved in the implementation of barter from inception, through to production, negotiation and selling of goods, the picture that surfaces shows us how much everyday life in Russia is unsteady and volatile. On some occasions, staff referred to 'just getting by', 'managing alone' and 'feeling in a vulnerable position'. On other occasions staff were evasive over the specific details of how this risky venture could assist in the operation of a prison colony.

Overall, I interpreted the diverse range of views on barter as a reflection of the amorphous lifestyles of contemporary Russians. The use of prison labour clearly has economic uses and from these uses, further social uses. It is these social uses that expose unique features of imprisonment in Russia that cannot be said to be evident in other large prison populations. Penal reformers and human rights groups often argue that to be sentenced to confinement is the punishment and that prisons should not serve additional pain through degrading conditions, unnecessary solitary confinement, bullying and other adjustments to the prison culture that can problematise rehabilitation. Added to the potential obstacles in prison socialisation is the problem of administering imprisonment during transformation from one type of government (in this case, a totalitarian society) to another. The criminological literature on imprisonment has yet to grapple with these issues in-depth, probably because the classic prison texts were written at a time when world order was organised according to ideological divisions of East versus West and communism versus capitalism.

It is worth while to mention here how prison staff and prisoners coped with the current use of barter and other more general concerns. The prisons literature debates how prisoners who are serving long sentences, in particular, navigate the prison space by constructing various identities that they share with others who are incarcerated (see Mathieson 1990; Jewkes 2003). Prisons are often described as constraining and limiting worlds (see Westwood 1990; Schmid and Jones 1991) where the 'authentic selves' of prisoners emerge only upon release from prison. Prisoners not only construct new ways of living but they also must contend with understanding the image of the prison and how the hallmarks of imprisonment as places that control the flow of movement and impose restrictions impact on their subjective reality. There is a whole range of ways that prisoners cope and the overall consensus from international research is that a new prisoner will adopt reflective practices wherein he or she absorbs, and then refers back to, the prison culture by paying attention to physical details and different social behaviours (see Jewkes 2003; Oleinik 2003). This was not borne out by everyone who participated in my study. With the onset of globalisation and the 'end of ideology', penal politics is entering a new epoch where boundaries are permeable to ideas from elsewhere. Combine the fluidity of prison borders with the relentless scrutiny to ensure that conditions meet 'international standards' and you will find that the routine of prison life in Russia has become ordered around multifarious identities from Russia's recent past and the West and – importantly – a daily routine of ensuring that the prison, in all its manifold parts, survives.

In this prisons project, prisoners would construct identities around their sociodemography (their status as fathers and brothers and their professional background) and prison officers mainly around their professional background and previous professions (a good number have chosen employment in prison because it was a more stable profession than, for example, education or the military services). One prison officer summed up the overall feelings about imprisonment well:

I used to work as an engineer. I had a great job, but when the USSR collapsed, I had to re-establish myself. I was no longer employed by the public sector because the public sector was the state. When the state went, my job went. So I lost a big chunk of my life and I didn't know what to do or what to identify with. And I needed to work. I had to forget about it and move on. It is difficult you know, psychologically, switching hats. I joined the prison service because I knew that compared to other jobs, it offered a good pension scheme.

Underpinning this typical construction of coping with the new penal pains is not how prison becomes a space for socialisation through interaction with various other structures or behaviours but, rather, how the change in the identity of the wider political and economic conditions has created different fates for Russian citizens. Nowhere was this more evident than in the use of barter as providing for a micro-economy. As Rusche and Kirchheimer (1939) illustrate, when the prison functions, to all intents and purposes, for economic motives, the 'social' features of confinement are played down and the primary objective is to administer economic concerns. This was particularly evident in the talk of 'surviving' in the prison. While the issue of personal survival during imprisonment is not unique to Russia, the emergence of survival within an unstable barter economy is. The term usually refers to the coping and psychological issues that prisoners address during custody such as maintaining contact with families, partners and friends, and surviving possible brutalities from staff or prisoners. Cohen and Taylor (1981: 53) describe imprisonment as 'disturbing the orderliness of life' in much the same way as the death of a loved one does. They argue that the prison environment is extreme and the prisoner must survive the extreme conditions by secondary socialisation or 'prisonisation', to quote a term used originally by Clemmer (1958). Survival skills are essential post-release where often-cited difficulties include trying to cope with the extreme cultural changes of life after imprisonment.

These aspects of survival are indicative of all prison systems and Russia is no exception. In Russia moreover there is the additional burden of trying to survive while working to ensure that essentials (heating, educational and industrial materials and staff wages) are provided. This is about balancing economic survival with psychological survival. Without a doubt, economic survival contributes to the goal of rehabilitation since keeping the body alive is probably a necessary condition for the maintenance of mental health. But in Russia keeping the body alive *through work* is a necessary condition for the maintenance of the establishment as well as the mental health of the prisoner. Hence psychological survival is very much dependent on economic survival. To a degree, prisoners acknowledged this but staff struggled to grasp fully that Russian prison colonies are increasingly relying on prison labour – yet again – to provide resources, and less on state subsidies: 'My main problem is imagining what the day-to-day situation would be if we received fewer and fewer funds, or if fewer prisoners worked. We have no way of knowing the future' (prison officer, Omsk strict regime).

I hope that the discussions outlined in Chapters 3 and 4 have highlighted the complexity of Russia's penal transition by drawing attention to how prison personnel and prisoners have responded to the current penological crisis by pursuing a range of rationales that aim to fill the void in penality that followed the collapse of the Soviet penal monolith and by installing different economic programmes that aim to stem the shortfall of government funds. My research has uncovered that important issues remain in Russian criminal justice regarding how prisons are legitimated and how prisoners are supported, and my intention was to highlight these issues in the present day through an analysis of the ideological and economic dimensions of prison labour.

In terms of reaching for a theoretical pathway for explaining what is going on in Russia's prisons, I believe that attention should focus on how knowledges of penality and technical assistance travel across time and space from Western penal realms to transitional societies. In the chapters that follow I develop these points further by opening up a critique of how penality is evolving in that country. For example, a pivotal resource for 'ideologising imprisonment' is both Western knowledge and re-embedding local discourses such as Marxist/Leninist orthodoxy. Both sources of knowledge have been instrumental in the formation of penal policy; in providing signs and signposts for prisoners and prison officers; in creating social networks beyond the penal realm and in aiding senior managers to attend to the business of justifying imprisonment as something that is more 'European' and less 'Soviet'. Equally important are the findings on barter, which tell us that in the current climate, prisoners are working under extremely stressful economic conditions. As Russia attempts to shake off its Gulag past and move towards democratic structures it is globalisation, as a process of knowledge transfer, that is coming to have some influence over the management of penal systems around the world (see Newburn and Sparks 2004). Thus, the findings on Russia might be illustrative of shift in how we come to form a view of prisons in societies marked by upheaval.

In the remainder of the book I will analyse the findings on penal identities and barter in Russia's prisons. Chapter 5 looks first at the process that has led to the creation of specific vocabularies in the rationales for prison labour. In mapping out a theoretical pathway, I import the most recent findings from my prison research in Kemerovo and Omsk regions as I found the prisons assimilating a new penal vocabulary of human rights. Nowhere in my findings from the 1999 study could I trace the post-Soviet changes in the language of penality as derived from a human rights discourse (although certainly, there were notable improvements in human rights practices and officials talked of humanity in imprisonment). Chapter 6 continues the analysis of the findings and I examine the utilisation of barter in relation to human rights legislation designed to protect prisoners from exploitation.

In Chapter 7 and in the concluding chapter I make a political connection between penal identities and barter. My main argument is that the paradoxes arising from barter, in that it may be contravening human rights norms, coupled with how the locally-established identities are evolving in the present day, reveal something about how prisons in transition are governed globally. The path of penal development in Russia is, I argue, dependent on Western norms, particularly human rights (aid, technical support, performance targets and consultation). While I do not wish to criticise the principle of human rights, the business of 'improving' prison systems around the world could be construed as an imperialistic invasion that has the effect of suppressing national penal propensities which is: a particularly problematic proposal for societies in transition.

Notes

1 Throughout the 1990s, when the archives opened, *The Times Literary Supplement* presented heated and prolonged debates between leading international scholars on the size of the Gulag in relation to Russia's historical and contemporary political culture (see *The Times Literary Supplement* 6 November 1992; 26 March 1993; 17 March 1994a; 7 April 1994b; 14 April 1994c; 21 April 1994d; 1 December 1995; 9 October 1998; 28 January 2000a; 2000b).
2 Source: chief of Omsk region, interviewed in 2003.
3 Because these are prisons and there were restrictions on the size of production, the holiday cottages were much smaller. They were equipped with basic facilities and were comfortable.

4   It is not known if Omsk Gas is involved in trading with other prison establishments in Siberia or elsewhere.

5   This title was created by the director of prison industries.

Chapter 5

Penal ideology in transition: identification in geographical spaces

The governance of crime in transitional states, in what has been referred to as an anxious age, has become a major focus of inquiry for analysts of crime and criminal justice policy (see Teitel 2000; Crawford 2003). It is increasingly the case that following greater world security (and insecurity), informal social control relates to and connects to formal social control policies that have converged around risk. But what of the governance of prisons during transition? As Chapters 3 and 4 have demonstrated, the new modes of penal ideology and penal practice in Russia have significantly recast the process of administering imprisonment during transition.

This chapter will position the penal identities outlined in Chapter 3 within an analytical framework which describes how penality in Russia has followed three ideological transitions which I characterise as 'occasions in penal identification' because they are junctures marked by incomplete and unfinished changes in penal principle and penal policy, or are what Melossi terms as 'cyclical representations of penal vocabularies' (1985, 2000). As I describe each of these occasions, my intention is to indicate how ideas about punishment are reconstructed from a range of biographies: from locales where there is greater political and economic stability and also from reliable and familiar social and political environments. My argument is that in societies in transition, there is a proclivity to transfer knowledge from dominant political spheres rather than exchange knowledge. I argue that the current situation in Russian prisons has given rise to a crisis in penal identification where local knowledge that could be moulded into a rationale or penal identity is subverted. The consequence is that custodians and prisoners become increasingly removed from the social, personal, emotional and ideological realities that come to be imposed on incarceration.

The discussion in this chapter seeks to reanimate the debate on prison labour with a direct observation of how the political and economic conditions in societies *in transition* come to determine and shape modes of penality. My findings also add to recent discussions on how transferring criminal justice knowledge across borders is constituted and maintained by illuminating, through the lens of Russian prisons, how penal policy 'travels' to less stable societies. I outline the concept of 'penal identification' in the section following. I then describe each occasion in turn in terms of how the interplay between branches of knowledge and penal practices is performed in transitional penal sites. I will conclude the chapter by considering how a universalist doctrine of human rights might be subverting localised penal ideologies.

Identities and social research

For decades, social theorists have endeavoured to elucidate knowledge on how identity is maintained and constructed. One conceptual problem in theorising identity arises from its dual operation at the psychic level and as a practice within the social field (Erikson 1974; Hall 1996; Bauman 2001). The arguments encourage us to use one in order to make sense of the other. For example, one argument is that following the break-up of the medieval social, economic and political order, the modern world became a more complex structure where individuals were seen, not as autonomous or self-reasoning individuals, but instead as persons 'mediated' by the culture of the world inhabited. Modernity, argues Giddens (1990), brought a conceptual shift in favour of the 'social'. As with Blumer's classic symbolic interaction theory (1969), and Goffman's conceptualisation of a social world in which individuals negotiate formal order, these shifts give rise to the 'me' of the world being modified in a continuous dialogue with the identities outside in the cultural world. Identities, therefore, bridge the gap between the outside world and the inside world and assist individuals in aligning their subjective feelings with objective spaces (Goffman 1961). What Hall (1992: 276; 1996) has argued is that, hand in hand with modernity, is a process wherein identity 'stitches' the subject into the cultural structure and in turn stabilises both the self and the social world.

A postmodern view is that 'old identities' (those that stabilised the modern world) are in decline and new identities have emerged that lead to fragmentation of modern life (Giddens 1994). The cultural landscapes of gender, race, sexuality and nationality are transformed giving rise to a displaced sense of the self in the social and cultural world and also in the personal world leading to crisis and uncertainty in how individuals and institutions are represented. An alternative argument is that the institutional changes brought about by the onset of globalisation, broadly defined as a process whereby nation-states are linked by multifarious interconnections where decisions, events, ideas and activities readily flow across territorial boundaries, have led to cultural dislocation and cultural voids (Laclau 1990). The process of obtaining an identity has, therefore, become more fluid, variable and open ended. In essence, boundaries have become insignificant. Identities are re-formed through new narratives where the psychic and the social are played down in favour of the historical. The continuous transformation of identity produces subjects who utilise contradictory identities at different times and in different locations. Not only that, any attempt to promote a unified identity is 'fantasy'; a comforting notion because it allows the subject to construct a personal narrative that is complete and secure (Hall 1992: 277; 1995). Identities are multifarious and perplexing sources of comfort and also – importantly – they are fleeting. Of non-modern societies, referred to in the literature as 'traditional' or non-Western societies (see Giddens 1990, 1994), it has been argued that identities are managed 'from within' according to quite different principles wherein *tradition* is honoured as a way of validly negotiating the disturbances of modern life. Tradition, therefore, cements traditional societies together.

It is unlikely that social theorists will be able to square up by what mechanism identity is constructed: whether identity is already constituted in the 'self' (the unconscious) or the 'social' (ideology) or whether the 'historical' determines identity, or how each gives way to the other in identity construction. The particular approach I wish to take in understanding developments in Russian prisons draws on different aspects of all the above. Here I am drawing on the work of Stuart Hall (1996) and Zygmunt Bauman (1989, 1993, 2001) wherein the authors continue to 'think with identity' (Hall 1996: 3) but in a regenerated format. Hall (1996) and Bauman (1989, 2001) argue that the conceptual difficulties in understanding how identity is manifest can be reduced if attention is focused instead on *identification* which is always in process and never complete and which has a pivotal relationship to modern forms of political agendas or to a political location. For example, given that Soviet penal culture was constructed from the political and economic identity of Marxism/Leninism, a discussion of post-Soviet penality might benefit from an analysis of how those involved with imprisonment identify with its broader philosophical goals.

In the context of imprisonment the dynamics of penal allocation and administration operate in response to powerful forces in the wider political culture, and I hope that Chapter 2 has shown that the goals of prison labour are mediated by the wider political milieu. Understanding how political and cultural conditions impel drastic changes in Russia's penal system is complex because at the core of Russian society is an erosion of the political and economic structures that were the defining elements of Soviet identity. Nowadays, the lives of Russians have become saturated with uncertainty and insecurity. Russia is currently swept up into a process read by Western societies and Russia's political elite as 'modernisation' (Malia 1999). But Russia's modernity is uncertain because the identity of society that is embedded in vacuous and loosely bordered forms has created a diverse culture whose elements are based on a fusion of different branches of knowledge, different 'pasts and presents'. These events have impacted on the discursive practices in prisons and also on how personnel and prisoners see and feel imprisonment.

Theorising Russia's penal identities

As commentators such as Parenti (1999) and Wacquant (2002) have separately noted, prisons are often reconceptualised in order to draw meanings from the discursive practices which are mediated by political and economic events. In Russia, in the absence of mainstream critical discourses on punishment, the reflections, practices, normative structures and self-constitution of the prison world must be continually reinvented or restylised by custodians and captives. It is my contention that the identities 'character reform' and 'social reform' are constructed from recognised origins or shared characteristics with another group (internal and external) which then allows the prison system to lay roots within the broader political contours of society as it undergoes a transition.

The framework I will utilise is called the 'occasions of penal identification' because, over the last 13 years, the penal system is evolving through different definitions in the process of 'becoming' a coherent, homogeneous and rational system. Bauman (2001) has noted that social systems do not keep their shape once and for all. Russian prisons have been dismantled and replaced with new ideals that stand up to a logic that translates in a global political and economic context. For example, while the more individualised approach to offender treatment programmes as found in Smolensk was very different from the massive development of cognitive behaviour therapy that emerged in the West in the 1990s, these developments were intended among other things, to fill the time that might otherwise have been occupied with work.

When I refer to identification, I am attempting to offer a logic to Russian imprisonment which shows how prisoners and prison officers have assimilated a range of ideas to create a form of knowledge that they carry in their heads and also implement in practice. Making sense of imprisonment in Russia today is, as the following quotation from a prison officer shows, an emotionally troubling business:

> I don't know what to think anymore about imprisonment. I am confused and I don't know how to feel anymore about anything. I mean, I spend my life not really knowing what is going on. I also don't know what to believe in anymore. We come to prison to work, but for what … I feel really insecure about myself and why I am working in this rotten place. Something is missing.

Identification bears similarities with identities in that it permits a construction of new identities from a range of narratives that sustain the public and personal worlds. Where my framework departs from studies on identities is in two separate but intimately related areas. First, where identities are essential precursors in coping with the pains of imprisonment, I see identification as shaping the path of development of penal systems during *transition*. Secondly, I do not view events in Russia as emanating from a single source that is from the social or from the psychic or from a symbiosis of the social with the psychic. I view events as emanating from a 'collision' of the historical with the political and economic. The process of creating identifiable concepts and structures is determined by the broader contours of the nature of the collapsed ideology and by the material demands and resources, such as the decline of prison labour. Consequently, there is a degree of indeterminacy and instability. And there is fear that without new constructions, all social and prison life is hollow. Each identification, moreover, unfolds from narratives that are created from a tension between the local (debates on local order and how the fracturing of dominant narratives impact on penal forms) and the global (integration into the European community; funding the penal system; spatial dispersal of prisons).

The occasions of penal identification are neither total nor speculative but are instead open-ended articulations that evolve through different phases but which also unite 'feelings' about imprisonment with particular practices to create new knowledges of penality. The end result is that at each stage, an identity has been 'stitched' into the social fabric of prison and inside everyone's mindset, creating a theoretical agenda that can be utilised to navigate the disordered world of penal politics. In the sections following, I hope to show how the social order of modern Russian prison life is articulated in the process of 'identification'.

The first occasion of penal identification: the death of Soviet penal identity

When the Soviet Union collapsed it marked the death of Soviet penal identity and the beginning of a crisis in implementing prison labour, as there was not enough labour to employ prisoners. The gruesome Soviet penal history, moreover, rendered complex how prison labour should be determined and administered. This period marked the beginning of the first occasion in penal identification, which I judge as between 1991 and 1996 when the prison system functioned according to an unknown discourse. Imprisonment remained the most widely practised sanction, but it lacked an ideological foundation. Rather than describing the Russian prison as in transition, a better way to describe it in this period would be as in turmoil as the term transition implies a sense of direction. At this time, very few officials had a grasp of what could fill the void left by the collapse of communism. This situation raised technical and political difficulties in defining the parameters of penal ideology thereafter and emotional obstacles for prison officers in how they understood life in prison. Indeed outside the prisons, the mood was changing. There was a great deal of anxiety that the stability that had shaped the lives of citizens for almost an entire century had given way to a collapse of most public institutions. And with the lack of a clear yardstick that would enable Russians (in prison life and in everyday life) to compare their own situation with what emerged outside Russia, the insecurities and uncertainties were increasingly impossible to reconcile.

The first occasion is interesting in exposing how an unstable prison system can be characterised as between the past and the future. The past configurations of Soviet penality produced particular political and economic outcomes that were incongruent to Western contemporary penal systems. The penal system's bureaucratic structure coupled with the history of forced labour meant that the perspectives that underpin the modes of penality in Russia in the future would require modification to transform the prison system into an institution where the outcomes would be tolerable or even desirable. But what of the space in between: the present? I have already made reference to how the reform of the penal system was predicted on a reformed criminal justice system. But the main momentum for change came from the political movement to ensure that the democratic co-ordination of the civil and criminal procedures was in line with those in Europe. As with many other transitional societies when the doors of the prison system opened, a degrading, overpopulated and inhumane penal environment was exposed. Considerable evidence emerged which revealed the Soviet penal system to be far more gruesome than previously realised with severe ill-treatment of prisoners, appalling conditions and dilapidated establishments provoking international condemnation. As Chapter 2 has shown us, between 1991 and 1995, the prison system underwent some incremental reforms in an attempt to 'un-stitch' Soviet forms of penality: the different elements of Soviet identity were removed from criminal justice legislation and the first post-Soviet penal code was established in June 1992.

This period did not mark conceptual shifts in how punishment should be determined – imprisonment continued as the main form of penal sanction – although it certainly marked a recognition that the historically specific penal practices and normative structures would perform under a different rubric. Kalinin (2002: 6) argues that one piece of legislation dating from 1993 'defined new aims, objectives, principles and direction of the work of corrective colonies, prisons and remand prisons'. Yet, while the legislation was progressive for its time, upon closer inspection of the Russian documentation, it was clear that the central focus of prison legislation was a commitment to meeting international norms, minimum standards and the extension of prisoners' rights. The opening up of the prison system, unsurprisingly, created tension between reformers and the authorities with the latter arguing that there was little that could be done to further penal reform because of chronic under-funding and the collapse of the command economy. I hope that it is apparent from the reforms outlined in Chapter 2 that no clearly defined or unified penal ideology emerged to replace Marxist/Leninist discourse. Thus, the legislation remained open to various interpretations. While thousands of prisoners languished in Russia's jails with nothing to do, the question of the objectives underpinning penal policy was thus unresolved.

The conception of a modern prison system derived from improving human rights. I want to reassert here that while I do not criticise the positive evocation of human rights, the point I wish to make is that there was very little critical debate on the forms that penality might take in the post-ideology phase. The immediate 'transformation of justice' occurred within a broader political movement to globalise rights and to make human rights abuses less likely and, later, this gathered momentum within the Council of Europe which was preparing for Russia's entry.

Thus, the question of identifying what a modern prison should look like was determined by external sources – that is, in the ways that prison officials imagined the system to be seen by others. This gave rise to a scenario wherein international political scrutiny dominated discussions on Russia's prisons. A period of particular difficulty were the years 1993–5 when the establishment of a reformed concept of imprisonment was delayed further by a poorly managed economy; an increasing prison population which grew quickly from 722, 363 persons in custody in 1991 to 1,017, 372 in 1995 (an increase of 40.7%[1]); difficulties in establishing a new democratic culture and the militaristic management culture in the prisons which was a hangover of a Soviet mindset. It was clear that the system could not continue as it was. However, it was by no means obvious at that stage in what direction it would change or how it would be achieved (see King and Piacentini 2004). Draft versions of penal codes appeared but they hardly constituted a dramatic departure from the old codes except with regard to prison visits and access to families.

Feelings about imprisonment

The feelings of prison officers and prisoners regarding how they were expected to conform to a new set of policy arrangements in the immediate period following the collapse of the USSR have not been explored by either academics or penal reformers. During this research, prison officers have, however, recalled that period. As one senior prison official interviewed in Kemerovo put it: 'To question the policy was to interfere with the government's plans for penal reform.' Moreover, the majority of the respondents I interviewed in 1999 and 2003 stated that while the collapse of the USSR was a momentous occasion for Russian people, their status as prison officers was unaffected. One prison officer stated: 'It took years for any real change to take effect as many senior prison managers continued to hold senior positions.' The chief of Kemerovo region added:

It was a chaotic period in some sense, but in an another sense, nothing really changed in the prisons and we still came to work in the same uniforms under the same ministry. We didn't really think about 'ideas' or 'ideology' and so on because the economy was unstable in the first five years.

Consider this comment:

No one really thought about ideology. You just get on with it. I am pretty sorted emotionally anyway and I certainly didn't give communism a thought afterwards. I think that there must have been some guys who were upset when the USSR collapsed. Most people, I think, were too busy just trying to survive.

That the collapse of one ideological construction had little impact on officers' sense of self was apparent from the interviews. When asked about how the collapse of Soviet penal identity impacted on their views of crime, the majority of prison officers stated that in the early years of *perestroika*, they were indifferent about the regime's previous exploitation of the term 'criminality' to secure a labour workforce. One senior prison officer defended Soviet criminal justice vehemently: 'I do not remember all the details of life back then. My views on crime did not change immediately. I still pursued the previous regime's criminal justice goals.' This was markedly different from my research in 1999 where prison officers had developed various interpretations of crime causation.

The recollections revealed that during the first occasion, the wider economic chaos coupled with the lack of direction in how to change the system dictated how prison officers experienced incarceration. In short, constructing a new personal and social world that prison officers could identify with was submerged under very real everyday concerns about how to survive the collapsing economy.

One of the spheres where positive reform could have been achieved in establishing a punitive mentality is in the area of addressing past atrocities meted out by the regime and its use of forced prison labour. As I have already indicated, King (1994) laid out several 'assurances' to staff over the forced labour issue (see also King and Mikhlin 1994). Significantly, these assurances were about how the West would interpret real events on the ground. King's work was ground-breaking but it does invite us to reflect on how almost immediately after the collapse of the USSR in 1991, Russia's prisons were measured as legitimate against Western standards (both academic knowledge and norms). Surely of crucial importance to the formation of a rationale or identity in institutions in transition is to ground fresh ideas and insight within the divisions, strife and violations of the past in order that a culturally specific reconstruction can commence (see McEvoy and Mika 2002).

The literature on transition and justice in South Africa and Northern Ireland serves as a particularly useful guide for understanding how the slogans of the past can be placed formally within a transformative process. Research conducted in countries undergoing transition indicates that criminal justice systems do face major obstacles in confronting new values particularly when crime control strategies have been utilised to deploy oppression (Priban and Nelken 2001). Under the auspices of seeking both justice and making political compromise, special commissions and inquiries have aimed to transcend the divisions of the past where violations of human rights led to a legacy of fear, hate and revenge. Legal experts argue that the total shift in the political conditions from justice as state repression and inhumanity, to democracy and humanity can only be 'secured' if there is some reconciliation with the past. The crux of the debate is that for fresh approaches of justice to emerge that reflect internal sensibilities, constructive debates or inquiries into past practices can operate to bring some clarity on what a modern-day criminal justice system should look like. And while there has been much debate on the state's role in societies where previously it was used to disable democracy, it is not *impossible* to reform prisons by being constructive with the past (see McEvoy *et al.* 2002).

In Russia, criminal justice in the immediate transition period was unstable and conceptions of penality were grounded in ensuring that the system becomes more humane. Alliances were formed between local non-governmental groups and bodies such as Penal Reform International and the Moscow Centre for Prison Reform (with Western support and encouragement, MCPR was emerging as a forceful voice). There was, however, very little communication between the central prison authority and prison managers in the vast penal system as to what constituted 'humanity' and there was poor provision for information on alternative ideas.[2] One of the regional chiefs whom I interviewed stated that the ongoing negative publicity of the prisons sapped morale: 'When I think of the *perestroika* years, I think about the fact that nothing was achieved and no one was consulted. What kind of penal system did we have then? We had one that was in chaos and where people outside Russia thought that we were backward.'

The narratives underpinning Soviet ideology that secured a penal identity for almost an entire century were not utilised to connect the past to the future. On the one hand, it could be argued that debates on penal ideology would evolve from reforms of the criminal justice system. On the other hand, however, the impetus for change was coming from experts who brought to Russia the obligations to outside bodies. Reform, therefore, was external to Russian penal sensibilities. Unlike South Africa where the dominant values of apartheid were not only dismantled but also challenged through an internal Truth and Reconciliation Commission, in Russia a precedent to utilise the resources of history, language and culture in the process of constructing a modern penal system did not emerge. A moment for critical self-reflection was lost and the question 'How is penal ideology constructed?' was out of sight, temporarily.

The second occasion of penal identification: theoretical improvisation

It is during the second occasion of penal identification, which I estimate as between 1997 and 2002, when penality was reconfigured by the wider political and economic conditions. I judge that the path of development evolved through an interesting transition phase where there was some collision between history and contemporary politics. On one side are the fresh approaches that emerged – the penal identities – that were based on different knowledges and which created ideal-type penal practices and policies. On the other side are the international conventions that Russia had ratified. These developments give rise to tension between, first, how prison officers and prisoners devise theoretical improvisations to create a range of conceptual vocabularies that can be utilised in the penal system and, secondly, how penal policy travels across borders (from the West). While these findings might not be typical given the scale and scope of the penal system, they do show how local penal sensibilities can emerge from the rubble of the collapse of an overly powerful political culture.

From 1995 onwards, Russia was in a severe economic and political crisis. As events became more disordered in criminal justice, so too was there great uncertainty with regard to the size of the prison population and the lack of criminal and civil procedures. While there were attempts to reform the penal system, in the absence of a strong central dynamic, coupled with mounting economic debt, the Russian government could not manage the penal system. So by the middle of the 1990s, the prison system lacked a central dynamic in its management structure and its policy framework. The devolved regions were expected to take responsibility for many of their own penal policies and practices.

In the second phase the prisons responded to the unknown discourse by reinventing penality from the single-concept theory of Marxism/ Leninism to a more individualised format. This was particularly interesting because the norms and values that emerged were judged by prison officers to be 'real and legitimate', but also 'unsafe and insecure' because each identity operated outside direct political patronage. Uncertainty and insecurity have been described by Crawford as 'late modern conditions' (2003: 33). The modes of development in this phase resemble closely, but not entirely, postmodern penality. I do not wish to enter into the well versed debate on what constitutes and explains post-modern penal shifts. Suffice to say Russia entered into a new order that we could interpret as post 'one kind of theory' where the object of analysis shifted towards new rhetorics and realities.[3] The emergent new penal order was complex; a kaleidoscope of ideas based on ideology building that combined (and also confused) different branches of knowl-edge (religion with psychology, market approaches with communist ideals). The new order also conflated concerns between regions (Smolensk and Omsk) with those between nations (the West and Russia). Taken together the resultant governing architecture of the prisons was uneven and unstable although it did enable a level of expediency in the administration of punishment.

Unlike Western criminal justice systems where governments have invested in areas where they might effect change in order to produce ordered environments, the events in Russia are revealing how prison officers and prisoners square up some penological insecurities, namely, filling the penal void. First, 'identity' has refigured certain dilemmas that faced prison officials following the collapse of the USSR. For example, what kinds of sanctions should be used to bring about rehabilitation? How should imprisonment be discussed? What penal policies should we institute to guide establishments? I hope that my findings show how prisoners and prison officers have resolved these questions through re-embedding traditional social norms in some areas, from localised knowledge and also, on ideas emanating from the West that were coming to have some influence on prison regions located near Western Europe. Secondly, 'identification', in so far as it is concerned with instituting a quality to imprisonment, is saturated with concerns about whether a prison should have an ideological purpose, whether it is a solution to crime and whether it can operate as a symbol of state power. These are dilemmas for any penal system, but they must rate as being of the greatest difficulty for Russian criminal justice officials to resolve due to the history, size and scope of the penal system.

In the section that follows, I will explore how the voids in penality that followed the collapse of the USSR have had various impacts on the massive penal system. I will then go on to explore how those points in the physical geography of the penal system, where ideas first permeate, influence the new modes of penality.

Voids in penality as an explanation for new penal identities

The evidence presented on the identities, 'character reform' and 'social reform' shows us that Russian prisons are in the midst of a new epoch where the picture is complex, but also exciting. The penal policies, programmes and ideas, coupled with the professional background of staff, indicate that imprisonment in Russia in the mid-1990s was a wide-open field. The prison system I found in 1999 (and to a lesser degree in 2003) was individuated from the centre and management had been delegated to the regional administrations. The hallmark of these new penal forms that is most distinguishable from the old order of prisons is that the new identities marked the end of the interplay between the state and the penal realm. The old procedures of punishment have fallen apart and given way to prisons that are excluded from direct political backing and influence. Of course, then, prison labour would have to adapt as the complex linkages between prison labour and the political and economic structures have withered away.

'Character reform' in Smolensk has emerged principally from changes in the economy. The collapse of the Soviet economy has resulted in the region being unable to compete with cheaper imports from the Far East leading to the closure of factories and reduced work opportunities for many of the region's citizens. In Smolensk, prison labour was in rapid decline and where work was offered this was concentrated in light assembly. With little else to offer that could be interpreted as 'meaningful', and which would reflect the vaguely defined norms outlined in national and international prison rules, the punishment meted out was found to be much more distinctive, legitimated by reference to a body of scientific knowledge – somewhat outmoded – that focused on therapeutic remedies for the stigmatised prison community.

The economic decline that has blighted much of Russia's contemporary development had not impacted in Omsk in the same way it had in Smolensk because Omsk region has abundant natural resources, raw materials (forests and arable farming) and accessibility to rail and road networks throughout Russia (southern republics of Kazakhstan, Uzbekistan and even northern Mongolia) to produce a healthier industrial outlook and a market for prison-produced goods. There was much more work for prisoners so alternatives to the *work ethic* were not relied on as much. However, that one region is unable to sustain work for prisoners such that it imports alternative programmes does not explain fully why Smolensk has adopted a template of individualised reform programmes, and Omsk an agenda that links the offender to the community. The findings suggest that the adoption of these identities is more revealing of a tension between the centre and the periphery and also of how Western penal policy punctures borders.

The spatial dispersal of prisons as an explanation for new penal identities

Historians and political scientists who have devoted their careers to unravelling the mystery of Russia refer to western Russia as 'European Russia', as it is in the cities to the West where trends and influences become etched in the sensibilities of local cultures that border Europe (Malia 1999). Given Russian proclivities for adopting worldviews, the prison regions that are close to the West are likely to implement strategies that reflect Western norms and practices. The argument being inferred here is that Western influences travel to Smolensk first and Omsk later due to its location. Not only that, the central prison authority, which is located near to Smolensk in Moscow, was found to have reactivated its influence and control over the region due to the exposure of the prison system to international observers.

Trends show that since 1995 the decline of work for prisoners in Western Europe has led to the introduction of supplementary treatment programmes such as cognitive behaviour therapy and offender-focused treatment (see van Zyl Smit and Dünkel 1999). Smolensk region is following this trend where the use of religion involves a competition between the Russian Orthodox Church and Chuck Olson's Prison Fellowship to capture the souls of a captive, but largely idle population and where psychology is an attempt at persuading prisoners to mend the error of their ways, aided by a new generation of young, middle-ranking staff trained in psychosocial techniques in the institutes in Western Russia (Ufa, Ryazan, Tompsk and Vladimir). Furthermore, in Russia, the Orthodox Church has become popular once again and church leaders appear regularly alongside government officials to speak out on the moral matters said to be 'afflicting' post-Soviet society (crime, breakdown of the family and reduced standards in education, to name a few). As a distinctly non-Soviet institution, the Russian Orthodox Church has emerged as a dominant force in Russian society and has filled that space for mediation with the state.

The decline of work and the re-positioning of the Orthodox Church do offer insight as to how prisoners, staff and the institutions build and incorporate ideas that they then turn into solutions. There was also evidence of an imbalance of support and guidance from the centre to the regions that could be explained as a consequence of Russia's devolved system of governance and, in particular, the scrutiny that the Russian prison system is under from international observers to achieve minimum standards. Herein lies the collision between history and political developments. The movement to reform the prison system is not balanced with a consistent process of monitoring (which is understandable given the sheer size and scope of the penal system). Prison officials from Moscow visited the Smolensk region once a month compared with a twice-yearly visit to Omsk region. Human rights monitors visit the regions in Western Russia more frequently compared with the regions in Central and Eastern Russia (although they do attempt to cover the whole country as much as possible). In addition, it is tacitly assumed in norms such as the United Nations Standard Minimum Rules (1955, 1995) and, moreover, the European Prison Rules (1987) that where work is not available, then alternative treatment programmes will be implemented. Russian officials viewed the introduction of alternatives to work, therefore, as an attempt to integrate into the democratic structure, a pan-European system that shares a common penal identity: 'We are following the rules set out in the EPR. It's fine if we don't have prison work, we can implement alternatives and this way the Council of Europe will be satisfied. For us, this means that we can continue moving closer to Europe.'[4]

Responsibility and oversight from the centre are greater in Smolensk compared with Omsk because this region is more exposed to influence and scrutiny from the West. No exact figures on the allocation of funds to all 69 prison regions were available at the time of the research. An estimation of the financial support given to the regional administrations was provided by Assistant Deputy Prisons Minister, General Alexander Zubkov, who stated in an interview that the central prison authority exercised 'greater involvement' in the regions near Moscow. During the fieldwork for this book, this involvement came to be understood as an authoritative influence and control over Smolensk region compared with Omsk. As mentioned earlier, senior officials visited Smolensk regularly. Consequently, there was greater scrutiny of programmes in that region. While this brought important advantages (some funds, nominal support, a sense of urgency to tackling real problems in the prisons), there were some disadvantages. First, there was less autonomy for Smolensk region as a whole compared with Omsk. Secondly, the absence of any real autonomy has created a state of indeterminacy for the region. The region has been left to fend for itself, as it currently does not receive full state support. Thirdly, the colonies remain under the glare of the Moscow administration. The vague, and sometimes incoherent, opinions towards the central government suggested that staff felt constrained by the Moscow authority.

In Omsk, as Western penal sensibilities have taken longer to travel to and then permeate the colonies, the region has reacted to the collapse of

Soviet communism by maintaining some of the traditions of the Soviet period. Here the nostalgia of the past has collided with the political and economic scene to create 'narratives of the self' (Hall 1992) which unified the social world of the prison with the emotional world of the individual and, ultimately, created new modes of penality that are more certain and which reflect economic and (recent) ideological sensibilities. Moreover, prison officers stated that the central government had abandoned the regions that were distant from Moscow and the general consensus among prison officers in Omsk was that the central authority 'mollifies' the West. As one governor of a penal colony in Omsk stated to me clearly: 'We do not have a system that is consistent. We rarely hear from Moscow. When we do, it is all about Europe.'

By 1999, the traditional order of Soviet imprisonment had been swept away. How I have read the nature of change is first as a period of rupture, discontinuity and chaos, where the uncertainty and insecurity of the social standing of the prison could not be faced point-blank and confronted directly since the roots of the problems in the prisons were stuck in areas that were far beyond the reach of prison officials and managers. A rational solution surfaced towards the end of the 1990s (at the end of the twentieth century) whereby individualised branches of knowledge or social positions (that is, identities for the social world of the prison) connected the people to the institutions. The second occasion of penal identification is notable because the new penal identities do not unify the entire system (and it may be that in other regions alternative identities have emerged). Rather, it is under the circumstances of fragmentation and weak governance that these individualised identities can be articulated together.

I discovered positive attributes among the disparate penal identities in Russia. First, they unhinge the previous discourse by offering new articulations of what prisons should be for and also what Laclau (1990: 40) refers to as 'the re-composition of the structure around particular nodal points of articulation'. For example, the consensus was that the implementation of the Community Liaison Partnerships in Omsk was unproblematic because they were organised around a modified version of Soviet penal ideology that was concerned with how punishment is rooted in sustaining ties with the community. The penal policies in Omsk, therefore, eased the path of development from old penality to new penality. These new 'thicker' penalities acquired a greater meaning because the prison establishments could take on a recognisably modern form. Secondly, cut off from the centre, the penal identity that I found in Omsk reflected local cultural sensibilities and provided for a language and discourse that were beyond contemplation and instead were rooted in local ties and attachments. Following the new recomposition of penality, and as Bauman notes, 'the words, which by the act of naming, create the realities they name' (2001: 52), prison officers and prisoners were able to attend to the question: 'Why do we punish?' with some authority, as the rituals had become solutions that were later habitualised and institutionalised.

In the recent contemporary period, developments in the social and political culture have impacted on the adaptations that emerged during the second occasion of penal identification. One explanation of the route that Russia's penal transition is currently taking can be found in the political discourses that arise from harmonisation and convergence of political systems. It is within this 'epistemic community' (Karstedt 2004: 21) where knowledge is transferred across borders via political networks and professional and social movements. Following Russia's entry into the Council of Europe, the central mechanism whose institutions are the streams of influence, there has been a concerted effort to put pressure on Russia to adhere to the principle of human rights. Substantial progress was made in this regard (although human rights violations in Chechnya remain an area of considerable concern). The drafting of new criminal codes, procedure codes and correctional codes was based on the principles of the Council of Europe. During the second occasion where different layers of meaning – historical, Western, sociological – were tangled together, so too was the Russian government ratifying a number of important conventions. As King and Piacentini (2004) note, hundreds of legislative Acts or amendments were made in an attempt to bring criminal justice procedures in line with Europe.

How do these developments measure against the characteristics of the changes in the second transitional phase? I judge the movement to administer human rights in Russia as counter to the individualised penal identities that emerged in the late 1990s. Character reform and social reform reflected the cultural variations in each region, whether there was enough employment for prisoners and the situation regarding central funding. While ideas emanating from Western penal locales have permeated Western Russia, it is within the trajectories of international criminal justice, particularly penal reform, where penal systems in transition are evolving through significant adaptations.

The resultant penal politics constitutes a third phase in penal identification which I identify as being the current period. Through examining Russian prison labour, I have uncovered interesting developments in how societies in transition follow Western criminal justice trajectories. I shall confine remarks here to how these very recent developments relate to the previous phases in Russia's transition. In

Chapters 7 and 8 I discuss in more detail how attempts to universalise penal ideologies are leading to Western notions of penal propriety dominating the modernisation of Russia's penal system.

The third occasion of penal identification: the universalisation of penality

Following a period of prison custody, re-entering the community to seek employment and resume relationships can be a bewildering experience. Consequently, former prisoners risk becoming disenfranchised as they re-emerge into the social world. In Russia, the symbiotic relationship between the prisons and the communities was unique in that through wheeling and dealing of goods and services, the boundary between 'community' and 'prison' became blurred, and this porosity minimised the social exclusion of former prisoners. Back in 1999 the prison officers I interviewed would often explain penal punishment to me using language and concepts that were not unfamiliar. But the big themes that emerged in 1999 do not mean much now and Russia's prison system is consciously aspiring to a new set of rules. A fresh discourse based on universal human rights is redefining the contours of imprisonment. How Russia came to import a human rights agenda is discussed in more detail in Chapter 7. However, several points about human rights are necessary here where they relate to this final transition phase and so that the scene is set for what follows later in Chapters 7 and 8.

The 'bait' of human rights[5]

The development of human rights standards in prisons is not a new phenomenon. With a pioneering missionary zeal, John Howard set about transforming penal systems around the world. Later, following the atrocities of the Second World War, the United Nations was established with the principal aim of not only inspiring nations to improve the living standards of citizens, prevent wars and secure economic prosperity, but also to recognise that prisoners' rights, better prison conditions and access to judicial defence form part of a body of principle in maintaining standards in prisons around the world. Nation-states are expected to subscribe to a human rights doctrine because principally – and problematically, as I will later argue – it is viewed as a force for 'good'. That world communities 'aspire' to a doctrine of human rights is evident from the raft of international treaties and obligations that have been incorporated into national legislation. A key feature of human rights is its universal application as a mechanism for justice standardisation which has developed as a principal expression of consensus. This is all fine and good but, as I have shown, the modernisation of contemporary Russia is evolving along a bumpy road and the diffusion of ideas across borders seems messy because transfers can represent an exchange of moral values as well as material practices.

The human rights agenda has been fundamental to the third phase in various ways. First, as an agenda, it is ready-made and can be adopted relatively easily, as it is a trend that is emerging across prison systems around the world (although its application is much more difficult to implement). Secondly, the development of human rights has also been concurrent with the movement to welcome Russia into the international community, so it is seen as a politically astute move; it is a rejection of Soviet repression. Thirdly, human rights have been instituted following a period of recentralisation of the management of the prison system and the establishment of criminal and civil procedures. It is therefore associated with a period of stability and centralised penal policy that many find familiar. This version of penality follows a decade of transition, blurred demarcation following decentralisation and turbulence where the system was loosely coupled and 'border-less'. It follows from a rather rapid process of improvisation of penal ideologies that metamorphosed into temporary penal identities or simple ways of seeing punishment. Now the prison system has found a solid script – a penal vision – which officials can present to the international community.

At the beginning of the twenty-first century the third occasion of penal identification marks a new era of centralised penal power, but with a twist: the new orthodoxy is imbued with values that are to be regulated by bodies outside of the national jurisdiction.

And human rights are having a positive effect. It is undoubtedly the case that conditions have improved right across Russia's prison system. However, it has led to a dilution of the penal identities that marked the second occasion and instead, reflects what is being imported. In 2003, I found that the Community Liaison Partnerships that had been set up in 1999 in Omsk had been abolished. In 2003, the chief of Omsk region said to me in an interview: 'We have abandoned the programmes for the time being because we had to focus on our human rights strategies.' When asked about the kinds of strategies now in place, he answered: 'Well there are none, it's all the norms and stuff and paperwork.' I am not suggesting here that there has been a radical break in the social development of Russian prisons as there still remain psychology booths, prison labour, barter, some training and religious activity. I attribute the evolutionary change to political and economic developments that began with the collapse of Soviet communism and finally ending with a process where the aim is to reach *continuity* between penal systems. This continuity relates to the contemporary governance of societies in transition and how continuity then transfers into the penal realm. For example, the transfer of 'technical support', expertise, new Assistants for Human Rights and international consultants which are intended to support existing mechanisms has to some degree had the opposite effect and has destabilised local penal sensibilities while introducing managerialist approaches to prison performance. Relatedly, the passion with which punishment was administered has been replaced by regimes of control.

I found it extremely fascinating to observe how the language of human rights has travelled to countries like Russia. In Chapter 7, I describe how, nowadays, human rights are viewed as many things: an ideological filler, deskwork, a foreign policy and also about respecting the lives of prisoners as citizens. Prison officers revealed a further dimension that has been discussed by Bauman (2001: 54) in relation to crime control strategies that aim to create: 'good societies, better fit for decent and dignified life'. I came to understand human rights doctrine in the penal environment as the promotion of 'good punishment': 'We are told to make things better because we have failed in the past.' 'I get depressed when I think about our past system. It was really bad.'

In conclusion, the third phase sees the limits of penal sensibility transcend institutional aspirations. Nowadays, the focus is upon prevention rather than engagement and local problems in the administration of imprisonment are deemed to require international solutions. The penal system appears to follow no solid script of its own and has operationalised concepts in a fragmented manner. Amid the messy business of developing a penal discourse during the second occasion, I found a penal system that was based on discipline and rehabilitation. I believe that the penal principles back then revealed that prison officers recognised how post-Soviet imprisonment could be realised. The utilisation of a range of confusing knowledges of crime gave promise of fresh insights into the personal biographies of the inmate populations (as either in need of a psychological cure or social rehabilitation). Nowadays, Russia's prisons are increasingly distancing themselves from critique because of the regulatory nature of human rights as measured in terms of performance indicators, but also the new global arrangement is so persuasive morally that very few of us 'bad mouth' human rights.

In the closing chapters, I argue that universal human rights operate as a counter-narrative to the existing modes of penality which could be rendered inhumane (in universalist terms) should the *external* arrangements adopt this view. For example, according to the chief of Kemerovo region, which we should remember is located 4,000 km east of Moscow and borders Mongolia: 'From the kind of food we provide, to ensuring that there is order in the prison, everything has to first meet the European Prison Rules.' This comment draws attention to the temporal and spatial dimensions of punishment that are inherent in cross-cultural prison research of this type.

Notes

1   There are no figures available for the rate as per 100,000 of the population.
2   Source: General Alexander Zubkov in conversation, February 1999.
3   I do not argue here that the transition from modern penal systems to postmodern as outlined by Hallsworth (2002) with regard to Western penal forms is in evidence in Russia. For example, how pain delivery is reduced; how proportionality is introduced in penal sanctions; how regimes are organised according to 'productive expenditure'; and how statutory due process emerges paving the way for postmodern conditions. As Penna and Yar (2003) carefully note, it has yet to be established whether 'penal modernity' in the West was a coherent and unidimensional phenomenon. Interestingly, their thesis could be read in the Soviet context where the bureaucratic structures of penal management sought to create a coherent entity that did 'entertain an image of itself' (Penna and Yar 2003: 472). Whether this means that Soviet penal forms were 'modern' is a question that requires rigorous empirical and historical investigation. I would frame the Russian penal system as Malia has done with contemporary cultural forms, which he describes generally as 'uncertain'. I cite some of the underlying principles of postmodernity in penal systems that are in evidence here in order to generate further debate on how the conceptual dimensions of 'premodernity', 'modernity' and 'postmodernity' translate into a Russian penal context.
4   Source: Colonel Alekseii Vasilievich Voronkov, Junior Prisons Minister in GUIN, interviewed in June 2003.
5   Source: the chief of Omsk prison region described human rights as sometimes appearing as 'bait'.

Chapter 6

Prison practices that test the limits of human rights norms

Chapter 5 presented a theoretical vocabulary that revealed variations in how the prison world was read and then administered that I subsumed under three main headings. Following the collapse of the Soviet Union, severe human rights abuses were exposed and there was uncertainty over what kind of prison system was likely to emerge in the future. On the threshold of yet another century, prisons in Russia appeared entrenched in polarised versions of rehabilitation arising from different ways of conceiving the individual (one focusing on the self, the other on social citizenship). This was the period when Russian prisons corresponded to a discipline model. How the prison system set about modernisation paved the way for an inevitable third stage. The argument that I introduced in Chapter 5 is that local penal sensibilities are passed over in favour of importing Western approaches of a specific kind: universal human rights. This development reflects changes in the international environment where global forces are determining the fate of national states due to more open economies (including Russia's) (Esping-Anderson 1998). However, the erosion of national sensibilities should not be exaggerated. One of most powerful conclusions arising from penal reform in Russia is that consensus-building has improved the situation on the ground (see also Coyle 2002). But there remains a huge discrepancy between existing modes of governance and universal demands for homogeneity over what constitutes 'humane punishment'.

In this chapter I want to return to the primary focus of the book which is post-Soviet prison labour. There is a tendency to view imprisonment in Russia as a space where violations of human rights are commonplace. A wide range of evidence shows this to be the case and penal reformers have been relentless in calling for better conditions in the penal system. Those behaviours categorised as occurring within that trajectory are therefore labelled as 'inhumane'. In my opinion, this is a simplistic approach that reduces penality to 'success' or 'failure', 'good' versus 'bad'. Of all the changes in the penal system in Russia, the one which perhaps appears to be the 'worst' is the *necessity* of at least some prisoners having to work to survive. New uses of barter have created self-sufficient, penal micro-economies and this might lead to the maintenance of a very high prison population. By using barter, there is a considerable chance that resource provision is prioritised over other aims of imprisonment, such as treatment.

None the less, all such charges of exploitation that do not chime well with international norms need to be placed in a local context. The characteristics of barter may mean that prisoners are more likely to be engaged in work that reflects local employment. Thus, prison labour is arguably rehabilitative. This challenges the tacit assumption in international legislation that where prisoners are forced into working, they are therefore being exploited. Consequently, I want to examine the question that the qualities of international norms that promote humanity in punishment are weakened when applied to Russia's penal system, specifically, the barter system. This raises a second important political question that I explore in the remaining chapters: are there imperialistic overtones in the international movement to harmonise penal systems according to human rights?

The peculiar role of barter in prisons

The problems that have beset Russia's prison system throughout the 1990s have been less of a simmering crisis and more about a high degree of exposure of appalling conditions and human rights abuses. Notwithstanding popular perceptions, the degree of change in the prison system, however, has been significant: the prison population has been tumbling downwards, conditions have improved and there has been greater regulation of, and transparency within, the management structure.[1] Yet, levels of poverty and deprivation have arisen dramatically, and relentlessly, in Russia. I imagine that most prison systems around the world do not rely on *contributions* from families, local communities and small and large commercial businesses to keep prisons operational. As one senior prison official remarked: 'Every day, I worry about finding ways to ensure that my prisoners eat the recommended bread allowance.' This poverty is not confined to the penal realm; such extraordinary conditions can be found everywhere. Unlike the prison system in the US where the current economic conditions are revealing of a different kind of penal economy, in Russia, the economic issues that overwhelm the penal system concern making the system function to a minimum standard.

The shrinking safety net of the state has led to the use of barter, a so-called 'primitive' exchange mechanism that operates through wheeling and dealing, bargaining and trading. Barter is an interchange based on quid pro quo or, put simply, a 'swap'. Since barter is based on transference, it is associated with giving, sometimes with honour and most of all with displaying possession. Distinct from a sale or purchase, barter can also be about trickery and cheating because it is based on a coincidence of wants. It could therefore be used to trick parties into believing that goods for exchange are necessary or, at least, desirable. Corporate barter also exists. There are currently over 450,000 companies (retailers, services and manufacturers) in the US who trade under a business-to-business network.[2] These examples of the varied economic contexts that can sustain barter use highlight its complexity and power both as an exchange mechanism and as a means for ensuring that individuals possess things and social positions (barter is utilised in Nepal to negotiate social positions in tribal communities; see Fortier 2001).

It is arguably the case that in normal circumstances, barter is far less controversial, particularly when its use reflects more basic goods-for-goods transactions (see Figure 4.1, Chapter 4). But because barter is a penal micro economy, necessary to the business of 'doing imprisonment', its role is far more complex. Barter has given rise to social and economic network groupings, facilitated by a group of private enterprises, by people and local businesses who have become inextricably linked to the prisoners' struggle to survive. The emergence, and pivotal role, of the Official Penal Sponsor whose task is to negotiate with the central prison authority how the prison establishment's funding is controlled, is a highly contestable role to perform in prisons. No less significant is that prisoners can survive because of barter and this surely must impose a greater burden on the captive population in Russia because prisoners carry the burden of trying to survive while working to ensure that essentials such as food, clothing, heating, wages and industrial materials are provided for.

In good years, the prison system does not require additional financial support from barter as the benefits of the state subsidy go to investing in treatment provisions, better wages and improving conditions. In the years of under-investment, money has withered away. Consequently, the social and penological benefits that funding brings are significantly reduced. Hence, the objective of the prison is to utilise labour to its maximum potential so that industrial enterprises can provide the basics. Ironically, like the far wealthier US penal system, in Russia a high prisoner workforce such as that found in Omsk is generating a successful economy that resembles a 'prison industrial complex' (without the increases in spending; see Schlosser 1998). In what follows I present two competing outcomes of the current situation in the economic sector of Russian prisons: whether high prison populations might be maintained and whether exploitative practices occur as a result of enterprise-based penal policy, and also (or whether) current practices reflect a unique form of social welfarism.

Prison labour and exploitation

The currency of Russia underwent hyperinflation followed by collapse in 1998, so reciprocal trade took on a greater role than it had during the Soviet years. The private sector has become integrated into the penal realm through barter exchanges which are utilised to link resources to outputs and outcomes. As I have already shown in Chapter 2, the debates on the emergence of the private sector focus attention on how in circumstances where the private realm is allocated a penal adminis-trative task, the state's role as the principal dispensing mechanism of a punitive mentality is eroded. The question of retaining a moral ascendancy over penal allocation and administration remains the most persuasive of the debates against the privatisation of punishment in the UK, in Western Europe, in Australia and in America. In Russia such debates are viewed as the indulgences of a community where the order of social life wavers little and where politics is powerful but robust. As one senior official impatiently remarked:

> These are trivial questions. It intrigues me that there are these debates and dialogues about who should be building prisons and delivering imprisonment. Who cares! It is about survival. Having decided not to send us money and having decided not to provide resources for prisoners and staff, the state has left us with no option but to seek help from families and business.

A subtle reading of this quotation sees Russian prison personnel concerned more with making the system work to a minimum standard than the criminological questions from the various Atlantic crossings of different modes of criminal justice. The single biggest problem facing Russian criminal justice practitioners is that there is an unstable financial sector which has affected the state's course of action, its formal and informal means of controlling the public sector and how it applies practical solutions or wisdom to produce desired consequences, in all areas of social and political life. As I said earlier, Russia's penal poverty is a mirror image of widespread levels of poverty throughout Russian society (although it should be kept in mind that the larger Russian cities have been transformed dramatically since 1991 with shopping malls, modern housing and fashionable stores). Recent research conducted by Vincentz (2000) reveals that the public institutions in Russia are now bearing some of the problems of the financial sector. Public services on the whole operate without the kinds of legislative frameworks, policies and guidelines that are designed to make public services accountable in the West. Although barter was not part of official penal policy, or formal procedures, it has none the less gone through a process of *normalisation* due to its overall use in Russian society and also because the chronic under-funding produced no alternative solutions: 'People are desperate' (chief, Kemerovo prison region). While prison personnel did not view barter as a preferred course of action, its very necessary integration has resulted in it becoming a pragmatic income provider. One colony governor talked of barter in terms of its sagacious and prudent qualities:

> We will always barter. We use the language of 'swapping' and 'trade'. Everyday, I ask my officers if they have anything to barter. There is definitely a barter-speak: 'are we trading today?' Or I will ask the *zeks* [prisoners], 'What can we trade up today?' I like using barter because we can control it, whereas the state subsidy is notoriously unreliable.

Another senior official remarked that barter is embedded in the routines of punishment. Consider this comment: 'Through "pure" resource provision, barter has become part of how we think about imprisonment ... about what prisons are for.' I judged these comments as illustrative of how barter has become both rhetoric and a survival mechanism and that these two aspects are entwined. They are mutually constitutive as a discourse and a practice or as a thought and an action. In Omsk region, for example, the use of barter has gone way beyond its typical use in goods-for-goods exchange. Some companies are acting as the Official Penal Sponsor to the colonies by paying some of the debts to the central government (Figure 4.2). In 2002, Omsk regional prison headquarters produced a draft framework for innovating barter transactions with private companies. The chief of Omsk region did not feel obliged to disclose barter contracts to the central prison authority: 'How I run my region is between me and my staff and the funders of some of the resources. Moscow is not involved.' What is clear is that as well as ensuring a minimum level of well-being for the prisoners and staff, barter is a sufficiently well run enterprise that it secures the institutional governance of the prisons.

The economically self-sufficient prison establishments, particularly in Omsk, do continue to rely on state subsidy. However, the structural changes across the prison colonies affected by barter are significant. First, as far as prison officers at the Omsk sites were concerned, the central prison authority has abandoned its responsibility for managing the colonies, so staff welcomed any other support and guidance that could be provided. Business leaders from Omsk Gas, which provides machinery in exchange for cheaper labour in one of its plants, are already involved in committees that meet to discuss improvements to prison industries. At first glance, this might seem like nothing more than knowledge-sharing between traders who identify and then label needs as 'priority for inmates' (food, clothing and materials for prison work); 'priority for staff' (goods that can be exchanged for household goods and food); and 'priority for the institutions' (refurbishment materials). However, it should be borne in mind that private prison operators are in the business of profit-making incentives (see Hogan 1997; Newburn 2002). If these incentives can be realised through the provision of cheaper labour, then the private business in question will favour a continuation in, and increase of, imprisonment rates which Davis (1999) has argued can progress further the exploitation of prisoners' work. In the regions in Russia where the private sector provides more resources to the prisons compared to the state, private enterprises might become influential in providing financial and political support to those regional governors (not the prison chiefs) who adopt a 'tough on crime' state of mind. One need only look to the US where there is a wide literature on the topic to observe how prison capitalism is at the forefront of penal functions (see Parenti 1999). There is evidence that this has led to accelerated prison population rates and also a labour force who are denied access to real wages (see Mauer 1999).

When considering whether the economically self-sufficient prisons are contributing to the maintenance of a high prison population, it should be kept in mind that none of the criteria for evaluating the impact of private sector involvement in the prison realm in Russia has been placed on the public record for scrutiny and as far as it is known there has been no academic scholarship into the relationship between the prisons and the private sector in Russia. In an attempt to begin a theory-building process, I would like here to identify several qualitative issues concerning the interface between high prison populations and heightened private sector involvement in Russia's prison establishments.

First, the very high prison population in Russia could be explained as a hangover from of the Soviet period. The Moscow Centre for Prison Reform has campaigned for the release of unknown numbers of victims who were sentenced to custody when they were children and young people in the 1940s. Human rights experts argue further that it has been the overuse of imprisonment for relatively minor crimes due to the lack of a structured sentencing system that can explain the rise in Russia's prison population (Coyle 2002).

Secondly, there may be structural changes in the economically self-sufficient prisons that concern whether private companies will be required to provide genuine reform or just physical improvements to the prisons. The emergence (and possible re-emergence in the future) of Community Liaison Partnerships in Omsk suggests that Russia is not moving in the direction of countries like Australia where concerns have been voiced over the absence of 'social learning models' in prisons where the private sector has emerged (Moyle 1995: 58). Thirdly, the self-sufficiency of the prisons might lead to structural changes in the community. The community might benefit from high prison population rates, as the vital prison economy contributes to the stabilisation of the local economies. Local people, therefore, have a vested interest in the utilisation of custody as a penal sanction: the more prisoners working, the greater the opportunity to trade with the prisons which increases the standard of living for local communities (more of which later).

Social and cultural geographical research in Russia reveals that many hundreds of villages and small towns maintain a better standard of living through important reciprocal survival strategies or egalitarian sharing (Commander and Mumssen 1998; Seeth *et al.* 1998; Lokshin *et al.* 2000; Tchernina and Tchernin 2002). Without these networks the institutions that are involved in trading, such as the prisons, cannot accommodate the expectations of the trading partner. Thus ironically, in times of demand, the local community might have a good deal of praise for the prison community. This was certainly understood to be the case from one prison governor in the rural eastern Siberian region of Kemerovo: 'I know all the locals here because they trade with us. They don't beg and we don't beg, but they share our view that we need each other. It's demand sharing.' Indeed, prison survival on the margins (in rural settings) has been identified from this research.

One other possible scenario is worth considering if a far more stable private sector in Russia emerges under President Putin. While the private sector does not dominate Russia's penal landscape in any comparable way to the US, it is worth considering some points about private sector management of penal matters. Should private enterprise rise in prominence in the prisons and, for example, set the hours of prisoners' work, have a say in the types of work undertaken, staff recruitment, health, safety and wages, then this might create conflict between Russia and the Council of Europe because such a trend mirrors, to an extent, the neoliberal penal policies increasingly embraced by the UK and already firmly established in the US (but which are treated with caution in Mediterranean Europe; see Newburn and Sparks 2004).

Although national criminal justice legislation sets the amount of hours prisoners can work to a level that meets minimum standards, those regions that are more autonomous from central government may ignore these guidelines and intensify the workload, fearful that if they do not then the barter contract and all the resources will be terminated (see Piacentini 2004a). Private companies might soon lobby for certain types of skilled prisoners to be sent to those regions. Valuable tradesmen and women may be refused parole on the basis of skills being needed. These existing social relations do not appear to run in tandem with existing standards to modernise and civilise the use of imprisonment within those countries currently in the queue to join the European Union. Prisoners are, therefore, under pressure to work hard. Their wages are linked to output in Omsk – an interesting prison region where in a nod to the Soviet period a sign hangs on a wall inside one of the massive industrial warehouses: 'The more you work, the more we eat, the happier we are.'

It is too early to conclude that a mutated version of Gulag forced labour is in operation in the present day as the political outlook and economic stability of Russia are improving (Cockburn 2002). However, it is worth while to make some introductory remarks concerning the remnants of the Gulag.

Work to live?

An often-cited problem to do with the resettlement of former prisons in the prisons literature concerns setting unrealistic targets and rushed-through initiatives (see Simon and Corbett 1994; King and McDermott 1995). Prisons in England and Wales, argues Simon (1999), do not currently support prisoners' needs. Moreover, prisoners are sent the wrong signals about work and often leave prison unmotivated. Where programmes do not match those found outside, states Simon (1999), it is better to do away with them altogether. In contrast to Simon's (1999) study, in all the prison colonies that I have visited since 1997, the vivid picture that emerged was that prisoners were kept fully aware of the importance of work. The following quotation from an interview with a prisoner in Omsk shows where the stress clearly falls: 'I know why I work. I work to live. It's a struggle to survive here. We have to work harder than most but it is a challenge.'

There was, however, a minority of prisoners who felt that if they were forced to work in order to survive, then this would inhibit social and personal rehabilitation: 'I work my life away in here and for what? Some stale bread, a bowl of *kasha* [porridge]. I don't feel reformed. I feel over-worked' (prisoner, Kemerovo open prison). Another prisoner remarked that prison work was not only essential to personal survival but it was also about ensuring institutional survival:

> It's as if our work keeps everyone going. I mean there is bugger all else for staff to do except keep an eye on us working. And our work can increase the provisions. We can exchange stuff. That means that staff can keep a record of what we do, for the books. Yeah, prisoners work their asses off to give staff some paperwork.

That prisoners work to create paperwork was not a view that was rejected by staff. In fact, I often found personnel seeking out paperwork to overcome the prolonged periods of boredom. Indeed, even the overly bureaucratic Gulag system of the Soviet period was missed by some. Whether this was true for the officers who worked in the industrial zone was another matter. Faced with high prison populations, under-staffing and an antiquated surveillance system, their lives were spent juggling a range of tasks with few resources.

The reality in most prisons around the world is that prisoners must work where it is available. However, this tacit assumption does not allow for instances where the state is unable to meet the full costs of running the prisons in its jurisdiction. It is clear that while prisoner reform in a 'European format' is favoured among criminal justice officials who aspire to a pan-European criminal justice ideology, it is also a peculiar notion because it is an external penal sensibility. For Russia to ensure that the 'work to live' reality becomes dislodged from the daily business of prison administration, and to reduce the possibility of the label 'modern-day Gulag', then the central prison authority must increase the prison budget. The Junior Prisons Minister, Colonel Alekseii Voronkov, informed me, however, that this is not likely to happen for several decades.[3]

More complex than prisoners working to live is that introduced into prison administration in Russia today is a form of begging. Begging occurs primarily during exchanges with strangers and there is no expectation from begging that there will be an exchange of goods. Demand sharing, on the other hand, occurs among the prison and local communities (see Scott 1986). When the demand ceases, the exchange is affected leading to a dilution of the discourses that are associated with the notion of 'reciprocity'. How this happens is as follows. Barter represents two ends of a continuum of behaviour that could create conflict. At one end is the prison establishment that must navigate two opposing worlds. First, it must be seen to deliver punishment. Secondly, the prison establishment must adroitly manage local barter trade which can be obtained through very little cost but which also presents new moral imperatives to share out their largesse. At the opposing end is the community who are focusing on their economic interests and who petition for the production of goods that service their economic needs (extra grain from farming and more garden vegetables, for example). While there was no evidence of disagreement between those who needed goods and those who provided goods (because barter is the levelling device), the intercultural exchange could deteriorate if the economic relations – the most important of all the connections between prisons and the outside world in Russia – collapse or *if* the prison establishment resorts to begging during its barter sessions. Consequently the prison loses some of its power to punish and the client/private sector increases in prominence. That prisons might resort to begging in some way for resources from the local communities adds, therefore, to the many other pains of imprisonment that have been cited in the prisons literature.

Working to live certainly threw up a whole range of, contrasting feelings and opinions from staff and prisoners. I found that the nature of services and their distribution were modified continually to ensure better coping strategies: 'We can cope much better with the instability in our country if we can set up these pockets of networks between the local people and the colony' (governor, Kemerovo strict regime). I also found that the majority of prisoners whom I interviewed felt that the work they undertook was realistic in that it enabled prisoners to live, not in isolation, but in harmony with their social surroundings. One prisoner remarked: 'I feel that my work has a real purpose. I can see that, from my work, my life will improve here. I also have a responsibility to my fellow inmates. It makes me feel good knowing that my work makes a real contribution.' Others felt strongly that prison labour gave back a sense of purpose and identity to the prison community: 'Those who work the hardest are given the most respect from the officers and from the *zeks* [prisoners]. They are the strongest.' And another prisoner from Kemerovo region who worked directly with local farmers said to me: 'It's better to know that on this day you will work to produce something for the local farmer than to have a situation where you make toys just to fill in some target sheets.' While other prisoners viewed the situation with humorous irony: 'I am working to keep the prison working. That is it, I am working to keep myself in prison!' (prisoner, Smolensk strict regime).

The majority of prison officers argued that it was necessary, sometimes, to exert pressure on prisoners to work: 'I tell my men in no uncertain terms, "without your work, we will all suffer". They understand because we are a collective' (prison officer, Omsk strict regime). Under present circumstances it is unlikely that prisoners would openly complain and staff and prisoners discussed the state of the prisons frequently. Sometimes it seemed that prisoners were being blackmailed into working, which was strangely reminiscent of the long-gone era of the 1940s where prisoners were reminded continually of the usefulness of their work. Indeed, there was a sense that there was a 'meeting of minds' (so to speak) between the necessity of prisoners working and the desire by many to return to that bygone era of living to work because: 'At least in Soviet times, we had direction, real purpose and an ideology that we worked by' (governor, Omsk strict regime). Mostly, though, staff were mindful of how they informed prisoners that the self-sufficiency of the prisons was dependent on prison labour. The varied responses to the current situation suggest a need to consider how the requirement that the prison infrastructure is protected from collapse has introduced a discourse into the prison setting that links two struggles together: personal survival to economic survival.

There are two ironies about barter. One is that as in the Soviet period, prisoners are forced into working in the present day. The other is that the community is involved in the day-to-day activities of the prison. This could benefit prisoners in terms of learning skills that might be useful after release. Consequently, another view is that prison colonies, as they currently function in twenty-first-century Russia, are arguably rehabilitative. As the community becomes ever aware of the roles that prisoners play in providing them with essential goods, so the community – whether it is cognizant or not – becomes locked into the social relations of the prison. The ways in which barter contributes to social welfare provisions are explored in the next section.

Prison labour and social welfare

The growing volume of barter trade in Russian prison colonies has reduced some of the basic problems associated with the decline in central funding. Aside from the provision of resources, barter was a vehicle that facilitated the integration of the community into the prison realm. In my opinion, because of barter, and not in spite of it, the community provides a form of sociological patronage that insulates prisoners from social exclusion.

In very simple terms, local people and local businesses benefited from barter because they used it regularly to purchase a whole range of products (from manufacturing to buying clothes buttons). Leading from this, the community could then plan ahead which goods and services they needed as they were kept informed over timetables of production and product development. This was achieved as much by 'word of mouth' as it was by placing adverts in the prison service journal *Prestuplennie i Nakazannie* (Crime and Punishment). Most of the staff lived in the villages surrounding the colonies so they could inform their neighbours and friends. Since all the products were chosen specifically with the local community's needs in mind, the local community had a direct say in the prison industries (how many prisoners worked, where prisoners worked in the penal colony and prisoners' skills). The community was therefore genuinely committed to the prisoner workers; a unique scenario when it is considered that in the UK, the focus has tended to be placed on prison industries rather than on prisoner industries (see Reuss 1999).

As a consequence, if we consider a scale, at the top end of which would be how community involvement in imprisonment enables prisoner re-entry into society and a realistic opportunity for prisoner rehabilitation, then at the lower end of the scale (Smolensk) local people would assist that re-entry by visiting the colonies every day to find out if changes had been made to production and to also inquire as to whether the colony administrators would require new products from the general public. I observed many scenarios, all varied, wherein local people would negotiate supplements to their barter agreement. Rarely did I find that the colony declined the opportunity to trade for that extra piece of machinery, that extra winter jacket or an extra two-dozen eggs. Similarly, if the colony had not met targets, then prison officers would wheel and deal and add products to the barter contract: 'One time, we did not produce enough screws in the factory so we ended up giving away some of our chickens to the local farmer in addition.' The community was kept informed about changes that might impact on the local economy. For Russians who have been used to fluctuating rouble–dollar exchange rates and ineptitude from political leaders in the decade since the collapse of the Soviet Union in 1991, this basic level of support was highly significant. The situation of mutual need and demand sharing had created trust between the prison managers and the local communities. Moreover, where the central prison authority had 'let down' prison managers by failing to meet its commitment to provide the most minimal of resources, so the community has stepped in to create opportunities that have led to the survival of the prisons. It could be argued that in the early twenty-first century some Russian prison colonies are depending more on the local community than the state for vital support, resources and guidelines.[4] One client involved in barter said in an interview: 'They [colonies] always need foodstuffs, we need parts for machinery. It's a mutually beneficial relationship.'

At the upper end of the scale (Omsk) successful prisoner re-entry was enhanced further by the partnerships between the penal colonies and local businesses and community representatives. It was stated to me by the chief of Omsk region that social reform was achievable because all parties were committed to participation in the management of the prisons. Unfortunately, the CLPs have now been abandoned, and it would seem without good reason as they provided a niche for both knowledge-sharing on improving prison industries and for discussions about ways to provide through-care for prisoners once they re-entered the community.

Although security protocols usually mean that it is not possible to observe directly what impact imprisonment has on prisoners, custodians and communities, in most prison systems in the West there is a lack of consultation between the prisons and the local community on a range of issues connected to imprisonment (the administrative system, penal practices, the work of prison staff, the demographic background of prisoners and release). Such breakdowns in communication and dialogue are said to exacerbate the difficulties of the through-care process. Within mainstream Russian prisons, the opposite is happening. There are greater and more imaginative possibilities for the provision of through-care in that country due to the reciprocal relationship – the wheeling and dealing of goods and services between the prisons and the local communities.[5] Should the current obstacles in implementing better strategies successfully be alleviated (these include shortages of resources in prisons; increased prison populations; matching treatment measures to that which might be found outside prison and diversion of resources towards increasing security measures) then Russia may prove to be an interesting example of a society where the local communities take possession of those aspects of penal punishment that directly affect them.

In sum, when barter is examined for its economic and social benefits, it is difficult not to view it as creating the conditions for prisoner rehabilitation, as well as stability for the prison as a whole. Prisoners benefit by learning barter skills that can be used when they are released. The community benefits in that the prisoners are viewed as a group of individuals who are able to provide the means to sustain a basic standard of living. From what I have said so far, the best features of the penal system reveal its *raison d'être* as operating according to a model based on co-operation, knowledge-sharing, giving and taking. But lets remain cautious over the potentially exploitative practices arising from barter.

What makes any prison system vital is how it is governed. In the remainder of this chapter I would like to consider prison labour in relation to the international instruments that intend to protect prisoners and raise standards in prisons everywhere. I will begin by asking what the position with regard to international norms in this area of prison activity might be. The most obvious indications are that the international benchmarks for prison management in Russia cannot accommodate the benefits that barter and prison labour bring to prisoners and local communities. This leads to a second question that I continue to explore in the remainder of the book: are international norms workable in prisons in societies in transition? As they currently operate international norms are prison-specific as opposed to culture-specific. Thus, practices might be seen as infringements even though they reflect local penal sensibilities and correspond to cultural conditions.

Denying reality

International norms are vague and imprecise in how they protect prisoners from human rights violations arising from exploitative work practices. Generally speaking, should prisoners be forced to work as a consequence of a conviction in a court of law, or where there is supervision and control by a public authority, then they are not protected by international law. Prisoners cannot 'choose' not to work for if they do, they face additional discipline. Moreover, should prison labour fit in with the requirement of the institutional administration (that is, if the regime can present a case that there are institutional benefits from compulsory labour), then a prisoner loses the right to choose to decline work. National penitentiary laws or penal codes determine how 'requirements' and 'expectations' are to be determined. It is preferable, state the European Prison Rules (1987), that the state or public administration, and not contractors, supervise personnel, administer punishments and manage the prisons generally. Prisoners are not protected anyway where private individuals, companies and associations dispose their labour. And where the private sector is involved, the European Prison Rules do not offer guidance on the extent of this involvement, on how wages are to be paid, on the conditions of work or how prisoners can be protected. Clearly, then, prisoners in Russia are afforded no protection as their work benefits the regimes.

According to Neale (1991) and De Jonge (1999), current guidelines on prison labour in the United Nations Standard Minimum Rules and the European Prison Rules indicate a failure of international norms to protect against forced prison labour because, ultimately, prisoners have forfeited their right not to be forced to work as a consequence of the custodial sentence. Forced labour is, therefore, an additional pain of imprisonment. King (1994) reassured us that, as prison labour is more or less voluntary across the world, a scenario where prisoners are forced to work has not tested the conventional wisdom of international prison rules. As this book has shown, the situation in Russia is far from clear cut (as King suggests that it is). One view is that the situation of prisoners working to live in contemporary Russia is worse than the situation during the Soviet Union because Russia is attempting to move towards more democratic structures and at the same time seems to be regressing in its prison management due to the use of barter as a substitute for money.

At this stage it is worth while to consider the areas of international law that discuss prison labour as a positive element of custody. That prison labour should be a positive element of punishment is a tacit assumption of the prison labour rules in most jurisdictions (see Rule 71, part 1 of the European Prison Rules 1987). My research shows that prison labour in Russia can lead to personal development in three ways. First, prisoners learned survival skills that included not only how to trade goods, but also skills in farming (one prisoner in a penal colony in Kemerovo was known affectionately as the 'prison cowboy' because he was a ranch hand who toiled on the land, herded cattle and traded with other 'free' farmers). While the majority of prisoners did not barter their goods directly, their own individual skills in how to practise barter trade improved by observing how contracts were negotiated between prison personnel and local people.

Secondly, there were the 'realistic outcomes of work', cited by Simon (1999) and Reuss (1999), as essential for minimising reoffending. In all the colonies I visited, prisoners were aware as to why they were working, and they could leave prison with relevant up-to-date knowledge of the economic and social climate that they were being released into. Indeed the boundaries between the prison and the community were blurred: here were two arenas where individuals worked to live, where resources were woefully short and where widespread deprivation and instability had led to a form of symbiosis between two types of citizens. While these skills might not be best suited to an environment such as the UK where employers place emphasis on training qualifications, in Russian prison establishments such skills are absolutely vital to survive the current climate of instability. Since between 50 and 70% of barter contracts were between the prison establishments and the local community, the latter's involvement might also minimise the sense of bewilderment, lack of self-confidence, isolation and possible deterioration in interpersonal relationships arising from forced separation from loved ones – all cited as factors that can lead to recidivism.

Thirdly, there is a spatial dimension. There are no figures dealing with the geographical areas where ex-prisoners resettle. In the present state, with the majority of Russia's population living in the west and most of the penal colonies located in the north and in the east, it is very probable that an informal system of exile is in place. Hence, the wellbeing of former prisoners, their health, education and work will depend on the position of the prisons in the local communities (see Pallot 2004).

The 'positive element' component of prison work was found to extend to the realistic levels of support within the community. One possible scenario facing regional prison officials is that the unique relationship of demand-sharing between the prison establishments and the community may cease to exist in its current form should full state funding resume. The Russian economy has been stabilising since around 2000 and the management of the prison regions is following the model of greater centralisation (Cockburn 2002). While a full resumption to central funding is the preferred status quo both nationally and internationally (see Zubkov *et al.* 1998), it may impact negatively on the relationship between the prisons and the community because a complete cessation of support, services and resources will follow. What will be vitally important is how the community receives the prisoner group, once they are released, and how it regards the resettlement of offenders. If, for example, the community no longer has a direct involvement in the daily lives of prisoners, the latter might become isolated from the communities that they are eventually released into because prisoners are less involved with the community. In the long term, the local community may be antagonistic to the prison community with whom it has little interaction. New groups (local hospitals or schools) may surface and trade with the community. A particular point I wish to make here is that I found no evidence of communities protesting over prisons located near to residential housing or which accommodated a specific category of inmate (for example, sex offenders or special regimes). Of course, it would be naive to assume that all local communities supported the prisons in their area.

The resumption of full funding might also impact on local economies. The local economy regulates the prison economy. Certain trades, skills and work programmes might cease now that there is no longer a demand; local economies might collapse due to a loss of services provided by the prison establishments. None of this is given yet, and further prison research in Russia may yield answers to these questions.[6] Relatedly, it remains to be seen whether the situation on the ground will create a new policy reality for Russia's penal system. Efforts are concentrated instead in establishing a coherent reform strategy that includes instituting a rule of law, improving the depth of accountability in management practices (but issues of breadth of accountability are almost impossible to determine given the size and scope of the penal system), minimum standards and human rights.

In conclusion, while one of the biggest failures of the penal system remains its alarming human rights record, does this therefore negate all other debates on the path of development of Russia's penal system post-1991? My research shows that the governance of Russia's penal system is based on whether current practices are 'inhumane' or 'humane'. This was certainly reflected in the responses. On the one hand there is barter, an ancient exchange system that involves the community and gives promise of 'real work'. On the other hand are human rights norms and where there was talk of human rights, there was talk of little else. In their desire to create a more principled penal system senior prison officials are creating a rhetorical strategy that is verbose, repetitive and persuasive but which is based on penal propriety deriving from external norms. I have already referred to this period as the third phase in the transition of Russia's penal system (see Chapter 5). One senior prison official based at the central prison authority in Moscow summed up well the mood among prison officers:

> We aim to improve human rights of prisoners and ensure that all our staff have human rights training. I accept that barter is utilised, but it is all about how to ensure that we are seen to improve the system according to human rights norms. This is what we have to do now – no debate.

This was a common response where the emphasis was on 'being seen' to improve conditions. Consider the following answers to a question about how staff coped after the collapse of Marxism/Leninism in terms of how personnel justified imprisonment: 'We do not use imagery any more to explain imprisonment.' 'We are governing through human rights.' 'It is human rights that will lead to improvements.' When the last respondent was asked about what these improvements might be, he answered: 'Just more improvements in human rights. I cannot say what else.' The improvised theoretical approaches, the 'penal identities', were played down; prison labour as a vehicle for regime renewal or alternatively as an exploitative practice (which I have explored above) was seldom discussed. The Community Liaison Partnerships in Omsk were a practical accomplishment that could have been recognised under international norms as advanced given the local penal conditions. However, they have been abandoned in favour of paperwork that reflected new regimes of control.

A brand of penality that reflects powerful agendas of universalism and integration is defining how the prison defines *itself*, rather than locally embedded norms. Pratt's conceptualisation of punishment as a civilising process is in evidence here, but only to the degree that civilising is premised on a model of modernisation (see Pratt 2002). Instead the Russian scene presents those concerned with a social analysis of imprisonment with a new way of thinking about how prison systems respond to the dynamic of change. The issue of human rights is pertinent to current penal practices but it is also highly significant for the sensibility of the penal system. I have formed an opinion that the current global penal culture has resulted in Russia being categorised as a *failed penal society*. When failed penal societies are identified, the political and ideological boundaries between nation-states are strengthened because of the human rights monitoring and regulation process that demarcates those systems that administer 'good' punishments from those administering 'bad' punishments. These observations of the global penal culture that have come into view from my research into post-Soviet prison labour are discussed in the final chapters.

Notes

1 See *The Observer* (29 December 1996, 4 July 1999); and *The Times* (15 November 1997, 28 June 1998, 31 January 1999).
2 Source: Barternews.com accessed January 2004 (http://www.barternews.com/trade_exchanges.htm).
3 Source: interviewed on 4 June 2003 at GUIN headquarters in Moscow.
4 But short of large-scale prison survey, this would be very difficult to calculate as the Russian prison service does not provide a breakdown of resource provision for each establishment. With the new federal regions in place, however, it may be possible to calculate investment as per region at a future date.
5 I would like to thank Nils Christie who discussed these issues with me and who suggested further reading material.
6 Moran, Pallot and Piacentini are developing a research programme that examines the impact of the spatial dispersal of prisoners in Russia on reoffending, their domestic arrangements and integration into local communities where they serve their custodial sentences.

Chapter 7

Western borrowings: how human rights have 'travelled' to Russian prisons

The two key findings on the emergence of penal identities and the use of barter revealed how the penal system has reacted to the dynamic of change following a long spell of exposure to several contemporary transformations in the wider ideological and economic culture. A further development that was introduced in Chapter 5 was that a political culture of harmonisation is impacting on prisons wherein a tension was identified between localised penal modes and global developments. I have referred to this period as *the third occasion of penal identification* which was the process whereby a body of knowledge loosely defined as 'human rights' is shaping and guiding the contours of imprisonment. This chapter and the concluding chapter focus not on individual failures in human rights but on some of the bigger ideological and systematic problems regarding its emergence.

While it is impossible to identify any pure model of imprisonment, I would like to contend that in recent years, a process of universalism of penal ideology has emerged that is being driven by the political temper of the advanced industrial economies of the West. How this happens is complex. In a world of permeable national borders, identifiable projects that can unite common identities or 'joint interests' and fuse the social (culture) with the political (citizenship) are influencing policy. Nowadays, aspects of national governments have been systematically reproduced to create systems that co-operate, are culturally united or more ordered. This leads to a formulation of international and inter-organisational relations based on the notion of mutual dependency and interdependency. Networks of expertise, knowledge transfer (not exchange), interorganisation agency work are administered under the guise of 'modernisation'. It is commonplace for countries to look elsewhere to find out what works in reducing offending. It is also the case that across the international spectrum, prisons look elsewhere in the search for new knowledge about how to operate 'successful prisons'. This is particularly so for prisons in states of transition.

My second contention is that for prisons to be measured as successful, so too must there be prisons that are failing. My view is that universalism has led to a repositioning of boundaries in this otherwise loosely bordered political mainstream, creating positions of dominance for some states but also creating *failed penal societies*. That failed prison societies exist exposes a penal discourse that links prison systems together according to whether they administer 'good' punishments but also which allows for divergence and difference in demarcating those systems that administer 'bad' punishments. The discourse operates through refuting penality's general effects in favour of importing knowledges that are defined as benchmarks of 'success'. The discourse creates a tension between national propensities to punish and external forces (voluntary or coercive, the effect is still the same) leading to the formation of new ideological boundaries between nation-states and their power to punish. Not only that, the new politics of penality – human rights – tells us very little about why we punish.

To illustrate this process, I will utilise Russia's prison system as a case study. This chapter is structured as follows. First, I discuss the modernisation and civilisation of Russia's criminal justice system in the context of a global trend to transfer criminal justice modes to other jurisdictions. Secondly, the chapter discusses the possible reasons why particular theorisations about imprisonment have emerged in response to transformations in policy convergence. In Chapter 8, I conclude the analysis of the research by explaining a new parameter within criminology: failed penal societies.

Russia's path to penal modernisation

Russian prisons have become embroiled in a process of modernisation and penal reform. This process reflects two key changes in the wider political culture: the collapse of the Soviet Union and Russia's integration into Europe. The development of human rights is a consequence of these key changes, achieved primarily by means of a process of criminal justice policy transfer, discussed in the next section.

Criminal justice policy transfer

One of the most fascinating developments in international criminology in recent years has been the work undertaken on policy transfer. In considering such questions as *who* is transferring policy, *how* it is transferred and *what* is transferred, analysts of crime and punishment are distinguishing between policy content (the instruments that reflect policy) and policy as rhetoric or figurative language in order to ascertain how decision-makers approach transfer and whether policy transfer across nations enhances the rationality of policy decisions. Is it the case that the convergence of language and practices of crime control and the casual interchange between nation-states and fact-finding missions to countries enable effective operation of policies as defined by society vis-à-vis the state? Or does policy transfer amount to little more than ideas-pinching? For example, 'zero-tolerance policing' crossed the Atlantic and became more widespread within political discourse in the UK than in practice.

Of all the examples of a global complexion to criminal justice, confirmed by data across Europe, it perhaps 'zero-tolerance policing', monitoring sex offenders, increased managerialism, harsher sentencing and an expanding imprisonment rate, the state opting out of crime control through 'responsibilisation' initiatives (financial rewards for reporting drunk drivers or benefit fraud, CCTV and Neighbourhood Watch) in the UK and the US, and rising levels of fear of crime that have captured the attention of criminologists (see Newburn and Sparks 2004). These examples are good illustrations of how nation-states inspire copying, policy imitation or the reformulation of existing modes of criminal justice. Certain crime control strategies have travelled well across nations in Europe and from the US, while other policies have been diluted. For example, the concept of community crime prevention has been transferred and remodelled successfully from the US to the UK but was then adopted less rigorously in Germany (Karstedt 2004). Scotland's 30-year-old system of dealing with vulnerable young people has been borrowed by England to inform referral orders and youth offending panels. Restorative justice is also viewed as a successful model of how a penal policy can travel around the globe. In addition, countries such as Thailand and India have been model shopping and established community policing initiatives from Northern Ireland (Brogden 2003). Accordingly, policy transfer is not limited to nations who share linguistic, cultural, political and economic spheres but does, beyond doubt, transcend national limits.

These studies certainly prompt normative questions on how ideas are spread and diffused. Yet while the majority of studies compare the UK with the US and compare the UK with Canada and with Australasia (although some studies compare prisons within one continent),[1] most exclude an analysis of prisons in transition. On the hand, I find this perplexing. When one considers societies in transition, the main question that comes to mind is how new institutions and fresh ideas come to fill political, cultural, economic and social voids. On the other hand, however, it is not difficult to understand why researchers have yet to investigate how prisons in transition and how their modes of governance are affected by policy transfer developments. It is exceptionally difficult to conduct prison research in cultures where the systems of data collection and the process of gathering knowledge might be outmoded, unreliable and themselves in a state of flux. Although I cannot say for certain whether the study of imprisonment in Russia is one whose moment has arrived, the scope for understanding penality in Russia can certainly be broadened with a view to identifying trends in penal policy transfer and positioning developments in a global context.

Policy transfer in prisons

Briefly, then, in the literature on imprisonment, it has been argued that the general route of crime control in advanced industrial nations has followed the path of creating easy transfer conditions that enable an extra punitive political discourse to plug into an extra populist public, leading subsequently to expanding prison populations (Garland 2001). For example, there are strong similarities between the UK and the US governments in terms of how their penal policy is manifest particularly when we consider privatisation in both those countries' prisons. The injection into the prison system of an entrepreneurial zeal exemplified a new approach to penal policy in the US that led to speedy change in prison administration. The number of privately run prisons rose by 102, from 50 in 1993 to 152 by mid 2001, with a significant number of these private prisons located in southern and western states (Jones and Newburn 2004). This was followed by a slower growth in the 1990s due to effective lobbying from reform groups and trade unions over poor commercial management of prisons. Privatisation in the UK has gathered pace recently following a slow start in the 1990s when one contract for Group 4 security to purpose build one institution has grown to a dozen prisons being privately managed.

Although it is difficult to identify how the policy of privatisation has crossed borders, generally speaking the UK has aligned with the political culture of the neoliberal right of the US where punishment-at-a-distance is favoured over and above central government involvement in administering crime control (which is the main characteristic of mainland Europe's criminal justice sensibility). More specifically, different trajectories have emerged leading some scholars to question whether the path of development of penal policy in the UK mimics US penal policy. For example, the development is more to do with a transfer of the figurative language of penal policy (legislative changes) than the substance of policy (the administrative instruments) in the early 1990s. When the southern and western states in the US set about integrating the private realm (which was essentially a response to the legal requirements to reduce overcrowding and defray the costs of confinement), the UK prison population was actually falling. Privatisation in the UK was viewed much more as a symbolic gesture; a radical measure from a radical Prime Minister (Margaret Thatcher) who endeavoured to change the face of penal administration to ensure that government could govern with conviction. A further example is how the Australian and New Zealand governments have systemised UK criminal justice legislation which has included perceiving of crime as a product of an individual's pathology rather than a social condition or society's unfairness and restrictions on union power in prisons because the governments of those countries are distrustful of the criminal justice system's abilities to put certain objectives into effect (Pratt 2002).

What we can conclude from the recent work on transfer and penality is that these subtle nuances across Western locales should not be played down in the process of a comparative critique. And if we look at the literature on how analysts of the historical, political and discursive trends in imprisonment have understood developments in Western prisons as evidence of a Gulag model, an important – but provocative – question emerges about the degree of difference between the two largest prison populations in the world and their accompanying global penal ideologies over the mid to late twentieth century. Although the Soviet East and the contemporary West at two separate time periods functioned according to different political ideologies, there is a degree of convergence in penal sensibility. Special consideration should be given here to the work of Christie and Pratt, who separately ask a number of questions in relation to the policy and ideological similarities between the Soviet Gulag and the penal systems of advanced Western, industrial nations.

The Gulagisation debate

That Russia's Gulag has been conceptualised in a Western context is, I believe, extremely interesting not least because the political culture that created the Gulag was radically different from any comparable culture. In a heavily revised version of his text *Crime Control as Industry* (1996) Christie (2000) conceptualised prison expansion in advanced industrial nations as at 'Gulag proportions' where the prisons have evolved through a historical process, designed to elicit the control of individuals by the state. The features of Gulagisation apply specifically to the US but some elements have emerged in other industrial societies. These include a boom in levels of incarceration; prisons as centres of capitalism designed to produce an industry that manages crime; for-profit prisons to relieve the state of its unwanted population at the lowest cost possible; the mechanisation of justice to cope with the influx of raw materials (the captives) and the removal of democratic restraint. These features have created a culture where prisons become commodifications that are configured within an open market. Mandatory minimum sentences are served to remove discretion from judges who, faced with constraints in matching punishments to the needs of the offender and the community, must operate to the demands of the industry's conveyor. Consequently, the combined populations in prison, on parole and on probation reach the incarceration rate of the Soviet Gulags.

Pratt (2002) has developed Christie's thesis on penal expansion further and he argues that we have moved beyond Gulag-style prisons where the vested relationships between the state and bureaucratic organisations have undergone a process of change across countries that he loosely categorises as 'civilised'. Pratt's thesis is that a civilising process has emerged from the overly rationalised state bureaucracy of penal administration that characterised the Gulag style. To give punishment its civilising effect, emotive punishments have emerged out of popular concerns. Whereas once it was the marriage between bureaucratic structures and the state where punishment found its greatest expression, nowadays the 'new axis' is one that fuses political culture with a civilising, populist punitive mentality. Thus, it is the public conscience that is the principal driver of penal expansion. Pratt's 'prisons as civilising centres' are marked by a shift from public to private punishment where it becomes invisible, an almost twilight world marked by unpredictable forms of punitive populism (2002: 191). The hallmarks of the process that is occurring in Australasia, Canada, the US and the UK are that punishment is remote (driven by missions and goals), sanitised and unchecked by a public who are distanced from prison administration.

Christie and Pratt offer much to think about in terms of how we can understand modes of penality in Russia past, present and future. Christie's work, in particular, reveals how the growth of the prison populations in the USA and in Western Europe in the last two decades is certainly the most compelling *visible* evidence of Gulag-style levels where prison populations over-ran to limitless and excessive levels. Yet more recent figures would indicate a global limit to penal expansion in some jurisdictions that might reflect the evolutionary process correctly observed by Pratt where there are fewer incidences of the market oiling the wheels of penal expansion. In America, the prison population has been stabilising. In New Zealand, the prison population has fallen from 157 persons per 100,000 in 2001 to 62 in 2003. In Russia too, the average number of prisoners per 100,000 of the population has been spiralling downwards from 688 persons held per 100,000 in 2001 to 633 per 100,000 in 2003 (a reduction in absolute terms of 86,098, from 1,009,863 to 923,765), because prison labour does not play the important role it played previously in the expansion of the prison estate. Pratt attributes this movement to a post-Gulag penal era to changes in the role of the state in administering punishment. Pratt plays down the commercial corrections thesis and focuses attention instead on the transformation of penality from an ideologically driven enterprise to a warehousing enterprise. However, Garland (2001) and Newburn (2002) say something a little different – that massive prisons continue to exist because the penal industrial complex has a vested interest and entrepreneurial role in continued profits.

These important and timely works permit an opportunity for comparison with the actual Soviet model of imprisonment. In the Soviet Gulag at no stage do we find the state removed or weakened from penal allocation and administration. In Christie's Gulag, we see the state giving up penal delivery to the private contractors. The Soviet system reveals how the highest levels of human deprivations were tolerated because the state administered total control of the populace. In Christie's and, to a lesser degree, in Pratt's post-Gulag concept, the central state adopts a crime control strategy that is saturated with public opinion. The penal system of the USSR did not reflect the public's common sense because the populace were deprived of developing their own punitive mentality. Finally, throughout the entire Soviet period, it was the science of the expert that determined imprisonment and not public opinion. Hence when the political culture collapses, so too does the expert knowledge weaken, creating voids in penality as to what prisons should intend to achieve (see Chapter 5).

The notion of a post-Gulag mode of imprisonment gets somewhat lost in the translation back to Russia from its application to the West (which is ironic when it is considered that the point of origin of this term is in Soviet criminal justice!). While it might be correct that Russia's penal modernisation might in fact be following a similar path of development to Western prisons wherein the language of penality is being altered to reflect a more civilised discourse, whether Russian penal sensibility is being driven by public common sense is something that I would question. For example, the improvements to health and diet and other daily arrangements and the penal mantra of human rights *are* making punishment remote. These comments are not intended as a negative critique of Christie's and Pratt's theses. Indeed, both accounts of penality are certainly thought provoking. The civilising process in Russian prisons poses new dilemmas for the direction of international penal development. Russia is engaged in its own process of penal modernisation that does not reflect reduced state control. My view, is that the theoretical model that is better suited to Russia looks at developments as neither Gulag-like nor post-Gulag-like. Instead the model that I am offering maps out the different reflexive relationships between the local, the national and the global and how these influences come to shape the identity of prisons in transition. Nowadays, prisons in Russia have become abstract and a panoptic order or discipline order no longer features. In discussing the final evolutionary stage of Russia's penal transition, special consideration must be given to South Africa.

South African prisons and transition

The Institute of Criminology in South Africa has conducted research into the process of criminal justice policy transfer in South Africa. Their research shows how the establishment of a rule of law and constitutional legal framework has enabled accountability, demographic proportionality and equity of access to emerge. As McEvoy and Mika (2002) found in Northern Ireland and also Bowring (2002) in Russia, constitutional reform is the foundation to criminal justice reform. But what about the *process* of transference as this is what I am principally concerned with here – that is, what are the routes that permit entities and criminological ideas to travel to new foreign climates? In South Africa, a process of importing knowledge or 'foreign donor assistance' is occurring which has been met with resistance because it is not uniform across different criminal justice realms. Van Zyl Smit and van der Spuy (2004) state that prisons have received less exposure to international influences than policing because improvements in policing are associated with better law and order. The material interest of the investors or foreign donors might be jeopardised if South Africa was to become a haven for organised crime which could affect the physical safety of police officers. There is also an imbalance between juvenile justice reform and prison reform wherein the captive community is viewed as less morally deserving of improvements in their conditions than the needs of 'innocent children'. In an interesting, but less than optimistic conclusion, the research reveals that in South Africa, although prisons performed many of the injustices of the apartheid regime, they simply do not attract foreign funding. The evidence from that country indicates that policy transfer has arisen primarily from an interest in governing security because reform is embedded in an alliance between the state, the market and civil society (Shaw and Shearing 1998). This has created a scenario where donors' perspectives are affecting what South African reformers perceive to be of urgent priority (van der Spuy 2000).

Unlike South Africa, police reform in Russia is way behind penal reform despite corruption in the police reaching epidemic proportions and regulation of practices being woefully behind police reforms in other countries (see Robertson and Chistyakova 2003). Moreover, whereas in South Africa there was greater criticism of the process of importing knowledge across criminal justice institutions, I judge this to be less the case in Russia due to three reasons.

First is Russia's history and the gruesome concentration camp colonies that operated for nearly an entire century. As I mentioned in the Introduction, imprisonment is ingrained in the psyche and social lives of citizens. Nowadays, attitudes to punishment are debated across Russian media. I understood these debates as reflecting a specific cultural sensibility that on the one level views prisons as gruesome relics of Soviet repression but, on another level, is accepting of imprisonment as attaining a level of functionality. As one Russian penal reformer stated: 'One reason why we talk about prisons so much is because prisoners also worked on national projects and industry.' Prisons did not operate on the periphery but were mechanisms that contributed to the sustainability of Soviet life such that discussion of imprisonment is plugged into a wider discussion of transition and the kind of society Russia wants to become.

Second is Russia's geographical location. The movement to drive down the prison population has followed a period of exposure to the international community, particularly Europe. As Malia (1999) brilliantly observes, there are many divergent knowledges operating across and within Russia emanating from Europe and from Asia. Western ideas permeate Russia faster because it is Europe that is increasingly welcoming Russia into its remit. Becoming 'European' is viewed as a way of breaking free from the Soviet past and also represents the nostalgia that is commonplace for a pre-Soviet period where modernisation was embedded in Europeanisation (Blair 1999). This begs an interesting question about South Africa. From what direction is penal knowledge being imported into that country? Looking at the geographical location of South Africa, at the most southern point of Africa in the Southern Hemisphere, it would appear that the only route for penal policy transfer is downwards from other African nations. However, the countries in close proximity such as Botswana, Namibia, Mozambique or Zimbabwe all operate politically volatile, economically unstable and, in some cases, brutal regimes. The legislative frameworks in operation in South Africa (with the exception of restorative justice) arise from a colonial consensus and this reflects the overall colonial nature of the prison import to African countries more generally. For example, the legal system of Botswana is based on Roman-Dutch law, as is Namibia's. Zimbabwe's system has retained elements of English common law. There have been attempts to import the European Prison Rules to South Africa, but these instruments are seen as 'relatively uninfluential'.[2]

Third, and leading from the previous point, is political integration as opposed to market integration. South African criminal justice has evolved according to the latter. With foreign money from the UK, the European Union, Scandinavian countries, France and Belgium, technical and financial assistance was provided to the police. Van Zyl Smit and van der Spuy (2004) describe a melange of international policing academics, donor-assisted projects and home-grown professional academics who, with a mixed bag of methodologies, created a confused agenda of reform. The lack of coherent criminological ideas between experts and local officials led to a system that was less communitarian and more bureaucratic as the system focused on criminal statistics, catching criminals and punishing them more effectively. As ideas became more confused, so the market entered into the realm of sophisticated information gathering, creating new dimensions for crime control. Turning attention to Russia, it is structural factors which account for some of the changes in Russia's prison system. The appalling conditions in the overly populated prisons were the symptoms of the crumbling Soviet political and economic system. But the main impetus for penal reform was from the movement to integrate Russia into the European community. It was widely felt that the prison system needed to improve and reform its practices, but with regard to what kind of culture would emerge there appeared to be little feel for a local sensibility that could be reformed. Thus, it is the purveyors of the human rights message who have furnished the prisons with a new penal identity. The distinctive features of penal policy transfer in Russia are globalisation, universalism and human rights which I discuss next.

Globalisation and universalism

Ignatieff (2003) argues that, generally speaking, it is too simplistic to describe the constellation of human rights norms as part of the language of globalisation where moral and economic individualism advance the interests of the powerful. His argument is that campaigns by human rights activists against exploitative labour practices from giant global corporations are indicative of how 'human rights is embedded in the soil of cultures and worldviews independent of the West' (Ignatieff 2003: 7). I support this view but my argument is that global human rights in the context of prisons in transition anchors itelf in a particular way that is revealing of how local penal forms come to be constrained by global movements.

The evident transitions in the world not only mark a time of endings but also of new beginnings. During the first two occasions of penal identification the ideology and practices found to be in use were not uniform across the penal system. My data reveal that the third occasion of identification is revealing of an unexamined hegemony over non-Western cultures where social forms and precepts have been opened up to scrutiny. How might we understand this development? Is it the case that penality is humane and therefore 'good' so long as it is acceptable to advanced industrial nations (is barter inhumane)? Are Russian prisons now 'modern prisons'? How we come to interpret the evolution of Russia's penal system can be advanced through an exploration of the global political culture where the global economy and universal criminal justice policies appear to be influencing how Russia's penal system is exercising itself.

Globalisation has generated heated debate and a massive literature that reflects the various disciplinary orientations and prejudices of protagonists. It is not within the remit of this book to review the literature but for the purpose of understanding the path of development of the second largest penal system in the world, it is instructive to illustrate some of the key features of globalisation.

The key features of globalisation are that it has an economic, political and social basis. Globalisation leads to the integration of a range of hitherto demarcated activities across state borders. Most dramatic has been the increase in interconnecting economic phenomena leading to elevated political positions of transnational corporations. Developments in communications, in transport and in how production is organised have thus been exploited. But equally important is the prominence of intergovernmental and non-state actors who have been involved in assisting international institutions which, put simply, is beyond nation-states to organise independently (see Beeson 2003). Not only is economic activity organised across borders, so too is it the case that the sovereignty of national infrastructures becomes co-operatively organised (see Chayes and Chayes 1998). This can be looked at as the state retreating as other institutions assume responsibility. Such a dynamic diffuses authority away from national governments. An alternative inter-pretation put forward by political scientists is that the efficacy of systems and institutions is marked by *legitimate participation* of a range of actors in addition to state structures. Rosenau (1997) argues that we are currently living in a multi-actor world which is marked – and this is key here – by 'spheres of authority'. What distinguishes spheres of authority is their ability to evoke compliance.

In a study by Cutler *et al.* (1999) globalisation is viewed as two-pronged and is based on abandonment and replacement. States abandon responsibility, the authors argue, because of 'ideology' or 'lack of state capacity'. The authors believe that in a range of private and public spheres governments choose to, or are forced to, share authority. Braithwaite and Drahos (2001) argue further that we are stepping into a new epoch of 'information capitalism' where regulatory forms of knowl-edge depend on complex webs of dependency relations and influence. What emerges in the literature on globalisation is that the uni-versalisation of institutions is inextricably linked to rule-making, control and rule enforcement. In an environment where political communities have collapsed and fallen away from any nationally demarcated territory, questions arise as to how national policy or sovereignty can play a pivotal role. Authority, it is argued, is divided leading to a tension between national sovereignty and international expansion. Giddens' outline of the aesthetics of modern social order is in the context of how Western societies pursue the legitimation of power such that the state 'imposes itself on passive subjects' (1994: 56).

The institutional problems associated with globalisation are gaining increasing urgency, but it is unclear in what way issues can be resolved. However, I would like to cite here some key aspects of globalisation as they relate to Russia before considering globalisation and imprisonment in Russia. Drawing on the debates on globalisation, Russian social scientists have adopted various positions. Some believe that Russia's position in global political culture is weak because its sovereignty has been negated by globalisation (Kara-Murza 1999; Rozanova 2003). Others adopt a one-sided view that globalisation means Westernisation where 'atlanticist' modes of political and economic culture threaten the entire community of non-Western entities (Stepin and Bello 2001). This is a problematic viewpoint because it assumes that different value systems are always incompatible. Others, however, debate globalisation as neutralising difference through technological developments while also aggravating difference through sociocultural differentiation. Consider the following: is globalisation about creating a mega-society of singular, inter-related and interpenetrating worlds, or is it about clearing the way for free markets as Tolstykh (2003) and Bogomolov and Nekipelov (2003) respectively argue? What is interesting about the debate on globalisation in Russia is that the positions adopted vary according to their angle or vision about the collapse of the USSR. There is some common ground, fuelled principally by an anxiety about preserving Russia's autonomy over its political, cultural, economic and social agendas, and this sense of anxiety is not instantly clear from debates on globalisation in Western cultures. In a world where there is co-operation of nations, there is also a concern that the underbelly of globalisation (that which is based on force and hegemony) will aggravate adaptability to global conditions for states in transition (see Ilyin 2003 for some very interesting Russian viewpoints on the topic).

Globalisation and prisons

Prisons in transition also provide a particularly illuminating space within which to examine the relevance of ideas of globalisation in relation to human rights discourses. Generally speaking, there has been a transfer of styles of punishment that has flowed around the world through complex exchanges. Western modes of penal governance are extending their spread via globalising processes from the US to UK criminal justice and also to countries such as Holland where there has been a dramatic reversal of the Dutch policy of tolerance (longer sentences, substantial prison building, mass immigration and neoliberal market reform).

My research in Russia has shown that where nation-states collapse a void in penal ideology and administration is exposed. Tradition, therefore, makes prisons legitimate (occasions 1 and 2). But this can only be temporary and the vacuous states of penality in Russia have been particularly exposed to global influences. Sealed off so that the possible negative effects (high-risk punishments, alienation of cultures, distance and remoteness of rival political economies) are reduced, the local activities in Russian prisons are being determined by global ideas that, while being remote and intrusive to Russian prison personnel, have been appropriated by experts who are setting about civilising the prison system. Occasion 3 is interesting because expertise comes to replace tradition. Giddens' (1994) hypothesis, that all forms of social action and relations are then governed by expert decisions that come to be enacted on the basis of claims of one kind of knowledge or another (for example, 'this is good', 'this is bad') has some currency here, particularly where he argues that modes of power relations dictate everyday decisions that affect *worldwide* relations over and above *local* relations. Consequently, in the global political economy the 'other' does not answer back and is instead locked within a relationship of dependency (economic, ideological and social). Within this context of harmonisation, if a prison system is premised on correct or incorrect modes, then it is more than likely that the worldview will be that it has, at some stage, failed or is 'failing'. I will return to the notion of failure as defining the ideological boundaries between nation-states shortly. To sum up, analysts remain unclear as to whether globalisation is an umbrella term for concepts such as Westernisation, universalism and modernisation. I do believe, however, that the emergence of a universal doctrine of human rights shares distinctive features with a process of globalisation.

Human rights as Russia's new penal ideology

While recent trends in globalisation have enabled a more effective human rights process to emerge around the world, human rights have emerged slowly in prisons since the eighteenth century where social upheaval in particular places at particular times led Western govern-ments (the US, France and the UK) to preserve 'the rights of man'. Thus, human rights are Western in origin. Stellars (2002) and Ignatieff (2003) argue separately that a new worldview was required following the Second World War. Harmony needed to be restored, regimes needed to be stabilised and political danger kept at a distance. Human rights were seen as the essential prerequisite for a peaceful world. Human rights also offers enormous political benefits both to benefactors and beneficiaries: human rights are used to win domestic support for new policies and mobilise support for causes; they provide a moral foundation for New World orders and they can 'provide sugar-coating for unpalatable foreign intervention' (Stellars 2002: xiii). Nations, viewed once upon a time as global pariahs, can be reformed through a commitment to human rights. Therefore, while human rights *exist* at the level of abstract morality, they also *operate* at the level of politics and must therefore be subject to rules and political doctrine.

Looking at the European context, the striking creation of expressive unity as constituted in European political integration has taken on a bigger form of late and has been enhanced with talk of world com-munities (sometimes referred to as transnational communities) which have their most enduring traditions in the conceptual vocabularies embedded in the doctrine of human rights. Citizenship, inclusion, democracy, federalism and the strong emphasis on communities as cohesive entities are just some of the conceptual vocabularies that give promise of a meaningful and united international and also a pan-European ideology that unites different consciences with common political identities (culture with citizenship). Nowadays, aspects of national governments have been systematically reproduced to create systems that co-operate, are culturally united and more ordered in their commitment to human rights. The course of political integration has led to changes in the modes of governance where institutional contacts have been established with the principal aim of improving relations between sovereign states. Further changes have taken place in the assumptions that underpin integration. There is a sense that integration is a force for good and that nation-states are willing to expose national initiatives to international scrutiny.

Turning attention to imprisonment, as rhetoric, human rights are viewed as a stimulus to improve standards and conditions and national jurisdictions are guided in their national legislation by the European Prison Rules (1987) and the United Nations Standard Minimum Rules (1955). As a practice, human rights enable prisoners to voice domestic grievances over procedures, treatment and conditions where often prisoners' rights are vaguely defined. It is recognised that a human rights sensibility forms part of a body of principle that seeks to maintain standards in prisons around the world and where prisoners' rights, better prison conditions and access to judicial defence are recognised. Thus, when we declare our allegiance to human rights, we are appealing to make institutions work better. Human rights also permit some philosophical respectability in the multifaceted and heterogeneous world that exists today: 'It is preferred because it holds out a hope that universal values may be something other than the arbitrary products of power or particular cultural artefacts' (Langlois 2003: 514).

Who is transferring human rights and how

There are numerous ways in which a joint understanding has been developing between Russia and Europe, but several are directly related to prisons. These are technical support, new positions for prison personnel, changes in the rights of prisoners, changes in the language of penality and regulation.

Technical expertise and publications

The European Union and the United Nations do not offer funds or financial aid to the Russian government for improvements to its prison system. In recent years the movement towards harmonisation has come in the form of knowledge transfer (technical support, human rights education and handbooks on how to deliver human rights).

Tatiana Bukareva of the European Union Delegation for the Promotion of Democracy and Human Rights based in Moscow monitors programmes that have been established between non-governmental organisations (hereafter NGOs) and local prison administrations. Micro projects are being piloted in some prisons in Russia. These are small-scale democratisation initiatives which are intended to deepen local civil society groups' involvement in the promotion of human rights.[3] Three programmes are underway in three prisons in Chelyabinsk and they are being monitored by the EU. In one example, radio sets were given to prisoners in a pre-trial centre as part of a project controlled by a local NGO. Interestingly, when the project started the prison administration told the NGO that it was expecting funds so that they could purchase the radios themselves which is not possible under EU regulations. The radio sets were given after the end of the project on the basis that the prison had reformed its practices. Although Bukareva favours the involvement of international NGOs, their involvement in penal reform may be reduced in 2004 due to changes in the legislation regarding the payment of foreign workers in Russia. There are bureaucratic obstacles in transferring money into foreign bank accounts in Russia so, for 2004, technical support is being offered to local NGOs. Other examples are that local and international NGOs bid for EU contracts. In an interview, Bukareva stated: 'The EU is pressing for the presence of international NGOs.'

Some NGO participation was also found in Siberia in the 'Food in Exchange for Progress' programme. The Red Cross gives the colonies meat, butter, beans, vegetables, flour and rice. The aid was initially marked for prisons where prisoners have TB, but the programme has now extended to other prisons. The TACIS organisation also works within the federal ministries and not with NGOs, and identifies projects with the federal ministries. The project is then contracted out. TACIS's work is concentrated on communicable diseases in prisons (TB, HIV and AIDS education).

Penal Reform International (PRI) has been prominent in reforming the Russian prison system for 14 years. It has produced numerous pamphlets, initiatives and strategies for prison reform; a book on combating communicable diseases in prisons in Eastern Europe and exchange programmes between prison personnel in Russia and Northern Ireland and England. Operating without the unbridled idealism that can often feature in some international initiatives, PRI produces texts on human rights management and alternatives to custody as well as work on the social integration of women offenders and their children. Altogether, these programmes have provided knowledge and guidance on how to implement international standards in a practical fashion. The main point of entry into all these programmes is Western expertise and consultancy. The Moscow Centre for Prison Reform has also been engaged in a campaign to reform prisons since the 1980s and concentrates its efforts on overcrowding and the management of diseases in prisons. MCPR receives core funding from the Soros Foundation and further support from Penal Reform International. All these projects are carried out within the context of the international standards relating to imprisonment. It is clear from the evidence on how technical support is delivered that the process of knowledge transfer on human rights in Russian prisons is result based, where the NGO has to establish how it will meet the predetermined objectives.

New positions for prison personnel
The position 'assistant for human rights', created in 2002, has been introduced to enable the process of administering human rights. Each region employs one assistant (up to 30,000 prisoners and 12,000 staff) and it is not certain whether the role will be extended to each establishment. In Omsk and Kemerovo, staff who had trained under the Soviet system had taken up these positions before retirement. One assistant is a former secretary who worked in the prison system for 25 years. The human rights assistants I met had mixed views about their role, with one assistant showing concern that the prison authorities might 'get carried away with human rights'. Another assistant adopted the view that while human rights was a positive step forward in prison administration, the concept did not transfer well: 'It's not instantly obvious to us what the term "human rights" means. We don't understand the terminology and we have had to ensure that, when we translate it, we explain it in great detail.'

Other recent changes are that Russia also has its first Prison Ombudsman and student prison officers receive human rights training. The prison system has not allocated a specific human rights programme to employ trainers, education staff or other professionals who have experience of working with offenders in delivering rehabilitation programmes. There is some human rights training taking place, but this is limited to a few 'pilot regions'. Instead, most of the human rights administration is deskwork. Very few, if any, of these assistants have the opportunity to travel outside Russia.

Prisoners' rights

Prisoner access to legal advice through programmes set up between regional administrations and NGOs has increased across the breadth of the prison system. The EU administrators whom I interviewed informed me that most of the legal advice requested by prisoners is to do with visiting rights and improvements in conditions which are protected under international law. Prisoners are now offered access to the various EU and UN bulletins on their rights under international law. It is the responsibility of the assistant for human rights to oversee access to these documents.

Reforming the language of imprisonment

The reform of the language of imprisonment in ministerial papers attests to a new penal vernacular. This vernacular conveys a general discourse through which flows the penal identity of human rights. There is missionary zeal in the language adopted ('problems', 'assistance', 'pioneering good practice', 'lessons', 'best efforts', 'progression') that is flowing into national guidelines.

Regulation/inspections

The central prison authority (GUIN) inspects all prisons annually. The new Federated Regional Administrations are expected to inspect on a more regular basis and then report to GUIN authority in Moscow. GUIN then reports to the Council of Europe. Inspections from the EU are every five years. Aside from these transactions between the prison authorities and human rights institutions, my data also show that the narratives produced by prison personnel have altered since 1999.

When I returned to Russia in 2003, human rights were discussed by a prison community that believes that all it is doing is violating human rights. Yet I also found human rights talk as reaching, first, performance-indicator proportions and, secondly, faith-like proportions. Regarding the former, efforts to find fault with the system were accompanied by a raft of targets to meet, performance goals to reach and bureaucracy 'devised to manage the extra paperwork generated from the human rights monitoring missions' (chief, Kemerovo region). On the second point, prison officers' narratives were constructed around an assumption that penal success stories were found in nations that believed in human rights. I was principally concerned, therefore, with the question: what does it mean to believe in human rights in Russian prisons? Is it a belief like believing in a faith or is it belief like a hope? I found it be both these things and much more besides. I discuss the various human rights propositions next.

Localising human rights: prison officer narratives

Prison officers conveyed a diverse range of views about how human rights. The categorisations that I describe here reveal some un-comfortable questions about how human rights in prisons remain under-critiqued.[4]

Human rights as 'humane rights'

Some respondents argued that the care and positive custody of prisoners were key to better human rights practices: 'It is about the maintenance of standards. It's about ensuring we meet norms. We get sent EU bulletins now in Russian. We know the outcome that needs to be achieved.' Another officer added:

> I am not sure if it is good or bad. Human rights are important because they are about promoting care, respect and humanity for offenders so that they don't reoffend and so that they are treated better ... but there is more control ... we have to be seen to meet norms because for ten years we struggled to do so. We have a long way to go to meet international norms.

Human rights as administration

When once prison officers viewed their role as 'punishers', 'custodians', 'carers' and 'responsible for rehabilitation', nowadays the majority of respondents viewed human rights as deskwork: 'My job is to check the bulletins to see how many of our prisoners complain'; 'I am the Human Rights Assistant. My job is to fill in the necessary forms'; 'It is an administration job'; 'We have executive meetings to discuss human rights with the International Red Cross.'

These examples will suffice as illustrations of how prison officers talk about human rights and they certainly reveal that prison officers are aware of the terminology. However, when probed to discuss human rights as a way of thinking about the function of imprisonment, the responses suggested that human rights was about exposing the system and its associated problems.

Human rights as integrative shaming

Most often, respondents found it difficult to explain a principle of penality that was, as one respondent stated to me clearly, 'about making them feel bad': 'We are told constantly, "make it better", "this is bad" '. While other officers complained to me that: 'The Westerners come here to tell us how bad our system is and then leave'; 'There is a lot of disapproval about our system.' The governors of the prisons that I visited expressed clearly the problems faced by the establishments: 'When I think of human rights I think of the rights of the prisoners. But I must admit I don't really know what that means because we never focused on prisoners rights in our society.' Another governor added: 'Is it about the human rights of society? Never have we had to listen to other nations, but now we have to listen.' Another member of staff responsible for delivering human rights strategies said:

> I have forms to fill in every day. Do they have enough water? 'Yes.' Do they have minimum standards? 'Yes.' I cannot answer 'no' to any questions or we are in trouble with the regional chiefs. I see human rights as a list of criteria to meet so that we have, well, so that we meet European norms.

The responses indicated to me that there was an imbalance between what the prisons could do for themselves to improve human rights in the context of the local conditions and international pressure. This was of keynote: the impetus and enthusiasm for penal reform were not coming from inside the prison system.

Human rights as a metaphor for 'good punishment'

The sheer deprivation of Russia's prison system and its dependency on the West exposed a broad range of emotions and views on what could be described as providing for 'penal propriety': 'We've got to do better and implement proper practice. The law says human rights are at the top of the list. We've got to get it right.' Another senior officer added: 'You ask us whether we think about how we understand punishment in the new post-communist society. I never ask myself these questions. I get depressed. We got it completely wrong and we now have a big mess, a terrible system.' Other respondents' comments were: 'It wasn't all bad in the past. We did have some good work practices. Work was so important for prisoners'; 'Well it is all about making things better than before.'

These comments were typical of those I spoke to. Views on imprisonment could be categorised as correspondingly, good prisons and bad prisons. This suggested to me that penality has been reduced to this categorisation discourse rather than discipline or rehabilitation modes.

Human rights as an ideological filler

There are many reasons for the current problems in prisons in Russia. From an academic position, I considered the complex linkages between the ideological vacuum that followed the collapse of the Soviet regime and the development of a new ethos that was acceptable to the West. The head of one prison region that I visited stated: 'We used to have a principle of imprisonment. It was work and education. We've gone through great change and I don't know why we have prisons. They tell us that human rights are the most important thing to concentrate on and it's the only thing they talk about.' While others expressed defiant nostalgia for previous penal policies:

> I was born in the Gulag, my father was a prison guard as was his father. I feel that human rights are good for the West but not here. What do you Europeans know about us? We are not European. I can't define human rights because it is not something that we created. The Gulag was … great. I am a patriot for that penitentiary system.

One officer added: 'We have lost our past.' While regarding the collapse of penal ideology, another officer said: 'No, I never think about whether we are in a new phase, ideology is no longer important.'

These comments revealed an irony. Whereas at one particular time prison officers would exaggerate their own self-importance and argue that international norms were the instruments of capitalism, so it is that nowadays, instead of viewing human rights as a vehicle for the disempowered and disenfranchised, they saw it as a set of rules organised by the world's most powerful states. Prison personnel could not shut their eyes to the new reality of penal politics. This was particularly noticeable from comments that human rights was a 'Western idiom' or 'foreign politicisation'.

Human rights as unjustified interference

Prison officers understood that human rights yielded political benefits, which they forecast as the establishment of an easily identifiable penal ideology. It was the case, moreover, that prison officers were tuned in to the process of integration into Europe. Consider the following comments: 'When we are told by our colleagues in Europe that progress is being made, I feel that we are really getting somewhere'; 'We look at what is going on elsewhere and try and incorporate it into our system. The West is our starting point'; 'We're much closer to Europe now and we read pamphlets from the EU.' Others were more sceptical that 'foreigners' had formulated Russian penal sensibilities: 'What does Europe know? Why should we listen to you? We are in Siberia, we have our own Siberian human rights [laughs]'; 'I am annoyed that these are not our changes. We cannot possibly be like Europe.' While there are numerous examples that concretely illustrate that, for many personnel, human rights is an obscure, regulatory mechanism, I provide the following quotation because it illustrates the many facets of human rights in Russian prisons:

> Why do our prisoners need the EU? If you look at the bulletin from Europe, it's Britain, France and other countries where more prisoners are reporting grievances. Hardly any prisoners from Russia are mentioned. Our prisoners are fine. I can't stand NGOs, they just say all the negative stuff. They are righteous. They base their reports on an entirely aggressive and negative approach. There is so much pressure on us.

When we compare the feelings about imprisonment recorded in 2003 to those recollected by prison officers in the 1990s, several points are worth mentioning. The above accounts were typical of those I spoke to. Each account of human rights indicates that while human rights intend to improve the lives of prisoners, the majority of personnel viewed human rights reform as a commodity rather than as a way of thinking about the prison experience. I also found prison officers to be emotionally and intellectually cynical about the latest path of development. In the early 1990s many prison officers did not consciously break with their old sense of selves as 'Soviet' prison officers who conducted their work under the rubric of a dominant political ideology. Moving on ten years, new emblems of penal punishment have been imported into the criminal justice system. As a consequence, human rights are not viewed as created by Russian prison personnel for Russian prisoners. Moreover, despite the good intentions of NGOs who work tirelessly to make Russian prisons better, some prison officers were found to be jealously guarding the identities that were established in the second phase (as in Omsk and Kemerovo) because they felt that the sovereignty of the penal system was under siege. Others employed in regions close to the West orient their strategies towards human rights (as in Smolensk) because officers felt that they worked under the gaze of the Moscow administration. Thus, the talk about human rights was interspersed with fear – fear at what might happen should officers fail to meet targets. Far from being realised in practice, prison officers, I found, believed human rights to be mere window dressing.

In conclusion, I came to critique human rights penal reform in Russia as indicative of how a country becomes swallowed up by reform projects within which the prisons succumb to a notion of good punishment following a period of exposure to globalised penal trends and discourse. Jefferson (2003) also gives firm indications of this in his work on prison officer training programmes in Nigeria. He argues that global move-ments and their constructed links to penal policy arrangements are contained within the political discourse of integration. I agree with penal reformers with whom I have discussed the difficult issue of critique versus reform that in Russian prisons, something had to be done and human rights was an utterly necessary and practical starting point. However, this starting point is designed to produce regulatory forms of knowledge because the movement from retrogressive to progressive punishments is embedded in global arrangements that fuse together monitoring, regulation and political integration. Distinct from the intention of penal reformers is human rights policy implementation. The strategy of human rights is feeding into a larger political process of shaming or as one officer stated to me, 'making them feel bad' (prison officer, Kemerovo remand prison). The imperative to make the prisons better alongside the common response just mentioned exposed a paradox, that while there is clearly a potential for global movements to transform for the better, the governance of prison systems during transition, such actions undermine critique as connections between human rights and reasons to punish rarely feature.[5] This is because the features and logic of human rights doctrine are creating a culture that identifies *failing penal systems* according to imported knowledges (benchmarks). The phenomenon of failed penal societies is introduced in the concluding chapter.

Notes

1   See the special issue of *Ethnography*, 'Ethnography's kitchen', devoted to prison research, December 2002.
2   Source: Professor Dirk van Zyl Smit, University of Cape Town, South Africa, February 2004 in conversation.

3 The Department of Social Work at the University of Edinburgh has conducted an evaluation of prison conditions for mothers who gave birth in prison in Chelyabinsk in Russia in 2003. At the time of writing, the report had not been published.

4 Unfortunately I was not permitted to interview prisoners regarding human rights. It must be emphasised here that the omission of prisoners' voices on a matter that so crucially affects their experience of incarceration concerned me when writing the book. By the same token, the exclusion of prisoners does not, I believe, weaken the overall focus of the book. It just raises more questions about how imported knowledges of regulation and performance are qualified on the ground by excluding the critical mass of individuals to which that process of regulation principally applies (as well as providing for further research opportunities).

5 The 'rights without reasons' debate has been captured recently in Langlois' work on theoretical problems with human rights (Langlois 2003; see also Walker 1991).

Chapter 8

Beyond the metaphor: the phenomenon of 'failed penal societies'

In this concluding chapter, I would like to give final consideration to some of the uncomfortable aspects of penal development in Russia that have revealed themselves to me in the course of examining post-Soviet penality. As I stated in the Introduction, this book has taken me on a journey into the murky waters of imprisonment in a former totalitarian country. It is my hope that this study of Russian penal development has contributed to the ongoing developments in the philosophical, political and economic study of prisons. Fifteen years ago, the Russian prison system was committed to Marxism/Leninism. One of this study's key findings is that, nowadays, the universal doctrine of human rights has produced a *failed penal society*.

Over and over again, 'does prison work?' is a key question that has occupied (some say troubled) prison sociologists, penal reformers and politicians for decades. And since far more light has been shed on what is going on inside the prisons in places as far apart as Poland and Pakistan, criminological discussion on what we can expect from imprisonment has certainly been enhanced. The debates may draw attention to whether prisons are effective at rehabilitation (Scottish Parliament 2004) or whether woman-centred prisons are a sensible approach to reducing barriers to reform in prisons for women in the UK (see Lowthian 2002). Further examples include how inmate relationships inside prisons can be mediated by specific prison-adaptive mechanisms such as the utilisation of television (Jewkes 2002) and, in an illuminating snapshot of French prisons, Marchetti *et al.* (2002) argue that what we can expect from prisons in France is carceral poverty: an accentuation of pre-existing social deprivation in economic, cultural, material, physical, recreational and afflictive realms. Indeed, the recurring anxiety that imprisonment is a failure inheres in the majority of the academic literature that develops a social, political and cultural critique of imprisonment and cannot be said to be reduced to one type of society or culture. When it comes to the anxieties of prisons' failure in societies in transition, moreover, there are several additional and also more specific difficulties in determining penality's general effects. In what follows, I argue that *carceral disgrace* and *carceral discreditation* capture some of the conceptual and organi-sational features of failed penal societies.

Carceral disgrace

In every country in the world there are failures to hold to international obligations because human rights, as a principle of 'good worth', is difficult to enforce. The US government, for example, approves of a judicial system that sentences people to death, but disapproves of a regime, such as that which operated under the Taliban in Afghanistan, which stones women to death. This example illustrates one of the fun-damental problems of human rights in prison: how is it characterised? This is a particularly complex question for the political cultures of a range of different countries that operate outside the group of advanced industrial nations which have been discredited in the eyes of the international community. While no society in the world can be said to have a perfect penal system, nor is there a perfect model to copy, in the majority of the societies identified as 'failing', their prisons are filthy and overcrowded and they operate outside a rule of law. In some cases observers will acknowledge efforts to reduce overcrowding which in many countries has improved (Rodley 2000). But there is a sense that national standards fall woefully short of international standards and conditions remain intolerable, gruesome even.

How do these 'failings' come to be understood by those involved in prison administration? I have already mentioned that in Russia the brutalising spaces where appalling squalor and poverty unite prisoner with prison have shamed the system into making a commitment to penal reform. 'Russia's disgrace' (as one well-known Russian politician who campaigns for penal reform described it) has produced a range of emotions one normally associates with politesse. Shame, morality, protocol and convention lead to considerable confusion, defensiveness and apology from prison officers whose principal task is to interpret human rights on the ground. The prison officers' stories revealed that human rights talk is de rigueur but few understood what they were talking about. This was problematic because, as a consequence, there were some extraordinary claims made that human rights offered the promise of some sort of *carceral respectability* in the global political mainstream. It was as though penal talk of propriety in imprisonment kept the political dangers associated with political differences at bay. Thus, after a few years of one kind of penal identity that linked prisoner with prison according to a very specific discourse on 'what has caused crime' (based on historical and social foundations), in the third transition phase, prison staff and prisoners are drifting further away from instituting reasons to punish as the burden of what follows from disgrace looms large. With human rights committees exercising authority to adjudicate violations that are brought before them, a once-oppressive regime can now be shamed and controlled in ways that were simply not possible for the entire twentieth century.

Carceral discreditation

The second difficulty arises from the potentiality of human rights to impose an extra burden and it concerns *discreditation*. The turn towards democracy is altering the political, social and economic face of Europe and beyond. At the time of writing (spring 2004), ten countries will shortly join the European Union (eight of which were subsumed under the Soviet Eastern Bloc). This enormous political event described by Romano Prodi, the European Commission's President, as a period 'when countries will make their history by becoming one reality', is a consequence of a movement to end political fighting across Europe and to address the democratic deficit of the Soviet and Cold War periods by instituting citizenship rights, respecting the rights of minorities, political participation and marketisation (just some of the societal preconditions for entry into the European Union).[1]

A fundamental assumption of EU expansion is the political anchoring of nation-states to a transnational entity of becoming European (although the pre-existing national identities that are essential to who we are remain attached to the history of particular nations). Despite continued reservations over the democratised state of nations[2] it is European models of democracy that are widely believed to be the only political order that is legitimate for new accession countries. Thus, countries that are unfamiliar with the political and economic territory of democracy must then search for objective characterisations for their institutions (Rozanova 2003). New styles of governance based on democracy are being embraced because they ensure better global social, political and economic relationships. On the one hand, this makes sense. Even in countries like Afghanistan and Iraq, which have been ruined by decades of dictatorship, conflict and war and where civil society is still weak, the new interim governments have requested support from international NGOs and the hope is that indigenous tribes will play a part in new forms of justice (see Albrecht 1999; Watson 2000a). Russia, on the other hand, has no such past history which could be reformed from within. In the post-Soviet period, the system has followed no solid script of its own and perhaps inevitably, Russian prisons operationalise external concepts into the penal realm. If human rights is a paradigm for democratic principles, then its humanising effects (establishing a rule of law, a transparent and independent judiciary, democratic structure, to name a few) protect institutions from regressing. Europe is welcoming in new communities mainly through this route. The appropriation of human rights, therefore, amounts to political creditation of practices and institutions.

One must wonder how the expansion of Europe, where the stress falls on reforming political governance so that regression is prevented, impacts on imprisonment in states in transition. When we look at a country like Russia, the institution of human rights into prisons is historically unprecedented. Russia is not yet a member of the EU but the presence of an EU delegation in Moscow is highly significant. Its role is to ensure that as a member of the Council of Europe, Russia is instituting democratic principles that are valid and within acceptable limits for the governing European Union. As prisons are highly complex because they reflect diverse cultural sensibilities, styles of state power, public temperament and moral visions, what human rights doctrine provides for is standardisation of diversity and difference. As a rigid template of penal reform that has been described as a 'one size fits all' mechanism, it smoothes out political and cultural differences by uniting and inspiring nations to come together (and this is certainly in keeping with the ongoing global nature of political cultures). Thus, Russia's curved penal spaces no longer feature (see Watson 2000b for a particularly interesting critique of transition). Instead, the rigid template means that Russia must guarantee that it administers civil punishments by submitting to monitoring and regulation from NGOs.

I accept that carceral disgrace and carceral discreditation are evident in prisons everywhere where every type of deprivation of liberty raises the question of legitimacy. Yet, these twin contentions are highly significant for prisons in societies in transition not only at the material level but also at the political level. The losses will be greater for societies in transition because these contentions determine the path of penal development. Prison institutions become discredited when they are named as undemocratic, ineffective and unaccountable to transnational organisations and institutions. Thus, prison systems in transition will be charged with not complying with international norms. Beyond prisons is the power to name and shame governments. This is clearly the most powerful aspect of human rights: its enforcement mechanism. The consequences of naming and shaming are that it becomes harder to secure aid and international loans and can lead, in some cases, to political isolation (Zimbabwe, Iraq and South Africa are some recent examples). Relatedly, the sense that Russia is a failed penal society is woven into more complex narratives of how Russian prison personnel come to understand their position in the global penal community. When discussing the appropriation of human rights, personnel did not gaze at internal practices and processes. Instead, their perceptions suggested an external essentialist stance where they configured human rights as external to models of penal punishment that reflect a national cultural sensibility due largely to the technocratic and managerialist logic of international norms that are conditioning and predisposing the prison officers to act in certain ways.

For failed penal societies, there are various consequences arising from importing norms such as human rights. These consequences are discussed below along with a critique of the impact of human rights on penal identities and prison barter that I have discussed in Chapters 3 and 4.

Doing something is better than doing nothing

While I have contested the progress of penal development in Russia, clearly doing something is better than doing nothing. In Russia, human rights doctrine has put the often-quoted statement 'prison is as punishment and not for punishment' on the agenda when previously to utter these words might have led to incarceration. This, in itself, is progress. Improvements in human rights have also thrown light on what is going on inside the prisons and this new knowledge opens up closed worlds. Armed with this knowledge, bodies promoting human rights have reduced the amount of cruelty and unmerited suffering of people in prisons. Often, national jurisdictions operate prisons at their own discretion, so to impose a system of regulation provides standards against which the national laws can be scrutinised and issues raised on what goes on in prison besides incarceration. Nations can also be held accountable through publication of activities in prisons and media activity.

Without human rights, prisoners would not see their rights judicially recognised. Because of human rights, the position of prisoners has been enhanced to one where there is the assumption that they are citizens as well as inmates. As Coyle (2002) notes, as there is very little prison research conducted in societies in transition, cataloguing terrible human rights abuses certainly prompts criminological discussion of how prisons can be enhanced. Such an approach, moreover, gives promise for critical penological scholarship as prisoners become sources of knowledge on penal development and are not viewed merely as subjects in the research treadmill.

The widening gap between reform and critique

With the exception of a significant reduction of the prison population and improvements in conditions, the boom in human rights has not, unfortunately, been fed by many intellectual accomplishments within Russia in understanding the role of imprisonment in that country. I believe this to be one of the costs of human rights. The sociology of imprisonment is rarely analysed in-depth and there is very little critical or theoretical debate about the legitimacy of imprisonment in Russia as the country undergoes modernisation. Prison officers are rarely con-sulted, which might be explained by the sheer size and scope of the penal system and the difficulty in communicating the message on the ground with very limited resources. However, no prison can be reformed in a vaccum and when prison reformers in Russia exclude the role of prison officers from their discussion of better human rights (as one reformer did during an interview), then human rights become an illusion. It can also lead to denial as evidenced in the nostalgia for Soviet penal models. I did not find evidence of personnel doctoring documentation to ensure that forms were filled in 'correctly', but, other criminologists have found evidence of this in the reform of Russia's police force (see Robertson and Chistykova 2003). Without the bearers of the message believing in the message and understanding its dimensions (while accepting its limitations), how can penal reform occur? As McEvoy (2003) has noted with regard to Northern Ireland's criminal justice system, although human rights work should be about a better understanding of the objects of inquiry, in attempting to make a difference, we should also be wary of political and sociological non-engagement. The same can be said for Russia. While there is some debate on reducing custodial sentences, these debates are controlled within concerns to alleviate overcrowding in order that norms are met. Though vitally important for advancing penal reform, the international pressure to reduce overcrowding is not sustained within a discourse on the desirability of imprisonment generally.

In this regard, there are marked differences between Russia and the UK, for example, over the state of critical scholarship. The recent literature on punishing particular groups such as women or young people in the UK reiterates the point that punishment must be appropriate to the social and personal biographies of local cultures (Carlen 2002; Muncie 2004). Penal ideology, it is argued, is determined from pre-existing notions of gender, race and class and consequently prisons can be disadvantageous (see Carlen 2002; Hudson 1997, 2002). The question regarding what prisons are for has exposed a failure of prisons not only to reduce crime but to aggravate social, political and economic deprivation because the prison needs of different groups have not necessarily led to culture or gender-specific practices. I would like to add another dimension to that debate by echoing van Zyl Smit's comment about penal reform in South Africa: how do we create normality in abnormal societies? As human rights is an elusive concept to many prison personnel, consequently, its institution into prisons renders obscure the reality of imprisonment in Russia and the complexities of that form of censure. Thus, the often-asked question of 'what are prisons for?' is not only thus unresolved, it also paves the way for a further question: 'who are the punishers?' Or, 'in whose name do prisons function?'

Disempowerment of knowledge

Leading on from the previous point, in academe there is a seeming tendency of human rights advocates to disconnect human rights talk from a substantive discussion of punishment that has taken on modern forms. This is due largely to the political aspects of human rights; human rights defence is about taking sides and mobilising protest to stop abuses taking place. Further research is required to assess whether human rights mark the natural conclusion to Russia's penal transition, but some further comparisons with Western prisons are useful here. Writing on penal reform in Canada, Hannah-Moffat (2002) argues that simply changing the content of regimes to be more women centred or, in this case study, humanity centred, often leaves structural and institutional frameworks unchallenged. I would add that in Russia human rights have led to a virtual demise of locally produced, home-grown ideological formats (such as character and reform and social reform; see Chapter 3). In my study, human rights have been integrated into the penal discourse, but have tended to obscure and then to some extent silence how we see social relations in prisons. Although Russian prisons are in a state of flux, in one sense the prison remains static because it must continue to function as a crime control measure: prisons remain for discipline, punishment and security. Yet, prison personnel in Russia have to some extent become disempowered from instituting a knowledge framework that is specific to the cultural milieu because they view the wider political milieu as operating to make 'us' more like 'them'.

Recalling Chapter 3, I described how in the wake of the crumbling industrial monolith of prison labour, new penal identities were constructed by staff and prisoners based on localised knowledge, local conditions (work and training) and a re-theorisation of existing trajectories amidst changes in global conditions. What emerged from that chapter was how the prison system came to be reconstituted while retaining its purpose. I judge that period – the second occasion of penal identification – to be a particularly fascinating episode in Russia's penal development. We can recall that during the second phase, diverse vocabularies of motive as to why we should punish were debated and then articulated clearly despite the surrounding political mainstream being marked by political disturbances, economic collapse and social discord. Some of the views on crime causation were extreme (particularly from the respondents in Smolensk who advocated character reform), but they were, none the less, passionately argued by those involved in the mystifying and bewildering world of imprisonment. The system that characterised the second phase was based on discipline and also rehabilitation. I believe that the emerging principles back then revealed that prison officers recognised that a prison system might be based on crime predicaments which created space for some interesting (if contradictory) penal identities to take hold. Moreover, I would suggest here that the identities allowed prisoners to be conceptualised in a particular way.

Denying essential features

The utilisation of barter exposes clearly how human rights and international conventions might account for what is right, but they do not necessarily account for what is compatible with the cultural milieu. I have examined how prison barter was a pragmatic solution to reduced state investment in the prison system. It led to prisoner survival, sustained rural communities and resolved some of the systemic problems in the function and organisation of prisons and the ongoing problems of improving conditions of confinement. Put simply, prison barter reduced the erosion of the prison estate.

Through demand sharing prisoners and the community have redefined what prisons should be for. The prisons I visited were atypical of institutions in Western advanced industrial nations where punishment, security and discipline remain the principal goals. In Russia, on the one hand, the prison functioned to bring about socially constructed formations of what constitutes rehabilitation (the second occasion of penal identification) yet, on the other hand, the punishment and discipline functions were de-centred from the prison because of barter use. The absence of a punitive agenda was evident in the ways that all the prison staff organised the order of the prison day around whether there were sufficient foodstuffs. If foodstuffs were insufficient, a decision would be made about improving barter contracts; stretching industry across the prison population; how staff could wheel and deal goods during lunch-breaks; and, in some instances, whether prison industries could cover the staff wages bill. Only once staff had met the task of providing basic resources could the business of imprisonment (as resembling anything vaguely familiar to those outside Russia) be met: 'We can't even think about treatment or education, if we don't have pencils for prisoners to write their names.' Having offenders take responsibility for their personal survival tested the limits of conventional wisdom whereby there is the expectation that prisoners take responsibility for, or ownership of, their actions, and it was certainly the case, that Russia's penal culture is seemingly more resonant of rural communities in underdeveloped nations where citizens survive on the margins. Thus, is barter inhumane in universalist terms because prisoners work to live?

As I have already stated in Chapter 6, international norms as they relate to prison labour afford prisoners very little protection, principally because there is such a growing variety of public and private labour that it is very difficult to legislate against exploitative practices and also because prisoners are excluded as an exempt category from prohibitions due to their position as in receipt of a custodial sentence. Rather than spend more time debating international law, instead I would like to indicate how I judge it be *unfortunate* that the far-reaching role of barter as a mechanism that resolves some of the dilemmas prison life throws up is currently overlooked. First, barter use is a locally embedded practice that is 'real' and authentic' rather than 'obscure' and 'remote' could be inserted into a broad national discussion that addresses exactly what it is that the Russians are attempting to reform. There is certainly a gap in criminology in the area of how states of transition see and 'feel' imprisonment. For example, prison officials side-stepped the thorny question of forced labour despite the current polity of imprisonment whereby following the damage created by an entire century of excessive imprisonment, the prisons are being judged (but not understood) by a dominant praxis of human rights.

Secondly, positive examples of tentative schemas for new pathways into imprisonment can be found from other jurisdictions around the world where there has been a hybrid of enterprising schemes that are locally embedded with international democratically based participation (some excellent examples can be found from Kieron McEvoy's work on Northern Ireland's transition towards restorative justice). Elements of such a hybrid could be modified in Russia and fed into an international debate about the function and organisation of prisons in exceptional states (states in transition).

Thirdly, that barter creates supportive relationships between local communities and the prisons, often cited as a specific problem for prisoner reform in Western prisons, should not be overlooked by the international community. Barter offered a route of praxis in Russian prisons (for example, the capacity for barter to encourage community participation was profound). Although prisoners working for personal survival tests the limits of conventional wisdom on what we expect prisons to do, when positioned within the broader cultural milieu, the notion of 'working to live' makes sense.

The central prison authority is not addressing the current prison labour practices because Russian prisons have to improve their clothing and hygiene arrangements, their educational and work facilities, their order and their attitude about who is sent to prison and why. Moreover, to debate the utilisation of prison labour and barter is to debate how prison labour is administered, and this is Russia's proverbial can of worms as insecurities of past penal memories continue to haunt prison officials: 'Don't mention Gulag. I am not answering questions on Gulag. The Gulag is irrelevant to today's system.' This anxiety was evident in the government statements from GUIN in Moscow and supported by international penal reformers. The Minister of Justice, Yurii Kalinin, describes the challenging circumstances of reform as a consequence of Russia's complex and enormous penal history as well as its current poor economic condition (Kalinin 2002), while one leading international campaigner added in an interview: 'Russia does want to rid itself of the Gulag and there is a sense that there are to be no gratuitous or barbarous punishments.' In as far as the Gulag represented a bureaucratic system where millions were incarcerated for political ends rather than criminological reasons, then Russia has rid itself of that system. But in emphasising universal human rights as advocated by experts rather than demonstrably eliciting new knowledge and research that uses language that has been chosen (for example, words that have a symbolic power) because it relates to the cultural and economic conditions, the overseers of the penal system cannot confront the past, are less inclined to survey the prisons for views on the course of direction and more likely to deny the penal estate a chance to operate within its own economic and cultural milieu. I have already compared Russia with South Africa and Northern Ireland where recent positive change in the political conditions is rooted in a restorative process, inside which officials and politicians are expected to take responsibility for past actions. I do not wish to criticise Russian prison officials for their attempts to cope with the enormous task of penal reform, but it seems peculiar that championing human rights has led prison officials at the most senior level to deny the current symbolic features of prison (prison labour and barter) as relatively *reliable* mechanisms for survival.

The powerful agenda of human rights is altering how the system defines itself. I find this troublesome because the symbiotic, dialectical and pragmatic social relations do not feature in Russia's new penality. Instead, what features are new ideological boundaries that divide prisons around the world according to whether their prisons are 'good' or 'bad'. In the closing pages of the book, I would like to consider how human rights trajectories might indicate that states in transition must tolerate a new boundary of punishment.

The 'making us more like them' problem

International human rights have gained increasing power around the world. Its scope and remit, however, have become increasingly blurred in terms of how it is characterised and how it is mechanised. In prisons, a particular problem is the charge of hypocrisy levelled at more powerful nations whose prison systems may operate under tightly controlled, well ordered regimes but where human rights abuses have also been recorded (Ignatieff 2003). For example, the prison services of the UK governments (particularly England and Scotland) are facing cases being drafted for presentation by prisoners to the European Court of Human Rights over the practice of slopping out, described by the European Court as an inhumane and degrading punishment. Not only that, some dominant nations will proclaim human rights and hold states as allies where atrocities are commonplace in prisons. For example, human rights abuses are recorded regularly by Amnesty International in prisons in the US, in Saudi Arabia, in Jordan and in Syria despite these countries being allies to the UK. These are interesting vantage points from which to criticise the movement to humanise Russia's penal system. The US has the highest prison population in the world as a percentage of the total population. There has been a range of human rights charges levied at the American government that include the use of the death penalty, the imprisonment of children and discriminatory practices in courts leading to the overuse of incarceration for black and hispanic individuals. It is well known among penal reformers that the American government has resisted importing norms such as the United Nations Standard Minimum Rules for the Care and Treatment of Offenders into its national legislation. Nor does the American government support the ratification of other treaties that would lead to possible charges of violations such as the 1989 Convention for the Rights of the Child (which prohibits the imprisonment of children). Put crudely, human rights, as a body of knowledge designed to provoke reform, is inimical to American penal culture.

Human rights objections feature less in America's penal culture because international human rights contradict the US constitution whereby human rights derive their legitimacy from individual consent. That human rights norms have at their core the moral imperative to ensure that groups or persons do not actively persecute others or actively harm them means that national governments will always be held in check. And this is why human rights are contested in that country. The neoliberal complexion of American criminal justice is becoming increasingly self-evident with campaigns for a rights agenda where individual notions of freedom, individuality and responsibility for actions are perpetuated. This has created a culture that is growing in punitive excesses year in and year out.

Interestingly, such a penal sensibility is unpopular within the senior management of Russia's penal system. The overall view is that Russia should not adopt a position of increasing its prison population levels because: 'While we don't have a problem with America any more [laughs], we certainly do not want to go down that road which is the opposite of how the European Union sees our prisons evolving'.[3] This comment illustrates clearly how human rights are linked to Russia's integration into the European community (while betraying a humorous sarcasm over post-Cold War relations with the US). As I have already mentioned, Russia *is* listening to the international human rights movement and an important consequence is that the prison population has come tumbling down. Russia identifies with a European sensibility which has to a far greater degree resisted the tendency to adopt a punitive mentality that has sent prison populations soaring in some jurisdictions (notably the UK and the US). It does not necessarily follow, however, that the European sensibility that adopts the position that imprisonment should be used with restraint is, in fact, an accurate reflection of what is actually happening. The prison populations in some EU countries are increasing. What is interesting is that the European norms that Russia is ratifying serve to validate the penal system so that good political, economic and cultural fortunes follow. I am not arguing here that there is some conspiracy over human rights. As Stellars notes, 'human rights cannot be dismissed as a con trick' (2002: 1996). But there must be limits in how we challenge the human rights of regimes when the legitimacy of our own track record of human rights is questionable. This echoes Ignatieff's observations of global human rights that the more that Western norms set about saving or transforming the polity of failed societies, the more our own rights standards are put into question. There was evidence of this in Russia where prison officers reacted angrily when it was revealed that prisons in the UK do not offer conjugal visits for prisoners' families and spouses. As one officer stated:

> It seems to me that we have conflict with you then on human rights. You have an authority over us and yet you violate human rights too. The idea of conjugal visits is an essential right of the prisoner. We have it and you do not. I bet you never see our side, because that is not what you do – look inside our regimes, properly.

Russian prison personnel understood that human rights were total and non-negotiable (after all, what is their use if they are based on facilitating compromise?), but it is worth considering whether human rights can be managed in prisons when a critique on national penal sensibilities is largely absent. When it is considered that the constitutional order of the prisons is linked to mainstreaming penal discourse, this point becomes highly significant.

Mainstreaming discourses and new ideological boundaries: can the prisons survive?

In this book I hope that I have raised awareness of how Russia has responded to the voids in penality that followed the collapse of the USSR by subscribing to a penal discourse that reflects a global political sensibility (harmonisation, European and international integration, democratic movements and civil society) but which denies a political critique (see the prison officer narratives). The current global culture, I have argued, has created permeable borders and this has generated a debate on whether transnational movements take precedence over national sensibilities. Within Europe, 'enlargement' has become the defining feature of a European identity in the early twenty-first century. Political integration has been critiqued as enabling nation-states to have their sovereignty legitimated by a global agenda the benefits of which include increased cross-border trade and membership in the biggest 'club' in Europe. Human rights as a technique that aims to standardise penal ideological differences have, in practice, had the opposite effect in that national penal systems interact with more dominant penal estates around 'success' or 'failure' creating a tension between national propensities to punish and external norms. Consequently, outside prisons and in the political mainstream, ideological and political boundaries are being repositioned.

That different standards exist from one penal system to the next permits an opportunity for appreciating differences and similarities. It would be impossible, argue political scientists, to operate across cultures without not only a shared discourse but also common standards which make comparative approaches possible. Mainstreaming these standards and standards of conduct is an essential prerequisite for the expansion of global civil society in the broadest sense, argues Ignatieff (2003). With over a decade of great upheaval it is the establishment of a 'rule of law', as well as technological developments and innovations in industry that are said to be the hallmarks of civilised societies. The standards of civilisation share a common position with the standards of human rights – each seeks to improve society through an authentication of institutions and norms. But political, economic and social advancement reached through authentication has, I believe, an unfortunate application in penal systems. Authentication is a complex business because it is those states that operate in positions of political dominance which process the authentication of less powerful states and their criminal justice systems. It is succumbing to the process of authentication (styled as 'working together') as much as it is the outcome that is the salient prerequisite for better transnational relations. On a macro level this might not include enlargement per se but on a micro level it definitely includes enhancements in cross-border trade and political, cultural and social exchange.

There are no simple answers to the overwhelming problems facing post-Soviet, Russian prisons and those in the other post-Cold War nations. The current high alert over international stability and security is premised on keeping political danger at a distance. One view posited by human rights scholars, is that Western governments are justified in concluding that restoring stability (even where it is authoritarian) matters far more than paying attention to the self-determination of states. Yet, succumbing to regulation, human rights monitoring and penal reconstruction does not help us square up the issue of how we come to understand, justify and administer imprisonment. For nations in transition, streamlining penal discourse is linked to a global agenda that may have imperialist tendencies because it diverts attention away from unequal distributions of wealth and also power that underpin these rules of engagement.

The prison officer narratives and the examples of human rights reform programmes are about creating good penal systems and since the nineteenth century, penal reform has aimed at creating stable prisons. Human rights has also been played out by international politicians, by diplomats, journalists, prosecutors and advocates who see it as a solution to domestic problems and also as an international cause. Human rights is intended to reduce difference but, in practice, it creates subordinate positions materially, economically and politically because it is based on liberal power and on the management and regulation of economic, political and social practices. The new boundary of power as evidenced here is more nuanced than other forms of global demarcation such as trade practices or styles of government. It is based on political integration and keeping forms of political difference or political danger at a distance. If nations do not meet norms, then they can be kept at a distance (Turkey's delayed accession into the EU is a good example of political discreditation arising from carceral discreditation). Moreover it is the *appearance* of making progress which is the mark of political legitimacy. So long as nations can demonstrate a commitment to good governance, then change itself becomes secondary. This is particularly complex in prison institutions which, generally, are unseen and unfelt institutions. For prisons in transition, change is all the more problematic because the relations of political power that are shaping societies in transition are often kept hidden. Indeed, it was compelling to observe personnel in the complex and hidden world of Russian prisons with their checklists for things to do, guides on better management and replicas of penal knowledge from Western penal systems.

One issue worthy of consideration is that if all the efforts and energies are focused on human rights, in what I have called the failed penal societies, we may see an increase in prison populations. The question of why we punish, as I have shown, is largely absent from the rationalisation process to make prisons conform. Russia is committed to reducing its prison population, but the prison populations of the societies spearheading improvements to human rights (the advanced Western European nations) are seeing *their* prison populations increase at various rates. It will be interesting to monitor whether Russia mimics the managerialist and extra punitive agendas of some European nations where better ordered penal bureaucracies tie in with punitive populism to service tough law and order agendas (Davies 1985; Bottoms 1995; Gallo 1995).

If analysis of imprisonment increased their awareness of global politics and how this impacts on global penal politics they would observe how, since the collapse of Soviet communism it is far easier for the West to intervene in the affairs of failed societies, as the recent invasion of Iraq demonstrated. It will, furthermore, be interesting to observe how the penal systems of the interim governments of Iraq and Afghanistan evolve in their sensibility. In Russian prisons, these interventions have led to improvements but they have also served to blur rather than to clarify the most pervading questions about imprisonment around the world: why do we punish and a second, intimately related question, what works? For example, on the occasions when I have met penal reformers in Russia and the UK, from their anecdotal accounts of visiting Russian prisons there is a sense that reformers are aware that, in the advisory process, a level of diplomacy and political sensitivity is required. I would sometimes hear comments that include: 'The West can learn from you'. These rituals were an endless source of fascination and also provided much to reflect on. Indeed, while these events marked a great political moment: an end of one kind of history,[4] I was also intrigued by the broad-brush statements made by reformers that 'we' can learn from 'them' because I believe that the West is prevented from plugging into knowledge *exchange* because of cultural and language issues but also because of Russia's path of dependency. Quite simply, the West is not dependent on Russia for improving the lives of its peoples. The unique Community Liaison Partnerships that I found in Omsk, the utilisation of barter to sustain local communities (carceral and non-carceral) in all the 15 prison establishments that I have visited, the modified prison work ethic in open prisons in Kemerovo where prisoner cowboys manage the inmate farmers and even the emergence of small-scale religious support for former prisoners in local areas that for many fill the void left by the collapse of Marxism/Leninism might not reflect Western values, but they serve as differing visions of a prison life that accord with Russia's history and traditions rather than an ethnocentric view of 'what works'.

Although the implications for human rights discourse as shaping the contours of imprisonment in Russia may be contestable, the foundations for believing that we need human rights in that country are much more secure. Of significance is that we need to hold countries to account and without human rights there is very little else in the concealed world of imprisonment to remind us that some conditions are intolerable.

What is clearly evident, however, is that in the process of becoming mainstreamed into Russian prisons, human rights discourses have become a fighting creed against conflict. The prospect of carceral disgrace and carceral discreditation for failed penal societies means that there is very little time and space (literally) to export knowledge to societies with well ordered national rights regimes. Is this wise? All forms of power are open to abuse and the power of human rights as a legitimating force can become exploited by the benefactors as well as by the beneficiaries. Questions, therefore, remain on cross-cultural validity and legitimacy of penal forms where they emanate from outside the stable, well ordered regimes of advanced industrial nations.

Concluding thoughts

Where does the preceding discussion leave us? At the very least, this book, I think, has opened up an interesting and unexplored area of scholarship in criminology. The book has covered much ground in exploring how post-Soviet prisons have adapted to the dynamic of penological, economic and political change. The book has concluded by raising, albeit in a tentative manner, the question of whether standardisation of penal policy along the lines of human rights is a direction mapped out by powerful penal sites for failed (penal) societies.

It is hard, therefore, to avoid the conclusion that while a decent and humane prison environment is a very simple principle, its application is complex due to human rights discourse in Russian prisons remaining rooted in a Western discourse such as the European Prison Rules. All too easily, human rights have surrendered to too much cultural relativism. So what is needed? First is the need for *goal clarification*. The continuous process of change in Russian prisons could be supported and understood far better if a commission was in place that could clarify the many important goals in the transition to democracy. Goal clarification then gives promise for a meaningful political debate on whether international norms are workable in societies in transition. Secondly is the need to develop a *critique of prisons in transition* so that the thin veneer of defining what is *not* permitted in prisons can be thickened into a meaningful discourse about what is *good* about prisons in transition. Thus, there is an empirical need for a reformed social concept that can be utilised to explore pathways for understanding the prison systems of societies in transition.

Thirdly, and relatedly, more research needs to be done in prisons in transition or in societies where prisons operate under extraordinary political and economic conditions. I appreciate that present political conditions in some countries make the prospect of prison research extremely difficult and unsafe. But it is not impossible (the sociologist Andrew Jefferson, for example, is currently engaged in prison research in Nigeria). My particular concern is that without more prison sociologists engaging in research in such settings like Russia then empirical and theoretical scholarship is under threat. As one of the very few Westerners currently engaged in research in the Russian prison system, I observed that the prison officers' ever-increasing distance from a critique of imprisonment impacted on their views on social or criminological research and methodologies. For example, when I informed prison officers that I was not there on behalf of an NGO or the Council of Europe, relief gave way to confusion. If I was not there to monitor conditions, what was the purpose of my trip? No prison system can be reformed in a vacuum, but the emphasis on regulation (be it an assessment of performance indicators in England and Wales or human rights violations in Russia) closes off the possibility of a critique. Thus, we need to finesse our understanding of national penal propensities and be aware of our seeming tendency to traverse the world in the name of penal reform.

Finally, to repeat a point made earlier, the basic intuition of human rights is relatively simple to grasp because violations are often detected in the physical conditions. The social relations that characterise prisons in transitional societies should not just be about exposing inhumane physical conditions. They should also be about assessing the overall patterns of imprisonment, their institutional context, cultural attachments to penal sensibilities and the general causes and consequences of imprisonment in exceptional societies. It is the answers to *these* questions that could form the basis for deliberating fresh frameworks for punishment in transitional states.

Notes

1   Source: http://europa.eu.int/comm/mediatheque/video/files/ prodi_256_en.rm.
    Other features include transnational institutions affiliated to the World Bank; decision-making structures embedded in the Council of Europe; transnational economic linkages; and consultation between sovereign states.
2   The EU has decided to postpone Romania and Bulgaria's entry until 2007 and Turkey's entry date has yet to be decided due to the failure of that country to meet the criteria. Turkey's legislative frameworks do not take into account human rights, democracy and respect for ethnic minorities. In one of

his regular web-cam pronouncements, Romano Prodi stated that some of the problems over integrating new states concern dissatisfaction over benchmarks and criteria for joining, but that the great historical project of EU enlargement is worth these 'points of dissatisfaction' (see: http://europa.eu.int/comm/mediatheque/video/files/prodi_256_en.rm).

3 Source: Colonel Alekseii Vasilievich Voronkov, Junior Prisons Minister of the Main Prison Authority of the Russian Federation, interviewed in Moscow, June 2003.

4 There is always a degree of political wheeling and dealing going on between human rights reformers and authorities such that at times discussions bear a resemblance to the formality and grandeur one normally associates with treaty signing. No expense would be spared with gifts being offered, singing national anthems, dancing and many of the famous Russian drinking toasts. While on the one hand these occasions afforded me an opportunity to eat better and talk in English, it was never made clear to penal reformers what my role was and sometimes I found myself sidelined as the 'interpreter'.

Appendices

1 List of interviewees

The dates that are presented alongside the names show the year in which the respondents were interviewed and the positions they occupied at the time of the interview. Some of the participants have since left these positions and have either retired, moved to other criminal justice departments or to a different prison region. Consent was given to quote all real names. With the exception of senior prison personnel and officers who were interviewed in the 2003 trip to Kemerovo region listed below, all the staff who are listed are not included in the total in Table 1.4.

Government ministers at the central prison authority (GUIN) in Moscow

Colonel Alekseii Vasilievich Voronkov, Junior Prisons Minister of the Main Prison Authority of the Russian Federation, based in Moscow, interviewed in June 2003.

General Alexander Illych Zubkov, Assistant Deputy Prisons Minister of the Main Prison Authority of the Russian Federation, based in Moscow, interviewed in February 1999.

Senior prison officers from colonies in Smolensk

General Anatolii Alekseivich Sakharov, Chief of Smolensk prison region, interviewed in March 1999.

Major Dimitrii Ivanovich Ponamaryov, Head of Security, Smolensk prison region, interviewed in February 1999.

Major Andreii Alekseivich Vorantsev, Deputy Director of Education, Smolensk region, interviewed in March 1999.

Major Yuri Shildov, Head of Marketing, Smolensk prisons region, interviewed in February 2003.

Senior prison officers from colonies in Omsk

General Yuri Karlovich Baster, Chief of Omsk prison region, interviewed in February 1999 and June 2003.

Major Nikolaii Nikolaievich Voranev, Deputy Director of Education, Omsk region, interviewed in March 1999.

Major Anatolii Gregorievich Kyzov, Head of Marketing, Omsk prison region, interviewed in April 1999 and June 2003.

Major Alexander Ivanovich Badkin, Head of Security, Omsk prison region, interviewed in May 1999.

Lieutenant Nadezhda Alexandrovna Kuzvova, Head of Accounting for Omsk prison region, interviewed in April 1999.

Senior prison officers from colonies in Kemerovo

Colonel Valerii Sergeivich Dolzhantsev, Chief of Kemerovo prison region, interviewed in May 2003.

Deputy Colonel Aleksander Mikhailovich Gerasimenko, Director of Prison Industries for Kemerovo prison region, interviewed in May 2003.

Sergeii Alekseivich Churinov, Director of Prison Industries, colony number 42 for drug addicts, Kemerovo prison region, interviewed in May 2003.

Nikolai Aleksandrovich Kostukov, Governor, colony number 7, Kemerovo prison region, interviewed in June 2003.

Gennadii Anatoliievich Pomanenko, Governor, colony number 42 for drug addicts, Kemerovo prison region, interviewed in May 2003.

Aleksander Yurevich Stepanshchev, Head of Educational Work, colony number 7, Kemerovo prison region, interviewed in May 2003.

Vladimir Petrovich Vassilev, Deputy Governor, colony number 7, Kemerovo prison region, interviewed in June 2003.

Viacheslav Vladimirovich Zhulyayev, Director of Prison Industries, colony number 7, Kemerovo prison region, interviewed in May 2003.

Penal reformers and human rights organisations

Valerii Abramkin, Director of The Moscow Centre for Prison Reform, interviewed in May 2003.

Tatiana Bukareva, Head of the European Union's 'Initiative for the Promotion of Democracy and Human Rights in Russia', based in the headquarters for the European Union delegation in Moscow, interviewed in May 2003.

Professor Andrew Coyle, Director of the International Centre for Prison Studies, based in London, interviewed in December 2003.

Sandra Mounier, officer for the European Union's TACIS Programme, based in the headquarters for the European Union delegation in Moscow, interviewed in May 2003.

Other persons contacted

Sergeii Kovalev, Deputat of the Russian Duma (Member of Parliament for the Duma) and leading penal reformer, interviewed in June 2003.

General Sergeii Nikolaevich Ponomaryov, Chief of the Ryazan Prison Service Training Academy, based in Ryazan, interviewed in February 1999.

2   Research questions and prompts used to guide the interviews

1   What do you think is the purpose(s) of imprisonment?
2   How might prison labour contribute towards those purposes?
3   How do these relate, if at all, to the causes of crime in Russia today?
4   What are the problems associated with providing prison labour today?
5   Bearing in mind the above, what other programmes might be in place besides prison labour to achieve these objectives? If respondents were uncertain about a reason, the following prompts were used – psychology, religion, anything else? And how important are they?
6   What role might the wider or local community play in achieving these objectives?

Analysis of data

In order to manage the large amount of interview material the interviews were categorised into 'themes' that emerged from the observations of prison labour. The themes were as follows:

1   Differences between colonies or regions in the implementation of prison labour.
2   Perceptions and meanings about prison labour by staff and prisoners.
3   Alternative methods used to occupy prisoners.
4   Perceptions of the financial situation in the colonies by staff and prisoners.
5   The economic role of prison labour.

Other themes that emerged but which were not uniform across colonies and are not consequently included in the book were staff perceptions as to how they could improve their job and whether staff informed families about the financial situation in the prison system. The themes became 'analytical categories' for understanding the responses to the six research questions above. The responses to question 1 were classified into broad categories: those that emphasised rehabilitation, on the one hand, and those that emphasised punishment on the other (see themes 1 and 2). Theme 3 relates to questions 2 and 4 that aimed at disclosing the reasons for providing work. For example, if staff were of the opinion that work was not useful for rehabilitation, it could be expected that staff would implement alternative strategies that were useful. Themes 4 and 5 relate to questions 4 and 5, the reasons for providing work, as prison labour may be used for commercial purposes as is found in other criminal justice systems such as America and the UK. Theme 5 also relates to question 1 on the goal of imprisonment as in the Soviet era there was an economic purpose to putting prisoners to work and it was felt that it would be interesting to see if and how this thinking has changed in the post-Soviet period.

The next stage involved clarifying the themes theoretically by returning to the literature. By examining the purposes of prison labour, I could examine how close Russia is to Western models, first by looking at the positive perceptions arising from the utilisation of prison labour (humanity, justice, rehabilitation and minimum standards) and, secondly, by examining some of the concerns that have been raised over human rights abuses arising from prison labour (trends towards privatisation raise issues analogous to forced labour). Some verification of the findings came from analysing documentary sources, policies, initiatives and directives that were in place. I also used 'verification tactics' such as feedback (Ball 1984) where respondents would be presented with observations that I had gathered. It should be kept in mind that respondent validation of phenomena does not ensure validity or accuracy of the data – one valid finding cannot ensure another further validity (Denzin 1970). Subjects may be concerned to manipulate the impression of behaviour which is contained in data as a way of enhancing or protecting the subject of inquiry. In the nature of a single-handed research project such as this, however, it was not possible to test for reliability of categorisations (I had few research colleagues able to read Russian) and, for the purposes of an exploratory study such as this, my analysis will have to suffice, and must be taken on trust.

3 Aerial plan of a Russian penal colony

The Western Prison Region of the Russian Federation: general regime number 3, Safonovo, Smolensk

Key

——— Perimeter wall
- - - - - Barbed wire
↑ Access to industrial zone
– · – · – · · Rail track

▦ Public entrance to the colony
▨ Bomb bunker
■ Watchtower

▨ Living zone
▨ Industrial zone
▨ Administration building and processing of prisoners

Industrial zone

1 Building not used
2 Building not used
3 Building not used
4 All light assembly production
5 Manufacturing
6 Building not used
7 Building not used
8 Part of building not used (No. 8)
9 Parts for agricultural industries
10 Prison garage
11 Roofless building

Living zone

(a)–(f) Prisoner accommodation blocks and exercise yard.
1 Dining rooms for prisoners and colony kitchen
2 Psychology booths (3) rehabilitation services, entertainment facilities and unused vocational training workshops
3 Medical facilities
4 Recreational yard
5 Staff quarters

References

Abramkin, B.F. and Chesnokova, B.F. (1995) 'Sotsiokulturnie problemii penitentsiarnoi reformi v Rossii', *Sovremennstvovannie Zakonodatel'stvo i Praktiki Uchrezhdenii.* Moskva: Ispolnuyushikh Nakazanniya, Na Osnove Konstitutsii Rossiskoi Federatsii, Ministerstvo Vnutrennikh Del ('The socio-cultural problems of penal reform in Russia', in *Contemporary Law and Practice in Institutions.* Moscow: Department for Executing Punishment According to the Constitution of the Russian Federation, Ministry of the Interior, Moscow).

Adams, B. (1996) *The Politics of Punishment: Prison Reform in Russia, 1863–1917.* Dekalb, IL: Northern Illinois University Press.

Ahkmadiev, F.X. (1993) *Stanovlenie i Razvite Organov Sovietskoi Militsii Ispravitelno Trudovikh Uchrezhdenii.* Ministerstvo Vnutrennikh Del, Ufimskaya Vishaya Shkola (*The Origins and Development of the Organs of the Soviet Police and the Correctional Work Departments.* Ministry of the Interior, Ufim Academy).

Albrecht, H.-J. (1999) 'Countries in transition: effects of political, social and economic change on crime and criminal justice – sanctions and their implementation', *European Journal of Crime, Criminal Law and Criminal Justice,* 7 (4): 448–79.

Alcock, A. (1971) *History of the International Labour Organisation.* London: Macmillan.

Amis, M. (2002) *Koba the Dread: Laughter and the Twenty Million.* London: Jonathan Cape.

Amnesty International (1980) *Prisoners of Conscience in the USSR: Their Treatment and Conditions.* London: Amnesty International.

Amnesty International (1995) *United States of America. Reintroduction of Chain Gangs – Cruel and Degrading.* London: Amnesty International.

Applebaum, A. (2003) *GULAG: A History of the Soviet Camps.* London: Allen Lane.

Asanaliev, T. (1993) *Stanovlenie i Razvite Organizatsionno-Pravovikh Osnov Trudovovo Peresvopitaniya Osuzhdionnikh v USSR*. Moskva: Academiya Ministerstvo Vnutrennikh Del (*The Origins and Development of the Legal Organisation of Work and Re-education of Prisoners in the USSR*. Moscow: Ministry of the Interior).

Bacon, E. (1992) 'Glasnost and the Gulag: new information on Soviet forced labour around World War Two', *Soviet Studies*, 44 (6): 1069–86.

Bacon, E. (1994) *The Gulag at War: Stalin's Forced Labour System in Light of the Archives*. London: Macmillan.

Ball, S.J. (1984) 'Beachside reconsidered: reflections on a methodological apprenticeship', in R.G. Burgess (ed.) *The Research Process in Educational Settings: Ten Case Studies*. Lewes: Falmer Press.

Barclay, G. and Tavares, C. (2003) *International Comparisons of Criminal Justice Statistics 2001*. London: Home Office RDS.

Barternews.com (available at http://www.barternews.com/ trade_exchanges.htm).

Bauman, Z. (1989) *Modernity and the Holocaust*. Cambridge: Polity Press.

Bauman, Z. (1993) *Modernity and Ambivalence*. Cambridge: Polity Press.

Bauman, Z. (2001) 'Identity in the globalising world', *Social Anthropology*, 9 (2): 121–9.

Baumann, G. and Bales, K. (1991) 'Matagalpa Prison, Nicaragua', in D. Whitfield, (ed.) *The State of the Prisons 200 Years on*. London: Routledge.

Beeson, M. (2003) 'Sovereignty under siege: globalisation and the state in southeast Asia', *Third World Quarterly*, 24 (2): 357–74.

Blair, A. (1999) *The European Union since 1945*. London and New York: Longman.

Blumer, H. (1969) *Symbolic Interaction: Perspective and Method*. Englewood Cliffs, NJ: Prentice Hall.

Bogomolov, O.T. and Nekipelov, A.D. (2003) 'Economicheskaya globalizatsiya i krizis mirovogo ekonomicheskogo poriadka' ('Economic globalisation and the crisis of the world economic order'), in A. Veber (ed.) *Grani globalizatsii*. Moskva: Vagrius (*The Dimensions of Globalisation*. Moscow: Bagrius), pp. 92–127.

Borna, S. (1986) 'Free enterprise goes to prison', *British Journal of Criminology*, 26 (4): 321–34.

Bottoms, A.E. (1995) 'The philosophy and politics of punishment in sentencing', in C.M.V. Clarkson and R. Morgan (eds) *The Politics of Sentencing Reform*. Oxford: Clarendon Press.

Bottoms, A.E. and Wiles, P. (1998) 'Explanations of crime and place', in J. Muncie *et al.* (eds) *Criminological Perspectives: A Reader*. London: Sage.

Bourdieu, P. (1994) *Language and Symbolic Power*. Cambridge: Polity Press.

Bowring, B. (2002) '*Recent developments in the Russian justice system, Department for International Development.*' (Presentation given at the roundtable discussion on Russian prison reform, 28 November).

Braithwaite, J. and Drahos, P. (2001) 'The globalisation of regulation', *Journal of Political Philosophy*, 9 (1): 103–28.

Brogden, M. (2003) 'Community policing in transitional society.' Paper presented at the British Criminology Society conference, University of Wales, Bangor.

Buchholz, E., Hartmann, R., Lekschas, J. and Stiller, G. (1974) *Socialist Criminology*. Germany: Saxon House.

Buck, P.D. (1994) 'Arbeit Macht Frei': racism unbound, concentrated labour in US prisons', *Urban Anthropology*, 23 (4): 331–72.

Bunyan, A. (1967) *The Origins of Forced Labour in Soviet Russia, 1917–1921, Documents and Materials*. Baltimore, MD: Johns Hopkins University Press.

Burger, W. (1982) 'More warehouses or factories with fences?', *New England Journal of Prison Law*, 8 (1): 111–21.

Carlen, P. (1998) *Sledgehammer: Women's Imprisonment at the Millennium*. London: Routledge.

Carlen, P. (ed.) (2002) 'Women's imprisonment: cross-national lessons', in *Women and Punishment: The Struggle for Justice*. Cullompton: Willan Publishing.

Carlen, P. (2004) 'Controlling measures: the repackaging of common-sense opposition to women's imprisonment in England and Canada', in T. Newburn and R. Sparks (eds) *Criminal Justice and Political Culture: National and International Dimensions of Crime Control*. Cullompton: Willan Publishing.

Carter, S. (1977) *The Politics of Solzhenitsyn*. London: Macmillan.

Cavadino, M. and Dignan, J. (1992) *The Penal System: An Introduction*. London: Sage.

Chao, H. (1970) *The Labour Correction Code of the Russian Socialist Federated Soviet Republic, 1926 Prison Code* (revised English edn). London: Sweet & Maxwell.

Chayes, A. and Chayes, A. (1998) *The New Sovereignty: Compliance with International Regulatory Agreements*. Cambridge, MA: Harvard University Press.

Christianson, S. (1998) *With Liberty for Some: 500 Years of Imprisonment in America*. Boston, MA: Northeastern University Press.

Christie, N. (2000) *Crime Control as Industry: Towards Gulags Western style*. London: Routledge.

Christie, N. (2004) *A Suitable Amount of Crime*. London: Routledge.

Clemmer, D. (1958) *The Prison Community*. New York, NY: Holt, Rinehart & Winston.

Cockburn, P. (2002) 'Putin grapples with his nation's history, but is he getting anywhere?', *The Independent*, 23 May.

Cohen, S. and Taylor, L. (1981) *Psychological Survival: The Experience of Long-term Imprisonment*. Harmondsworth: Penguin Books.

Commander, S. and Mumssen, C. (1998) 'Understanding barter in Russia', in *The European Bank for Reconstruction and Development Working Paper* 37, pp. 1–38.

Connor, D. (1972) 'The manufacture of deviance, the case of the Great Soviet Purge, 1936–1938', *American Sociological Review*, 37: 403–13.

Conquest, R. (1960) *Common Sense about Russia*. London: Gollancz.

Conquest, R. (1986) *Kolyma: The Arctic Death Camps*. London: Macmillan.

Conquest, R. (1990) 'What is terror?', *Soviet Studies*, 39 (6): 546–8.

Council of Europe (1987) *The European Prison Rules*. Strasbourg: Council of Europe.

Coyle, A. (2002) *Managing Prisons in a Time of Change*. King's College, London: International Centre for Prison Studies.

Crawford, A. (2003) 'The governance of crime and insecurity in an anxious age: the trans-European and the local', in A. Crawford (ed.) *Crime and Insecurity: The Governance of Safety in Europe*. Cullompton: Willan Publishing.

Cutler, A.C., Haufler, V. and Porter, T. (eds) (1999) *Private Authority in International Affairs*. New York, NY: State University of New York Press.

Dallin, A. and Lapidus, G. (eds) (1995) *The Soviet System: From Crisis to Collapse*. Oxford: Westview Press.

Dallin, D.J. and Nicolaevsky, B.I. (1947) *Forced Labour in Soviet Russia*. London: Hollis & Carter.

Davies, M. (1974) *Prisoners in Society: Attitudes and After-care*. London: Routledge & Kegan Paul.

Davies, M. (1985) 'Determinate sentencing reform in California and its impact on the penal system', *British Journal of Criminology*, 25 (1): 1–30.

Davis, A. (1998) 'From prison slavery to the slavery of the prison: Frederick Douglas and the convict lease system', in B. Lawson and F. Kirkland (eds) *Frederick Douglas: A Critical Reader*. London: Blackwell.

Davis, A. (1999) 'Globalisation and the prison industrial complex', *Race and Class*, 40 (2–3): 145–57.

De Jonge, G. (1999) 'Still "slaves of the state": prison labour and international law', in D. van Zyl Smit and F. Dünkel (eds) *Prison Labour: Salvation or Slavery?*. Aldershot: Dartmouth.

Denzin, N.K. (1970) *The Research Act*. Chicago, IL: Aldine.

Depov, M.G. (1994) 'Sovremennostii Istoricheskie Aspekti Razvitiya Penitentsiarnoi Sistemi Rossii', *Ryazanskii Institut Prava i Ekonomikii, Byuletin*, Ministerstvo Vnutrennikh Del ('Contemporary and historical aspects of the development of the penitentiary system in Russia', *Ryazan Institute of Law and Economics Bulletin*, Ministry of the Interior).

Detkov, M.G. (1994) *Nakazannie v Tsarskoi Tyrmi': Sistema Yevo Ispolenie*. Moskva (*Punishment in Tsarist Prisons: The System and its Operation*. Moscow).

Deveraux, S. and Hoddinott, J. (eds) (1992) *Fieldwork in Developing Countries*. Brighton: Harvester Wheatsheaf.

Diamantopoulos, A. and Schlegelmilch, B.B. (1997) *Taking the Fear out of Data Analysis*. London: The Dryden Press.

Dostoevsky, F. (1860) *Memoirs from the House of the Dead*. (Reprinted Harmondsworth: Penguin Books.)

Dugin, A.N. (1990) 'Govorit Arkhiivi: Neizvestnie Strannitsi Gulag', *Sotsialno-Politicheskie Nauki*, 3 ('The archives are opened: the unknown pages of the Gulag', *Socio-political Science*, 3).

Elias, N. (1984) *The Civilising Process*. Oxford: Blackwell.

Empey, L.T. and Rabow, J. (1961) 'The Provo experiment in delinquency rehabilitation', *American Sociological Review*, 26 (1): 670–96.

Erikson, E.H. (1974) *Identity, Youth and crisis*. London: Faber.

Esping-Anderson, G. (1998) 'After the Golden Age? Welfare state dilemma in a global economy', in G. Esping-Anderson (ed.) *Welfare States in Transition: National Adaptations in Global Economies*. London: Sage.

Fenwick, C. (forthcoming) 'Private use of prisoners' labour: paradoxes of international human rights', *Human Rights Quarterly*.

Fitzpatrick, S. and Viola, L. (eds) (1990) *A Researcher's Guide to Sources in Soviet Social History in the 1930s*. Armonk, NY; London: M.E. Sharpe.

Flanagan, T.J. (1989) 'Prison labour and industry', in L. Goodstein and D.L. MacKenzie (eds) *The American Prison: Issues in Research and Policy*. New York, NY: Plenum Press.

Flanagan, T.J. and Maguire, K. (1993) 'A full employment policy for prisons in the United States: some arguments, estimates, and implications', *Journal of Criminal Justice*, 21: 117–30.

Fleisher, M.S. and Rison, R.H. (1999) 'United States of America: inmate work and consensual management in the Federal Bureau of Prisons', in D. van Zyl Smit, and F. Dünkel (eds) *Prison Labour: Salvation or Slavery?*. Aldershot: Dartmouth.

Fortier, J. (2001) 'Sharing, hoarding, and theft: exchange and resistance in forager-farmer relations', *Ethnology*, 40 (30): 193–11.

Foucault, M. (1979) *Discipline and Punish*. London: Peregrine Books.

Gallo, E. (1995) 'The penal system in France: from correctionalism to managerialism', in V. Ruggiero *et al.* (eds) *Western European Penal Systems: A Critical Anatomy*. London: Sage.

Garland, D. (2001) *The Culture of Control: Crime and Social Order in Contemporary Society*. Oxford: Oxford University Press.

Geertz, C. (1975) *The Interpretation of Cultures*. London: Hutchinson.

Giddens, A. (1990) *The Consequences of Modernity*. Cambridge: Polity Press.

Giddens, A. (1994) 'Living in a post-traditional society', in U. Beck *et al.* (eds) *Reflexive Modernisation, Politics, Tradition and Aesthetics in the Modern Social Order*. Cambridge: Polity Press.

Gilinskii, Y. (1993) 'Penitentsiarnaya Politiki v Rossii', *Ekonomiki i Organizatsii Promishlennosti*, 5: 45–8 ('Penal politics in Russia', *Economy and Organisation of Industry*, 5: 45–8).

Gilinskii, Y. (1998) *Crime and Deviance: Stare from Russia* (English trans.). St. Petersburg: Russian Academy of Sciences Institute of Sociology.

Goffman, E. (1961) *Asylums*. London: Penguin Books.

Gutman, Y. and Berenbaum, M. (1994) *Anatomy of an Auschwitz Death Camp*. Bloomington, IN: Indiana University Press.

Hall, S. (1992) 'The question of cultural identity', in S. Hall *et al.* (eds) *Modernity and its Futures*. Milton Keynes: Open University Press.

Hall, S. (1995) 'Fantasy, identity, politics', in E. Carter *et al.* (eds) *Cultural Remix: Theories of Politics and the Popular*. London: Lawrence & Wishart.

Hall, S. (1996) 'Who needs "identity"?', in S. Hall and P. du Gay (eds) *Questions of Cultural Identity*. Sage: London.

Hallsworth, S. (2002) 'The case for a post-modern penality', *Theoretical Criminology*, 6 (2): 145–63.

Hannah-Moffat, K. (2002) 'Creating choices: reflecting on choices', in P. Carlen (ed.) *Women and Punishment: The Struggle for Justice*. Cullompton: Willan Publishing.

Harding, R.W. (1997) *Private Prisons and Public Accountability*. Oxford: Oxford University Press.

Hawkins, D.F. (1985), 'Trends in black-white imprisonment: changing conceptions of race or changing patterns of social control?', *Crime and Social Justice*, 24: 187–209.

Henriksson, H. and Krech, R. (1999) 'International perspectives', in D. van Zyl Smit and F. Dünkel (eds) *Prison Labour: Salvation or Slavery?*. Aldershot: Dartmouth.

Her Majesty's Chief Inspector of Prisons (2000) *Annual Report and Accounts for April 1999 to March 2000*. HC 622. London: HMSO.

Hobbs, D. and May, T. (1993) *Interpreting the Field: Accounts of Ethnography*. Oxford: Clarendon Press.

Hochstellar, A.L. and Shover, N. (1997) 'Street crime, labor surplus, and criminal punishment, 1980–1990', *Social Problems*, 44 (3): 358–65.

Hogan, R.G. (1997) 'Exploiting and profiting from the poor; private prisons and convict labor.' Paper presented at the meeting of the American Society of Criminology, San Diego, California, November.

Home Office (1993) *National Framework for the Thorough-care of Offenders in Custody to the Completion of Supervision in the Community*. London: HMSO.

Home Office and Employment Department (1992) *Employment in Prison and for Ex-offenders: The Government Reply to the First Report from the Employment Committee Session, 1991–1992*. HC 30 (Cm 1837). London: HMSO.

Hudson, B. (1997) 'Social control', in M. Maguire *et al.* (eds) *The Oxford Handbook of Criminology* (2nd edn). Oxford: Oxford University Press.

Hudson, B. (2002) 'Restorative justice and gendered violence: diversion or effective justice?', *British Journal of Criminology*, 42 (3): 616–34.

Hughes, L. (1998) *Russia in the Age of Peter the Great*. New Haven, CT: Yale University Press.

Ignatieff, M. (1978) *A Just Measure of Pain: The Penitentiary in the Industrial Revolution*. Harmondsworth: Penguin Books.

Ignatieff, M. (2003) *Human Rights as Politics and Idolatry*. Princeton, NJ: Princeton University Press.

Ilyin, M.I. (2003) 'Politicheskaya globalizatsiya i mirovoe uprvalenie: institutionalye aspekti' (Political globalisation and global governance: institutional aspects), in A. Veber (ed.) *Grani Globalizatsii*. Moskva: Vagrius (*The Dimensions of Globalisation*. Moscow: Vagrius).

Ispravitelno Trudovoi Kodeks Rossiskoi Sovietskoi Federalnie Sotsialisticheskii Respublikii (RSFSR) (1926) Moskva: Ministerstvo Vnutrennikh Del (*The Corrective Labour Code or the Penal Work Code of the RSFSR*. Moscow: Ministry of the Interior).

Ispravitelno Trudovoi Kodeks (RSFSR) (1933) Moskva: Ministerstvo Vnutrennikh Del (*The Penal Work Code of the RSFSR*. Moscow: Ministry of the Interior).

Ispravitelno Trudovoi Kodeks (RSFSR) (1977) Moskva: Ministerstvo Vnutrennikh Del (*The Penal Work Code of the RSFSR*. Moscow: Ministry of the Interior).

Jacob, J.B. (1999) 'United States of America: prison labour: a tale of two penologies', in D. van Zyl Smit and F. Dünkel (eds) *Prison Labour: Salvation or Slavery?*. Aldershot: Dartmouth.

Jakobson, M. (1993) *The Origins of the Gulag, 1917–1934*. Lexington, KY: University Press of Kentucky.

Jasny, N. (1951) 'Labor and output in Soviet concentration camps', *Journal of Political Economy*, 59 (5): 405–19.

Jefferson, A.M. (2003) 'Reforming prisons in democratic, developing countries questioning a global (ising) agenda.' Paper presented at Euro Group (UK)/ Edge Hill-organised conference 'Tough on crime … tough on freedoms', 22–24 April, Chester.

Jewkes, Y. (2003) *Captive Audience: Media, Masculinity and Power in Prisons*. Cullompton: Willan Publishing.

Jones, T. and Newburn, T. (2004) 'The convergence of US and UK crime control policy: exploring substance and process', in T. Newburn and R. Sparks (eds) *Criminal Justice and Political Cultures: Exploring National and International Dimensions of Crime Control*. Cullompton: Willan Publishing.

Jupp, V. (1989) *Methods of Criminological Research*. London: Unwin Hyman.

Kalinin, Y.I. (1995) 'The prison system in the Russian Federation', *Prison Service Journal*, 97: 54–9.

Kalinin, Y.I. (1998) 'The prison in the Russian Federation.' Paper published for a conference in Moscow to mark the fiftieth anniversary of the Declaration of Human Rights in Russia in December 1998. Published in *Human Being in Prison*. Moscow: Moscow Centre for Prison Reform.

Kalinin, Y.I. (2002) *The Russian Penal System: Past, Present and Future*. London: International Centre for Prison Studies, King's College.

Kara-Murza, S. (1999) 'Sushchnost globalizatsii', in V. Inozemstsev (ed.) *Raspad tsivilizatsii*. Moskva: Polis ('The nature of globalisation', in V. Inozemstsev (ed.) *Broken Civilisation*. Moscow: Polis).

Karstedt, S. (2004) 'Durkheim, Tarde and beyond: the global travel of crime policies', in T. Newburn and R. Sparks (eds) *Criminal Justice and Political*

Cultures: Exploring National and International Dimensions of Crime Control. Cullompton: Willan Publishing.

Kauffman, K. (1988) *Prison Officers and their World*. Boston, MA: Harvard University Press.

King, R.D. (1994) 'Russian prisons after Perestroika: end of the Gulag?', *British Journal of Criminology*, 34 (special issue): 62–82.

King, R.D. (2000) 'Doing research on prisons', in R.D. King and E. Wincup *Doing Research on Crime and Criminal Justice*. Oxford: Oxford University Press.

King, R.D. and McDermott, K. (1995) *The State of our Prisons*. Oxford: Oxford University Press.

King, R.D. and Mikhlin, A.S. (1994) 'The Russian prison system: past, present and future', in R.D. King and M. Maguire (eds) *Prisons in Context*. Oxford: Oxford University Press.

King R.D. and Wincup, E. (2000) *Doing Research on Crime and Criminal Justice*. Oxford: Oxford University Press.

King, R.D. and Piacentini, L. (in press) 'The correctional system during transition', in W.A. Pridemore (ed.) *Ruling Russia: Crime, Law, and Justice in a Changing Society*. Boston, MA: Harvard University Press and Bloomington, IN: Indiana University Press.

Kneen, P. (2000) 'Political corruption in Russia and the Soviet legacy', *Crime, Law and Social Change*, 34 (4): 349–68.

Kommer, M.M. (1993) 'A Dutch prison officer's work – balancing between prison policy, organisational structure and professional autonomy', *Netherlands Journal of Social Sciences/Sociologia Neerlandica*, 29 (2): 130–46.

Kovalev, O.G., Ushatikov, A.I. and Deev, B.G. (1997) *Kriminalnaya Psikhologiya*. Ministerstvo Vnutrennikh Del (*Criminal Psychology*. Moscow: Ministry of the Interior).

Krone, D.G. and Reddon, J.R. (1995) 'Anger and psychopathology in prison inmates', *Personality and Individual Differences*, 18 (6): 783–8.

Kurasawa, F. (2002) 'The ethnological counter-current in sociology', *International Sociology*, 15 (1): 11–1.

Laclau, E. (1990) *New Reflections on the Revolution of our Time*. London: Verso.

Langlois, A.J. (2003) 'Human rights and modern liberalism: a critique', *Political Studies*, 51: 509–23.

Ledeneva, A.V. (1998) *Russia's Economy of Favours: Blat, Networking and Informal Exchange*. Cambridge: Cambridge University Press.

Liebling, A. (1992) *Suicides in Prison*. London: Routledge.

Lindlof, T. (1995) *Qualitative Communication Research Methods*. Thousand Oaks, CA: Sage.

Lokshin, M., Mullan-Harris, K. and Popkin, B. (2000) 'Single mothers in Russia: household strategies for coping with poverty', *World Development*, 28 (12): 2183–98.

Logan, C. (1990) *Private Prisons: Cons and Pros*. Oxford: Oxford University Press.

Lowthian, J. (2002) 'Women's prisons in England: barriers to reform', in P. Carlen (ed.) *Women and Punishment: The Struggle for Justice*. Cullompton: Willan Publishing.

Lynch, A.C. and Thompson, K.W. (1994) (eds) *Soviet Union in a World of Change*. Charlottsville, USA: Miller Centre University Press.

Malia, M. (1999) *Russia under Western Eyes: From the Bronze Horseman to the Lenin Mausoleum*. Boston, MA: Belknap/Harvard University Press.

Mandelshtam, N. (1972) *Hope against Hope*. London: Collins Harvill.

Marchetti, A.M. (trans. Nice, R. and Wacquant, L.) (2002) 'Carceral impoverishment: class inequality in the French penitentiary', *Ethnography*, 3 (4): 416–34.

Marvasti, A. and Smyth, D. (1998) 'Barter in the US economy: a macroeconomic analysis', *Applied Economics*, 30 (8): 1077–88.

Marvasti, A. and Smyth, D.J. (1999) 'The effect of barter on the demand for money: an empirical analysis', *Economic Letters*, 64: 73–80.

Mathieson, T. (1990) *Prisons on Trial: A Critical Assessment*. London. Waterside Press.

Mauer, M. (1999) *Race to Incarcerate*. New York, NY: New Press.

Mawby, R.I. (1999) *Policing across the World*. Berkeley, CA: University of California Press.

McAlister, B. (1999) 'Countdown to paradise', *Prison Fellowship Journal, Inside Change*, 1.

McEvoy, K. (2003) 'Beyond the metaphor: political violence, human rights and "new peacemaking criminology"', *Theoretical Criminology*, 7(3): 319–46.

McEvoy, K. and Mika, H. (2002) 'Restorative justice and the critique of informalism in Northern Ireland', *British Journal of Criminology*, 42 (3): 534–62.

McEvoy, K., Mika, H. and Hudson, B. (2002) 'Introduction: practice, performance and prospects for restorative justice', *British Journal of Criminology*, 42 (3): 469–75.

Medvedev, R. (1971) *Let History Judge: The Origins and Consequences of Stalinism*. London: London University Press.

Melossi, D. (1985) 'Punishment and social action: changing vocabularies of motive within a political business cycle', *Current Perspectives in Social Theory*, 6: 169–97.

Melossi, D. (2000) 'Changing representations of the criminal', *British Journal of Criminology*, 40 (2): 296–320.

Melossi, D. and Pavarini, M. (1981) *The Prison and the Factory*. London: Macmillan.

Metcalf, P. (2000) *They Lie, We Lie: Getting on with Anthropology*. London: Routledge.

Morgan, R. (1997) 'Imprisonment: current concerns and a brief history', in M. Maguire *et al.* (eds) *The Oxford Handbook of Criminology* (2nd edn). Oxford: Oxford University Press.

Moscow Centre for Prison Reform (1993a) *Prison Reform in the Former Totalitarian Countries. Proceedings of the International Conference in Petrovo-Dalneye, near Moscow*, issues 1 and 2. Moscow: Moscow Centre for Prison Reform.

Moscow Centre for Prison Reform (1993b) *Information Bulletin on Human Rights in Prison* 5. Moscow: Moscow Centre for Prison Reform.

Moscow Centre for Prison Reform (1998a) *Human Being in Prison*. Moscow: Moscow Centre for Prison Reform.

Moscow Centre for Prison Reform (1998b) *International Perspectives on How to Reduce Russia's Prison Population*. Moscow: Moscow Centre for Prison Reform.

Moscow Centre for Prison Reform (1998c) *Reforming the Concepts of Criminal Justice in Russia Today*. Moscow: Moscow Centre for Prison Reform.

Mosher, S.W. (1991) 'Chinese prison labor', *Society*, 29 (1): 49–59.

Moyle, P. (1995) Private Prison Research in Queensland, Australia: A Case-study of Borallon Detention Centre, 1991, *The British Journal of Criminology*, 31 (1): 34–62.

Moyle, P. (2001) 'Separating the allocation of punishment from its administration: theoretical and empirical observations', *British Journal of Criminology*, 41 (1): 77–100.

Muncie, J. (2004) 'Youth justice: globalisation and multi-modal governance', in T. Newburn and R. Sparks (eds) *Criminal Justice and Political Culture: National and International Dimensions of Crime Control*. Cullompton: Willan Publishing.

Neale, K. (1991) 'The European prison rules: contextual philosophical and practical aspects', in J. Muncie and R. Sparks (eds) *Imprisonment: European Perspectives*. New York, NY, and London: Harvester Wheatsheaf.

Newburn, T. (2002) 'Atlantic crossings: "policy transfer" and crime control in the USA and Britain', *Punishment and Society*, 4 (2): 165–94.

Newburn, T. and Sparks, R. (eds) (2004) *Criminal Justice and Political Culture: National and International Dimensions of Crime Control*. Cullompton: Willan Publishing.

Nove, A. (1993) 'Victims of Stalinism: how many?', in J. Arch Getty and R.T. Manning (eds) *Stalinist Terror: New Perspectives*. Cambridge: Cambridge University Press.

Observer (1996) Leigh, D. 'Children in the workhouse, gruel on the menu. Dickens? No, Russia in 1996', 29 December.

Observer (1999) Meek, J. 'The wasteland: Norilsk, a Siberian city built by slave labour', 4 July.

Oleinik, A.N. (2003) *Organized Crime, Prison and Post-Soviet Societies*. Aldershot: Ashgate.

Otto-Pohl, J. (1998) *The Stalinist Penal System*. Jefferson, North Carolina and London: Macfarlane and Company, Inc.

Pallot, J. (2004) Russia's penal peripheries: space, place and penalty in Soviet and post-Soviet Russia (forthcoming), *Transactions of The Institute of British Geographers* (December 2004).

Parenti, C. (1999) *Lockdown America: Police and Prisons in the Age of Crisis*. London: Verso.

Pease, K. (1994) 'Cross-national imprisonment rates – limitations of method and possible conclusions', in R.D. King and M. Maguire (eds) *Prisons in Context*. Oxford: Oxford University Press.

Penna, S. and Yar, M. (2003) 'From modern to postmodern penality?: A response to Hallsworth', *Theoretical Criminology*, 7 (4): 469–82.

Piacentini, L.F. (2004a) 'Barter in Russian prisons', *European Journal of Criminology*, 1 (1): 17–45.

Piacentini, L.F. (2004b) 'Penal identities in Russian prisons', *Punishment and Society*, 6 (2): 131–47.

Pratt, J. (2002) *Punishment and Civilization*. London: Sage.

Priban, J. and Nelken, D. (eds) (2001) *Law's New Boundaries: The Consequences of Legal Autopoiesis*. Aldershot: Ashgate.

Ragin, C.C. (1994) *Constructing Social Research*. London: Pine Forge Press.

Rahikainen, M. (1995) 'The fading of compulsory labour: the displacement of work hobbies in the reformatory school in twentieth century Finland', *Scandinavian Economic History Review*, XLIII (2): 251–62.

Ramwell, J.J. (1993) 'A visit to a Russian prison', *Prison Service Journal*, 90: 7–9.

Rawlinson, P. (1997) 'Hunting the chameleon: the problems of identifying Russian organized crime.' Unpublished PhD thesis, London School of Economics.

Rawlinson, P. (2000) 'Mafia, methodology, and alien culture', in R.D. King and E. Wincup (eds) *Doing Research on Crime and Justice*. Oxford: Oxford University Press.

Reuss, A. (1999) 'Prison(er) education', *The Howard Journal*, 38 (2): 113–27.

Robertson, A. and Chistyakova, Y. (2003) 'Policing in the former Soviet Union: Russia and Ukraine compared.' Paper presented at the British Criminology Society conference, University of Wales, Bangor.

Rodley, N. (1995) *Report of the Special Rapporteur, Mr Nigel S. Rodley, Submitted Pursuant to Commission on Human Rights Resolution 1994/7: Visit by the Special Rapporteur to the Russian Federation* (E/CN.4/1995/34/Add.1,16). United Nations Economic and Social Council.

Rodley, N. (2000) *The Treatment of Prisoners under International Law* (2nd edn). Oxford: Oxford University Press.

Rosefielde, S. (1987) 'Incriminating evidence: excess deaths and forced labor under Stalin: a final reply to the critics', *Soviet Studies*, 39 (2): 292–313.

Rosenau, J.N. (1997) *Along the Domestic-Foreign Frontier: Exploring Governance in a Turbulent World*. Cambridge: Cambridge University Press.

Rossi, J. (1989) *The Gulag Handbook: an encyclopedia dictionary of Society Penitentiary Institutions and terms related to the Forced Labour Camps*. NY: Paragon House.

Rozanova, J. (2003) 'Russia in the context of globalisation', *Current Sociology*, 5 (6): 649–69.

Ruggiero, V., Ryan, M. and Sim, J. (eds) (1995) *Western European Penal Systems: A Critical Anatomy.* London: Sage.

Rusche, G. and Kirchheimer, O. (1939) *Punishment and Social Structure.* NY: Russell.

Rusche, G. (1978) 'Labour market and penal sanction: thoughts on the sociology of punishment' (originally published in 1933, translated and reprinted in Platt, T. and Takagi, P. (eds) (1980) *Punishment and Penal Discipline.* Berkeley, CA.: Synthesis Publications).

Schlosser, E. (1998) 'The prison industrial complex', *Atlantic Monthly,* December: 51–7.

Schmid, T. and Jones, R. (1991) 'Suspended identity: identity transformation in maximum security prisons', *Symbolic Interaction,* 14 (4): 415–32.

Scott, J.C. (1986) 'Everyday forms of peasant resistance', *Journal of Peasant Studies,* 13 (5): 5–25.

Scottish Parliament (2004) *Inquiry into the Effectiveness of Rehabilitation Programmes in Prisons* (adviser Dr Laura Piacentini). Stirling: University of Stirling.

Seeth, H.T., Chachnov, S. and Surinov, A. (1998) 'Russian poverty: muddling through economic transition with garden plots', *World Development,* 26 (9): 1611–23.

Shaw, M. and Shearing, C. (1998) 'Reshaping security: an examination of the governance of security in South Africa', *African Security Review,* 7 (3): 3–22.

Shaw, S. (1992) 'A short history of prison privatisation', *Prison Service Journal,* 87: 30–2.

Silverman, D. (2001) *Interpreting Qualitative Data: Methods for Analysing Talk, Text and Interaction.* London: Sage.

Simon, F.H. (1999) *Prisoners' Work and Vocational Training.* London: Routledge.

Simon, F.H. and Corbett, C. (1994) *An Evaluation of Prison Work Training in London.* London: Centre for Criminal Justice Research, Brunel University.

Smartt, U. (1996) 'Industrial prisons: a new idea by Judge Tumim or Sir General Learmont in the 1990s?', *Prison Service Journal,* 106: 2–8.

Smith, C. and Wincup, E. (2000) 'Breaking in: researching criminal justice institutions for women', in R.D. King and E. Wincup (eds) *Doing Research on Crime and Criminal Justice.* Oxford: Oxford University Press.

Solzhenitsyn, A. (1986) *The Gulag Archipelago: An Experiment in Literary Investigation.* London: Horvill.

Sparks, R. (1994) 'Can prisons be legitimate?', *British Journal of Criminology,* 34 (1): 14–18.

Sparks, R., Bottoms, A.E. and Hay, W. (1996) *Prisons and the Problem of Order.* Oxford: Clarendon Press.

Stellars, K. (2002) *The Rise and Rise of Human Rights.* UK: Sutton.

Stepin, V. and Bello, W. (eds) (2001) *Dilemmy globalizatsii, obshestv i tsivilizatsiy: riski i illuzii.* Moskva: Variant (*The Dilemmas of Globalisation, Societies and Civilisations: Risks and Illusions.* Moscow: Variant).

Stern, V. (ed.) (1989) *Bricks of Shame*. Harmondsworth: Penguin Books.

Stern, V. (1998) *A Sin against the Future: Imprisonment in the World*. Harmondsworth: Penguin Books.

Super, G. (1999) 'The Namibian prison system', in D. van Zyl Smit and F. Dünkel (eds) *Prison Labour: Salvation or Slavery?*. Aldershot: Dartmouth.

Sutherland, E. and Cressey, D. (1966) *Principles of Criminology* (7th edn). London: J.P. Lippincott.

Tchernina, N.V. and Tchernin, E.A. (2002) 'Older people in Russia's transitional society: multiple deprivation and coping responses', *Ageing and Society*, 22: 543–62.

Teitel, R.G. (2000) 'Transitional justice genealogy', *Harvard Human Rights Journal*, 16: 69–86.

Times, The (1997) Phillips, A. 'Gulag is now a memorial to liberty', 15 November.

Times, The (1998) Franchetti, M. 'Stalin's forgotten prisoners', 28 June.

Times, The (1999) Franchetti, M. 'Daughter fights to clear Stalin's hitman', 31 January.

Times Literary Supplement, The (1992) Edition devoted to 'The Russian Revolution – 75 years on', 6 November.

Times Literary Supplement, The (1993) Lilla, M. 'A taste for pain: Michel Foucault and the outer reaches of human experience', 26 March.

Times Literary Supplement, The (1994a) Conquest, R. 'Playing down the Gulag: attempts to minimize the numbers of Stalin's victims', 17 March.

Times Literary Supplement, The (1994b) Arch Getty, J. and Rittersporn, G.T. 'The victims of the Gulag', 7 April.

Times Literary Supplement, The (1994c) Szamuely, H. 'The Russian archives', 14 April.

Times Literary Supplement, The (1994d) Conquest, R. 'Victims of the Gulag', 21 April.

Times Literary Supplement, The (1995) Pryce-Jones, D. 'The Gulag miasma', 1 December.

Times Literary Supplement, The (1998) Gordon, R. 'The centaur's ghastly tale: Primo Levi as Chronicler of Hell and essayist of nature', 9 October.

Times Literary Supplement, The (2000a) Hosking, G. 'The road to terror: how rhetoric became reality in the fearful years leading to Stalin's terror', 28 January.

Times Literary Supplement, The (2000b) Chown, J. 'Grounds for optimism: Russia's "barter of the bankrupt" – and how to end it', 28 January.

Tolstykh, V. (2003) 'Razmishliaya o globalizatsii: sotsialno-kulturniye aspekti' ('Considering globalisation: socio-cultrual aspects'), in A. Veber (ed.) *Grani Globalizatsii*. Moskva: Vagrius (*The Dimensions of Globalisation*. Moscow: Vagrius).

Tucker, R. (1992) *Stalinism: The Revolution from above*. New York, NY and London: Norton.

Ugolovnie Ispolnitelnie Prava (1997) Moskva: Ministerstvo Vnutrennikh Del, chast 70:203 (*The Corrective Labour Code*. Moscow: Ministry of Internal Affairs, Part 70:203).

United Nations (1955) *The United Nations Standard Minimum Rules for the Treatment of Prisoners*. New York, NY: United Nations.

United Nations (1995) *Basic Facts about the United Nations*. New York, NY: United Nations Department of Public Information.

Ushatikov, A.I., Shelamov, O.I., Kovalev, O.G. and Borisov, V.N. (1997) *Audiovisualnaya Psikhodiagnostika Osuzhdionnikh*. Ryazanskii Institut Prava i Ekononmiki, Ministerstvo Vnutrennikh Del (*Audio-visual Psycho-diagnosing of prisoners*. Ryazan Institute of Law and Economics, Ministry of the Interior).

van der Spuy, E. (2000) 'Foreign donor assistance and policing reform in South Africa', *Policing and Society*, 10: 342–66.

van Zyl Smit, D. (2003) (book review) 'Sentencing and sanctions in Western countries', *Punishment and Society*, 6 (1): 115–26.

van Zyl Smit, D. and Dünkel, F. (eds) (1999) *Prison Labour: Salvation or Slavery?*. Aldershot: Dartmouth.

van Zyl Smit, D. and van der Spuy, E. (2004) 'Importing criminological ideas in a new democracy: recent South African experiences', in T. Newburn and R. Sparks (eds) *Criminal Justice and Political Cultures: Exploring National and International Dimensions of Crime Control*. Cullompton: Willan Publishing.

Vincentz, V. (2000) 'The non-cash economy in CIS: in quest of policy recommendations', *Economic Systems*, 24: 51–4.

Wacquant, L. (2002) 'The curious eclipse of prison ethnography in the age of mass incarceration', *Ethnography*, 3 (4): 371–97.

Walker, N. (1991) *Why Punish?* Oxford: Oxford University Press.

Walmsley, R. (1996) *Prison Systems in Central and Eastern Europe – Progress, Problems and International Standards*. Helsinki: European Institute for Crime Prevention and Control.

Walmsley, R. (2000) *Research Findings No. 116: The World Population List* (2nd edn). London: Home Office Research, Development and Statistics Directorate.

Warren, C. (1988) *Gender Issues in Field Research*. London: Sage.

Waterhouse, L., McGhee, J. and Loucks, N. (2004) 'Disentangling offenders and non-offenders in the Scottish children's hearings', *The Howard Journal of Criminal Justice*, 43 (2): 164–80.

Watson, P. (2000a) 'Politics, policy and identity: EU eastern enlargement and east–west differences', *Journal of European Public Policy*, 7 (3): 369–84.

Watson, P. (2000b) 'Re-thinking transition', *International Feminist Journal of Politics*, 2: 185–213.

Westwood, S. (1990) 'Racism, black masculinity and the politics of space', in J. Hearn and D. Morgan (eds) *Men, Masculinity and Social Theory*. London: Allen & Unwin.

Wheatcroft, S. (1985) 'New demographic evidence in excess collectivisation deaths: yet another Kliuvka for Stephen Rosefielde?', *Slavic Review*, 44 (3): 505–602.

Williams, S. (1996) 'The new barter economy: an appraisal of local exchange and trading systems (LETS)', *Journal of Public Policy*, 16: 85–101.

World Prison Brief is available at http://www.kcl.ac.uk/depsta/rel/icps/worldbrief/

Wu, H.H. (1992) *Laogai: The Chinese Gulag*. Boulder, CO: Westview Press.

Wu, H.H. (1994) *Bitter Winds: A Memoir of My Years in China's Gulag*. New York, NY: Wiley.

Zubkov, A.I. (1974) *Teoreticheskie voprosii pravovo regulirovaniya truda osuzhdionnikh v sovietskikh ispravtel'no trudovikh uchrezhdeniyakh*. Tomskovo: Izdatel'stvo Tomskovo Universiteta (*Theoretical Questions on the Legal Regulations of Prisoners in Soviet Work Departments*. Tomsk: Tomsk University Publications).

Zubkov, A.I., Kalinnin, Y.I. and Si'soev, V.D. (1998) *Penitentsiarnie Uchrezhdenie v Sisteme Ministerstvo Yustitsii Rossii: Istoriya i Sovremennost'*. Moskva: Norma (*The Penitentiary Systems of Russia under the Ministry of Justice: Historical and Contemporary Development*. Moscow: Norma Publishing).

Index

central prison authority (GUIN) 3,
119, 162, 178
centralisation
prison management 141
Soviet penal ideology 36–7
character reform 55–66, 108, 117
character traits, and criminality 57
children, imprisonment of 4
choice, vocational training 46
civilisation standards 182
civilising process, of punishment 143,
150, 152
class relations, prison labour 35–6
cleaning work 75
CLPs *see* Community Liaison
Partnerships
collective unity, nostalgia for loss of
69
colonial consensus, penal knowledge
transfer 154
colonisation policy, Soviet forced
labour xii
colony settlements 4t
colony to bank transfers 93
commercial reasons, prison labour 71
common identity, between researched
and researcher 10
communitarian responsibility,
punishment as 40
community
attitudes to prison labour use 44
goal of imprisonment to preserve
68
community crime prevention, policy
transfer 147
Community Liaison Partnerships
(CLPs) 73, 74–7
abandonment of 123, 143
benefits 95
blueprint for probation service 78
implementation of 120
prisoner re-entry 138
re-emergence of 132
community-prison boundaries,
blurred 90, 141
community-prison relations

central funding 141–2
lack of in West 138
minimisation of exclusion 122
prison barter 91, 138
compulsory labour 45
*A Concept Paper for the Reorganisation
of the Penal System of the Ministry of
the Interior of Russia* 49–50
conjugal visit programme 90–1
Conservative Party, penal ideology 41
continuity, between penal systems 79,
85, 124
corporate barter 128
corporate business, prison labour
42–4
correctional colonies 3
Corrections Corporation of America
43
Corrective Labour Code (1997) 72, 92
costs, maintaining prisons 89
Council of Europe
penal reform xiv, 50, 121
private sector involvement, prison
labour 133
crime causation, perceptions
Omsk 68–9, 82
Smolensk 56–7
crime control, policy transfer 148
Crime Control as Industry 150
crime legislation, under Stalin xiii–xiv
criminal justice
authentication 182
insecurity and uncertainty, post
USSR 114, 115
market integration 154
policy transfer 147–8, 152
Soviet Union
corruption 29
prison officer's defence of 113
transition periods 114
criminalisation 28, 29, 34
criminals, as politically imperfect 57
cultural anthropological approach, to
research 12–13
cultural variations, penal transition
121